# GROWTH <small>AND</small>
# CONVERGENCE <small>IN</small>
# METROPOLITAN
# AMERICA

# BROOKINGS METRO SERIES

The Center on Urban and Metropolitan Policy of the Brookings Institution is integrating research and practical experience into a policy agenda for cities and metropolitan areas. By bringing fresh analyses and policy ideas to the public debate, the center hopes to inform key decisionmakers and civic leaders in ways that will spur meaningful change in our nation's communities.

As part of this effort, the Center on Urban and Metropolitan Policy has established the Brookings Metro Series to introduce new perspectives and policy thinking on current issues and lay the foundation for longer-term policy reforms. The series will examine traditional urban issues, such as neighborhood assets and central city competitiveness, as well as larger metropolitan concerns, such as regional growth, development, and employment patterns. The Metro Series will consist of concise studies and collections of essays designed to appeal to a broad audience. While these studies are formally reviewed, some will not be verified like other research publications. As with all publications, the judgments, conclusions, and recommendations presented in the studies are solely those of the authors and should not be attributed to the trustees, officers, or other staff members of the institution.

BROOKINGS
METRO
SERIES

Also in the Brookings Metro Series

*Laws of the Landscape:*
*How Policies Shape Cities in Europe and America*
Pietro S. Nivola

*Savings for the Poor:*
*The Hidden Benefits of Electronic Banking*
Michael A. Stegman

*Reflections on Regionalism*
Bruce Katz, editor

# GROWTH AND CONVERGENCE IN METROPOLITAN AMERICA

Janet Rothenberg Pack

BROOKINGS INSTITUTION PRESS
*Washington, D.C.*

*Library of Congress Cataloging-in-Publication data*

Pack, Janet Rothenberg.
    Growth and convergence in metropolitan America / Janet Rothenberg
Pack.
    p.  cm.
Includes bibliographical references and index.
    ISBN 0-8157-0247-7 (pbk. : alk. paper)
    1. United States—Population—Economic aspects.  2. United
States—Economic policy.  3. Regional disparities—United States.  4.
Metropolitan areas—Economic aspects.  5. Cities and towns—United
States—Growth.  I. Title.
HB3505 .P33 2002                                        2001006592
330.973'009173'2—dc21                                   CIP


9 8 7 6 5 4 3 2 1

The paper used in this publication meets minimum requirements of the
American National Standard for Information Sciences—Permanence of Paper
for Printed Library Materials: ANSI Z39.48-1992.


Typeset in Sabon

Composition by R. Lynn Rivenbark
Macon, Georgia

Printed by R. R. Donnelley and Sons
Harrisonburg, Virginia

# Foreword

ANALYSIS OF MORE than 200 metropolitan areas in the Northeast, Midwest, South, and West over the last three decades of the twentieth century shows convergence in per capita incomes, poverty and unemployment rates, and educational attainment. This convergence is largely due to improvements in the relative position of the South. Nonetheless, the South still lags behind the rest of the nation, as it has for more than a century. The very large differences in economic growth rates among the regions of the United States have important implications for the well-being of those who live in these regions.

Indeed, whereas much contemporary urban research focuses on differences in growth between cities and suburbs, Janet Rothenberg Pack argues that regional differences are critical. In some regions, such as the West, both cities and suburbs grow rapidly, and in others, such as the Northeast, both grow relatively slowly. The region in which a metropolitan area is located affects its prospects more than would improved cooperation between cities and suburbs. Her analysis also indicates that the forces behind regional growth are highly vulnerable to unforeseeable shocks, and therefore, a policy based on the experience of earlier periods is often inappropriate. Thus policymakers must contend with the implication that urban growth is not simply a matter of choice (policy or market forces), but also of idiosyncrasy, fate, and history.

Despite a vigorous national economy in the 1980s that had widespread beneficial results, some metropolitan areas continued to lose population and tax base, and to increase poverty and unemployment. The regional concentration of highly distressed metropolitan areas is great: in 1990, twenty-four of the thirty-one were in the South. (The very well-off metropolitan areas are more dispersed across the country: nineteen are in the South and West, fourteen in the Northeast and Midwest.) This suggests that policies targeted at promoting economic growth and well-being in whole regions should be developed to complement the city-focused strategies that are already widely discussed in urban policy literature.

Pack identifies broader policy prescriptions that can complement regional or place-based strategies. These include continuing federal expenditure and transfer programs, underpinned by a progressive income tax system; pursuing a robust economy that lowers unemployment rates and poverty; investing in educational improvement to enable workers to take advantage of economic opportunity; and supporting a market system that draws firms to places with suitable land and labor markets for efficient production.

In essence, Pack contends that the focus on population growth rates rather than welfare in much of the policy literature puts the issue backward. The clearest case in point is the South, where population growth rates have been high, yet many metropolitan areas trail behind the rest of the country in socioeconomic measures. Public policy—at the federal, state, and local levels—should properly be concerned with improving income, education, and employment levels; that is, with ensuring the well-being of the population.

Brookings is grateful to the Fannie Mae Foundation for financial support for the Center on Urban and Metropolitan Policy and to the Ford Foundation, the George Gund Foundation, the Joyce Foundation, the John D. and Catherine T. MacArthur Foundation, and the Charles Stewart Mott Foundation for support of the center's work on metropolitan growth and urban reinvestment issues.

The views expressed in this volume are those of the author and should not be ascribed to any institution acknowledged above or to the trustees, officers, or other staff members of the Brookings Institution.

MICHAEL H. ARMACOST
*President*

*January 2002*
*Washington, D.C.*

# Acknowledgments

I T MAY BE that no book is written without the help of institutions and other people. Certainly, for this volume, institutional support has been generous, and many individuals have provided important encouragement and assistance.

The Department of Public Policy and Management, the Wharton School administration, and the University of Pennsylvania granted a two-year sabbatical that provided the continuity so important to developing the basis of this volume.

The Brookings Institution—its Economics Studies program, headed by Robert Litan, and its then new Center on Urban and Metropolitan Policy, directed by Bruce Katz—where I spent the two years, provided significant support. This included a visiting fellowship; a fully equipped office with a view of the ground on which the weeping cherry tree once stood; helpful library staff and research facilities; and a knowledgeable and cooperative computer support staff. The opportunity to associate with Brookings colleagues who come to seminars with provocative questions and helpful comments and who engage in vigorous substantive discussion is genuinely appreciated.

Robert Litan extended the initial positive response to my research proposal and made available the resources of the Economics Studies program. Bruce Katz and his center provided more than monetary assistance. The numerous projects in which he and the center are involved (and in which I was included) provided not only a generally stimulating environment in which urban issues were the focus of attention, but also many useful ideas that have found their way into this volume—ideas he may not recognize (or, if he does, may not agree with).

Many helpful comments on the materials in chapters 1 and 2 were made at a conference in September 1998, "Urban-Suburban Interdependence: New Directions for Research and Policy," sponsored by the Lincoln Institute of Land Policy, the Great Cities Institute of the University of Illinois at Chicago, and the Brookings Center on Urban and Metropolitan Policy.

During my two years at Brookings, I was fortunate to have the skillful and careful assistance of Joseph McQuown and Hannah Zwiebel, research assistants in the Economics Studies program. And I do believe that behind everything was a lot of help—in ways I may not even yet realize—from Linda Gianessi, associate director of Economic Studies, for administration. When it came time to get this work into production at the Brookings Institution Press, Tom Lehr edited the manuscript, Meghan McNally verified the factual content, Carlotta Ribar proofread the pages, and Enid Zafran provided an index.

Not only did the public policy and management department, the Wharton School, and the University of Pennsylvania make my two-year leave possible, but it was in this supportive environment that I completed the volume. Wharton's Lippincott Library, headed by Jean Newland, the Wharton Computing Center, headed by Gerald McCartney, and the department of public policy and management staff, headed by Susan Roney, all contributed to the effort.

I have also been fortunate to have the assistance of three students at the university: James Lucania, Matthew Klein, and Vanessa Freeman.

Howard Pack, ever my most valued critic and consultant, has once again played a major part in the development of the volume. He has been a sounding board for ideas, never hesitating to disagree, and, given his unusual bibliographic storage capacity in so many intellectual areas, has often shown me a path I would not have known.

# Contents

## Tables

Maps *(color insert following page 22)*

# Data Note

TWO DATA FILES have been employed in this study: Richard Voith generously made available his extensive data files for 277 metropolitan areas (based on data for 656 counties). Wherever reference is made to 277 metropolitan areas, the data come from these files. The data were assembled for 1960, 1970, 1980, and 1990 from the U.S. Decennial Census of Population and Housing and City County Data Book tapes and CD-ROMs. Definitions of metropolitan areas for 1990 were used with appropriate adjustments of the geographic scope of the data for earlier years. In all cases metropolitan statistical areas (MSAs) were the unit of analysis.

The Voith files were matched with data from the U.S. Department of Housing and Urban Development's State of the Cities Data System (SOCDS). These data may be accessed from the HUD User website (www.huduser.org), which draws on data from the 1970, 1980, and 1990 decennial censuses. Population counts are updated to 1996 from Census Bureau estimates. Data on labor force come from the Bureau of Labor Statistics. The match of the Voith and SOCDS data resulted in a data set for 250 of the original 277 metropolitan areas. Where data are presented and analyzed for 250 metropolitan areas, they are derived from this matched data file.

The variables from the Department of Housing and Urban Development data used in this study are poverty rates, educational attainment, race, immigrant status, and industry of employment. All other variables come from Richard Voith's files. Chapters 3, 5, and 6 and part of chapter 2 draw on this combined file.

## CHAPTER ONE

# Major Shifts in Population and Economic Activity

Dᴇsᴘɪᴛᴇ ᴛʜᴇ ᴜɴᴘʀᴇᴄᴇᴅᴇɴᴛᴇᴅ prosperity of the 1990s, urban issues have sunk below the threshold of serious national policy discussion.[1] During the intense policy debates of the national presidential campaign of 2000, neither major-party presidential candidate offered a platform on the state of the cities or their suburbs. The one minor exception was Vice President Albert Gore's anti-sprawl position.[2] Voters entered voting booths more knowledgeable about anti-ballistic missile shields, the benefits of long-term trade relations with China, and the long-term rate of return on social security contributions relative to the Nasdaq index than about the continued deterioration of Camden, New Jersey, or East Palo

1. In describing a bill in the U.S. Congress in 2000 (subsequently adopted), David Boldt, writing in the *Philadelphia Inquirer,* notes that "urban aid has been off the table since at least 1992, the year of the Los Angeles riots." But as Boldt points out in the article, "the proposed legislation sets up no new programs, provides no new services, and largely bypasses the state and city bureaucracies. The benefits accrue directly to individuals, businesses, and community groups in the distressed areas." David Boldt, "Parties Toss Old Formulas in Fresh Effort to Help Cities," *Philadelphia Inquirer,* June 25, 2000, p. D1.

2. Vice President Gore talked about "an American movement to build more livable communities," and said, "In the past we adopted national policies that spend lots of taxpayer money to subsidize out-of-control sprawl. . . . [Such policies] suck the life out of urban areas, increase congestion in the suburbs, and raise taxes on farms." Timothy Egan, "The Nation Dreams: Dreams of Fields; The New Politics of Urban Sprawl," *New York Times,* November 15, 1998, Section 4, p. 1.

Alto, California. This stands in contrast to strong interest in earlier decades: the 1960s, when urban problems, eventually resulting in the Kerner commission report, were high on the national political agenda; the 1970s and early 1980s, when the divergent fortunes of the Northeast and Midwest (the Frost Belt or Rust Belt) and the South and West (the Sun Belt) generated intense discussion about the regional implications of the federal budget. Nevertheless, the absence of public debate does not mean that city and suburb, Sun Belt and Frost Belt, no longer provide important axes for policy or analysis.

Urban policy has become largely a state and local preoccupation, despite the continued urban efforts of the U.S. Department of Housing and Urban Development (discussed in chapter 2).[3] Some of the issues that are currently being raised at the state and local level have antecedents. The widespread attack on suburban sprawl has links to questions raised in earlier decades about how suburbanization affects society as a whole and whether this pattern of growth can be sustained environmentally. Some critics have suggested that suburbs should be required to help their core cities, perhaps by fiscal integration, but the dramatic improvements in the quality of life in many cities during the 1990s have muted these arguments. The still-unexplained drop in crime rates has reduced the urgency of some of these concerns. The growth of sectors such as Internet-related firms, whose main requirements are often low-cost loft space and a nearby Starbucks, has led to a reinvigoration of dilapidated areas in some cities—for example, "Silicon Alley" in Manhattan. During the booming stock market of the 1990s, young single persons who preferred cities to suburbs bid housing prices up, which led to a perception that cities were again robust and needed no special attention. The slowdown in 2000 tempered this perception somewhat.

Despite these phenomena, there are two major long-term trends that require analysis, namely, the continuing shift of economic activity and population from the Frost Belt to the Sun Belt and from the city to the suburb. To determine whether these trends are desirable and whether they should be the focus of public policy requires first documenting the process and then attempting to understand it. Public policy becomes relevant only if the geographic redistributions have undesirable consequences or if

---

3. Katz (2000) points to the growing state and local efforts to adopt "smart growth" plans. "In last fall's elections alone, more than 200 communities debated—and more than 70 percent adopted—measures to support smart growth," p. ix.

**Table 1-1.** *Share of Metropolitan Population and Income in Cities and Suburbs, by Decade, 1960-90*

Percent

| Decade | Population | | Income | |
|--------|-----------|---------|--------|---------|
|        | Cities | Suburbs | Cities | Suburbs |
| 1960 | 44 | 56 | 45 | 55 |
| 1970 | 40 | 59 | 39 | 61 |
| 1980 | 36 | 64 | 33 | 67 |
| 1990 | 34 | 65 | 30 | 70 |

Source: See Data Note (based on 277 MSAs).

undesirable consequences result from current government policies that distort normal underlying economic processes. Analysts who are concerned with cities often assume that some public policy is necessary to foster growth, often focusing on the potential contribution the suburbs can make. The perspective in this book is on the huge regional shift that has occurred in economic activity and population. As one measure, almost all of the fifty fastest-growing metropolitan statistical areas (MSAs) are in the South and West, and almost all of the slowest-growing ones are in the Northeast and Midwest.[4] It seems unlikely that even perfectly managed suburb-city integration will suddenly propel ten metropolitan areas of the Northeast and Midwest into the top fifty or remove ten from the slow-growth list.

Thus, my view is that urban issues in the United States must necessarily be considered in a regional framework—a perspective that was widely held during the 1970s and gradually abandoned. The remainder of this chapter provides the empirical documentation for these views.

## Urban Development: The Post–World War II Shifts

Two shifts in the locations of population and industry have resulted in a major change in the urban structure of the United States. The relocation from city to suburb (table 1-1 and figure 1-1) and from Northeast and Midwest to South and West (table 1-2 and figure 1-2) have brought to the

4. The terms *metropolitan area* and *MSA* are used interchangeably throughout this volume.

Figure 1-1. *Metropolitan Population in Cities and Suburbs, by Decade, 1960–90*

Percent

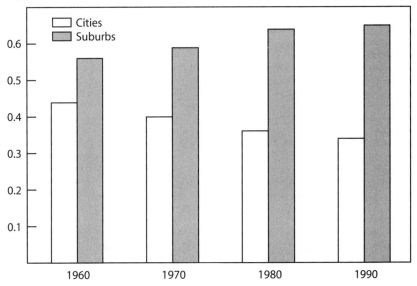

forefront the problems of cities, particularly the older cities of the Northeast and the Midwest.[5] The regional shifts in the distribution of the metropolitan population (figure 1-2) are striking. The metropolitan populations in the South and West have been growing steadily, while the metropolitan populations in the Northeast and Midwest have been declining.

Table 1-2. *Regional Distribution of U.S. Metropolitan Population, 1950–96*

Percent of metropolitan total[a]

| Census region | 1950 | 1960 | 1970 | 1980 | 1990 | 1990* | 1996 |
|---|---|---|---|---|---|---|---|
| Northeast | 34 | 31 | 29 | 26 | 24 | 22 | 20 |
| Midwest | 29 | 28 | 28 | 27 | 24 | 25 | 24 |
| South | 23 | 24 | 25 | 28 | 29 | 32 | 33 |
| West | 14 | 17 | 19 | 21 | 23 | 22 | 23 |

Source: U.S. Department of Commerce, Bureau of the Census.
a. 277 metropolitan areas; 1990* and 1996 based on 250 metropolitan areas.

5. The four census regions are Northeast, Midwest, South, and West. The states in each of these regions are listed in appendix A.

Figure 1-2. *Distribution of Regional Metropolitan Population, by Decade, 1960–90*

Percent

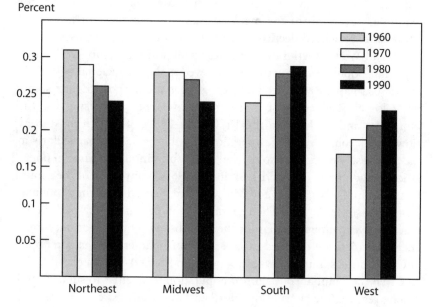

Between 1950 and 1996 the metropolitan populations of the Northeast and Midwest declined from 63 percent of the metropolitan total to less than 45 percent (table 1-2). During the same period, the proportion of the metropolitan population living in the West and South increased from less than 40 percent to more than 55 percent (table 1-2).[6]

These dramatic interregional shifts are graphically illustrated in maps 1-1 through 1-9 (see color plates), which show the population growth rates by quintiles for each of the metropolitan areas in the sample. Maps 1-1 through 1-3 show metropolitan area growth rates for the 1960s, 1970s, and 1980s; maps 1-4 through 1-6 show suburban area growth rates for the same three decades; and maps 1-7 through 1-9 show the

6. Data for 277 metropolitan areas are included in table 1-2 (facing). They contained 63 percent of the total U.S. population in 1990. Since they include all the largest metropolitan areas, they undoubtedly contain even larger percentages of personal income and total output. These 277 metropolitan areas are referred to as the metropolitan areas and their population as the metropolitan population (as if they included all metropolitan areas). For 1996, 250 metropolitan areas are covered, and the comparable proportions are shown for the 250 MSAs for 1990*.

growth rates for central cities for these decades. Both the regional central tendencies and the intraregional variation are clear. In the 1970s, for example, nearly all of the metropolitan areas in the Northeast and Midwest experienced decreases in population or small increases. In the South and West growth rates were nearly all positive. Although the metropolitan population growth rates showed a similar regional pattern in the 1980s (map 1-3), the declines were greater and the growth rates somewhat lower. The contrast in the suburbs is not surprising for the Northeast and Midwest in the 1970s and 1980s: although most grew slowly with some declining, several of the suburban areas, particularly in the Midwest, experienced somewhat more substantial increases in population growth (maps 1-5 and 1-6). In the 1960s many more of the suburban areas in the Northeast and Midwest experienced substantial population increases (map 1-4). The geographic population growth pattern for cities was very similar to that for the suburbs, with one important difference: the cities that declined experienced much larger decreases in population than the suburbs that lost population (maps 1-7 through 1-9).

Given the simultaneous shift of population from cities to suburbs and among regions, the cities of the Northeast and Midwest experienced the greatest declines in population, falling from 33.4 million in 1960 to 29.2 million in 1990.[7] During this same period, their total suburban populations continued to increase (table 1-3). In the South and West, the populations of most cities actually increased.[8] The data in table 1-3 are the basis for the preoccupation of urban scholars and policymakers with the decline in city population and the low growth rates in both cities and suburbs of the Northeast and Midwest (as well as with the differences between cities and suburbs, in per capita income and poverty, in all regions of the country, analyzed in chapter 3).

Just as population shifted from cities to suburbs and among regions, so too did total income. In 1960, 45 percent of metropolitan income was in central cities. By 1990 the proportion had fallen to 30 percent (table 1-1 and figure 1-3). In 1960, total income in the metropolitan areas of the Northeast and the Midwest was 62 percent of the metropolitan total. By 1990 the proportion had declined to 49 percent (table 1-4 and figure 1-4).

---

7. The period 1960–90 forms the basis for most of the data described in this volume.

8. This is due in part to the annexation of parts of the suburbs by the cities of these regions discussed in chapter 2.

**Table 1-3.** *Total Population and Population Growth: Region, City, and Suburbs, by Decade, 1960–90*

Units as indicated

| Area | Total income[a] | | | | Percentage change | | | |
|---|---|---|---|---|---|---|---|---|
| | 1960 | 1970 | 1980 | 1990 | 1960–70 | 1970–80 | 1980–90 | 1960–90 |
| All MSAs | 127,575 | 149,125 | 164,042 | 182,512 | 17 | 10 | 11 | 43 |
| Cities | 56,529 | 60,568 | 59,279 | 62,114 | 7 | –2 | 5 | 10 |
| Suburbs | 71,046 | 88,557 | 104,764 | 120,398 | 25 | 18 | 15 | 69 |
| Northeast | 39,173 | 43,229 | 42,752 | 44,116 | 10 | –1 | 3 | 13 |
| Cities | 16,142 | 15,705 | 13,896 | 13,892 | –3 | –12 | 0 | –14 |
| Suburbs | 23,031 | 27,524 | 28,856 | 30,224 | 20 | 5 | 5 | 31 |
| Midwest | 36,264 | 41,004 | 42,094 | 43,149 | 13 | 3 | 3 | 19 |
| Cities | 17,227 | 17,516 | 15,787 | 15,284 | 2 | –10 | –3 | –11 |
| Suburbs | 19,036 | 23,489 | 26,307 | 27,865 | 23 | 12 | 6 | 46 |
| South | 30,625 | 37,278 | 45,463 | 53,349 | 22 | 22 | 17 | 74 |
| Cities | 14,207 | 16,695 | 17,551 | 18,506 | 18 | 5 | 5 | 30 |
| Suburbs | 16,418 | 20,583 | 27,912 | 34,843 | 25 | 36 | 25 | 112 |
| West | 21,513 | 27,613 | 33,733 | 41,898 | 28 | 22 | 24 | 95 |
| Cities | 8,952 | 10,653 | 12,045 | 14,431 | 19 | 13 | 20 | 61 |
| Suburbs | 12,561 | 16,961 | 21,689 | 27,467 | 35 | 28 | 27 | 119 |

Source: See Data Note (based on 277 MSAs).
a. Thousands of dollars.

**Figure 1-3.** *Metropolitan Income in Cities and Suburbs, by Decade, 1960–90*

Percent

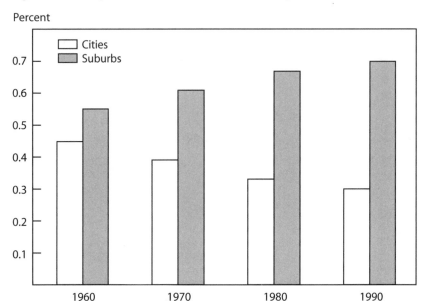

As a mirror image, the share of total income during this period in the South and West increased from 38 percent to 51 percent.

The geographic patterns of per capita income growth rates are shown in maps 1-10 through 1-18 (see color plates). Shifts in total income are described above. Per capita income is a very different indicator. It is possible to have declining population and declining total income but rising per capita income; that is, an increase in the welfare of the population. It is also possible to observe the opposite pattern: rising population and total income but slow growth or decline in per capita income. The maps show both of these. In the 1970s, the lowest rates of growth (including many declines) in per capita income in metropolitan areas occurred in the Northeast and much of the Midwest. By the 1980s, it was the metropolitan areas of the Northeast in which per capita incomes were growing most rapidly; the situation was the reverse in the Midwest. A similar pattern, particularly in the Northeast, characterizes the suburban portions and central cities of the metropolitan areas. These differences in population and per capita income growth patterns are important throughout this volume.

**Table 1-4.** *Share of Total MSA Income: Regions, Cities, and Suburbs, by Decade, 1960–90*

Percent

| Area | 1960 | 1970 | 1980 | 1990 |
|------|------|------|------|------|
| Northeast | 32 | 30 | 26 | 26 |
|   Cities | 13 | 10 | 7 | 7 |
|   Suburbs | 19 | 20 | 19 | 19 |
| Midwest | 30 | 28 | 26 | 23 |
|   Cities | 15 | 11 | 9 | 7 |
|   Suburbs | 15 | 17 | 17 | 16 |
| South | 20 | 22 | 26 | 27 |
|   Cities | 10 | 10 | 10 | 9 |
|   Suburbs | 10 | 12 | 17 | 19 |
| West | 18 | 19 | 22 | 24 |
|   Cities | 8 | 8 | 8 | 8 |
|   Suburbs | 10 | 12 | 14 | 16 |

Source: See Data Note (based on 277 MSAs).

During the 1970s, the far more rapid growth in total income and population in the Sun Belt states of the South and West than in the Frost Belt states of the Northeast and Midwest was a major urban policy concern.[9] The Sun Belt–Frost Belt literature documented the convergence of per capita incomes among regions that reflected the high growth rates in per capita incomes in the South—incomes that had been far below those in other regions. In contrast, the Northeast and Midwest grew more slowly. Between 1960 and 1990, the total income in the metropolitan areas of the Northeast and Midwest grew by 101 percent and 91 percent, respectively, compared with 234 percent and 216 percent in the South and West (table 1-5, last column).

One might reasonably think that such enormous shifts among regions influenced the development, form, and welfare of the growing regions as well as of the declining regions. However, it remains to be determined whether this is so and if so how these influences differed and why (see chapters 3 and 4).

9. See, for example, Coelen (1978); Haveman and Stanfield (1977); Jusenius and Ledebur (1976); Nourse (1968); Olson (1976); Pack (1980); Perry and Watkins (1977); Peterson (1977).

Figure 1-4. *Proportion of Total Metropolitan Income, by Regions, Cities, and Suburbs, by Decade, 1960–90*

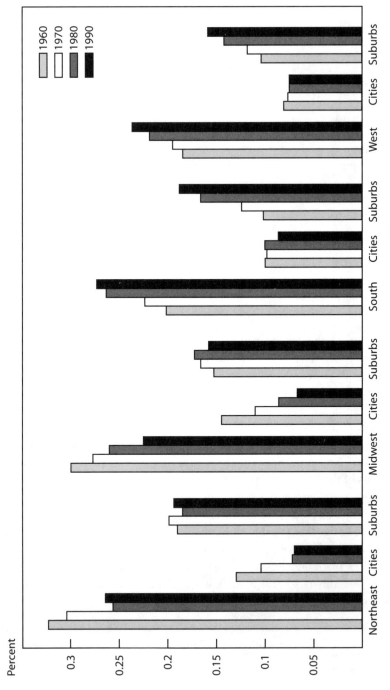

**Table 1-5. Total Income and Income Growth: Region, City, and Suburbs, by Decade, 1960–90**

Units as indicated

| Area | Total income[a] | | | | Percentage change | | | |
|---|---|---|---|---|---|---|---|---|
| | 1960 | 1970 | 1980 | 1990 | 1960–70 | 1970–80 | 1980–90 | 1960–90 |
| All MSAs | 883,427 | 1,294,485 | 1,546,296 | 2,173,290 | 47 | 19 | 41 | 146 |
| Cities | 393,478 | 506,438 | 514,136 | 651,980 | 29 | 2 | 27 | 66 |
| Suburbs | 489,949 | 788,047 | 1,032,160 | 1,521,310 | 61 | 31 | 47 | 211 |
| Northeast | 285,736 | 393,750 | 397,886 | 574,440 | 38 | 1 | 44 | 101 |
| Cities | 114,594 | 135,680 | 112,766 | 152,850 | 18 | -17 | 36 | 33 |
| Suburbs | 171,142 | 258,070 | 285,120 | 421,590 | 51 | 10 | 48 | 146 |
| Midwest | 256,421 | 358,940 | 402,820 | 489,540 | 40 | 12 | 22 | 91 |
| Cities | 120,080 | 144,060 | 133,410 | 144,860 | 20 | -7 | 9 | 21 |
| Suburbs | 136,341 | 214,880 | 269,410 | 344,680 | 58 | 25 | 28 | 153 |
| South | 178,159 | 289,715 | 407,750 | 594,430 | 63 | 41 | 46 | 234 |
| Cities | 87,260 | 128,318 | 150,640 | 186,750 | 47 | 17 | 24 | 114 |
| Suburbs | 90,899 | 161,397 | 257,110 | 407,680 | 78 | 59 | 59 | 348 |
| West | 163,112 | 252,080 | 337,840 | 514,880 | 55 | 34 | 52 | 216 |
| Cities | 71,544 | 98,380 | 117,320 | 167,520 | 38 | 19 | 43 | 134 |
| Suburbs | 91,568 | 153,700 | 220,520 | 347,360 | 68 | 43 | 58 | 279 |

Source: See Data Note (based on 277 MSAs).

a. Millions of dollars.

One of the purposes of this chapter is to present a broad overview of the major changes in urban growth over a fairly long period so as not to become entangled in excessive detail and idiosyncrasy. Despite these very large regional shifts, however, some regions and individual metropolitan areas showed substantial differences in growth rate from decade to decade. As indicated above, in the discussion of the maps, the most striking of these decadal contrasts occurs in per capita income growth between the 1970s and the 1980s. The average metropolitan per capita income growth was 14 percent in the 1970s and 19 percent in the 1980s. However, the change in growth rates was scarcely more than 1 or 2 percentage points in each of the regions but the Northeast. In the Midwest the average metropolitan growth rate in per capita income increased from 13 percent in the 1970s to 15 percent in the 1980s; in the South the average rate increased from 18 percent to 19 percent; and in the West the rate increased from 15 percent to 17 percent. In contrast, in the metropolitan areas of the Northeast the average growth in per capita income rose from 5 percent in the 1970s (lowest of all the regions) to 32 percent in the 1980s (the highest of all regions) (table 1-6).

It is critical to recognize these differences in each of the decades in the analyses in chapter 3, in which the effects of growth on the welfare of the population are estimated, and in chapter 4, in which the determinants of differences in growth rates are estimated. When such large relative (and absolute) regional swings in the growth of a major variable occur, it does not make sense to use averages over three decades.

## The Fastest-Growing and Slowest-Growing Metropolitan Areas

Identifying more specifically the metropolitan areas that are growing most rapidly and most slowly will help to anchor the emphasis on the importance of region in analyzing urban trends. Listed in tables 1-7 and 1-8 are the 50 metropolitan areas whose populations grew most rapidly (table 1-7) and those that grew most slowly (table 1-8) between 1960 and 1990.[10] It is not surprising to see that 48 of the 50 most rapidly growing regions are in the South and West (more than one-third of the 137 metropolitan areas in these two regions). Only 2 metropolitan areas from the

---

10. Growth is defined as (total population or total per capita income in 1990 minus total population or total per capita income in 1960) divided by total population or total per capita income in 1960.

**Table 1-6.** *Average Metropolitan Area per Capita Income Growth, by Region, 1970s and 1980s*

Percent

| Region | 1970s | 1980s |
|---|---|---|
| All 250 MSAs | 14 | 19 |
| Northeast | 5 | 32 |
| Midwest | 13 | 15 |
| South | 18 | 19 |
| West | 15 | 17 |

Source: See Data Note (based on 250 MSAs).

Midwest appear in the list: Columbia, Missouri, ranked 40th, and Lawrence, Kansas, ranked 49th. Moreover, the fastest-growing metropolitan areas are concentrated within a small number of states: 11 of the 50 are in California, 11 are in Florida, and 8 are in Texas.

There is also substantial regional concentration among the most slowly growing metropolitan areas (table 1-8): 38 of the 50 metropolitan areas with the slowest population growth are in the Northeast and Midwest (38 of 113 metropolitan areas in these two regions). Of the 12 remaining, 10 are in the South, with several bordering the Northeast or Midwest (in West Virginia and Ohio). The slowest-growing areas are also concentrated in a few states: 10 of the 50 are entirely or partly located in Ohio, 6 are in Pennsylvania, 5 are in Illinois, and 5 are in New York (see also maps 1-1 through 1-3).

It is not surprising that just as rapid population growth has been concentrated in the metropolitan areas of the South and West, so too has the growth in total income.[11] Of the 50 MSAs with the most rapidly growing total incomes over the three-decade period, only 5 are in the Northeast and Midwest. Among the 50 slowest-growing MSAs, 40 are in the

11. Since $(Y/P)(P) = Y$ (where $Y$ is total income and $P$ is population), it would take large changes in $Y/P$ to make the two groups—the fifty metropolitan areas with the fastest-growing populations and the fifty areas with the fastest-growing incomes—very different. The fact that the two groups are not identical is due to the places where relative $Y/P$ has changed radically. Thus, although there is not a perfect correlation, there is very substantial overlap between the fastest-growing and the slowest-growing metropolitan areas on the two dimensions: population and total income. Of the fastest-growing metropolitan areas, thirty-seven are among the fastest-growing in both dimensions; among the slowest-growing metropolitan areas, thirty-eight appear in both categories.

Table 1-7. *Fifty Fastest-Growing Metropolitan Areas, Population, 1960–90*

| Rank | MSA | Region | Growth[a] |
|------|-----|--------|-----------|
| 1 | Las Vegas, Nev. | West | 4.84 |
| 2 | Fort Pierce, Fla. | South | 3.47 |
| 3 | West Palm Beach-Boca Raton-Delray Beach, Fla. | South | 2.79 |
| 4 | Fort Lauderdale-Hollywood-Pompano Beach, Fla. | South | 2.76 |
| 5 | Sarasota, Fla. | South | 2.61 |
| 6 | Fort Collins-Loveland, Colo. | West | 2.49 |
| 7 | Phoenix, Ariz. | West | 2.20 |
| 8 | Riverside-San Bernardino, Calif. | West | 2.20 |
| 9 | Orlando, Fla. | South | 2.18 |
| 10 | Boulder-Longmont, Colo. | West | 2.03 |
| 11 | Reno, Nev. | West | 2.01 |
| 12 | Daytona Beach, Fla. | South | 1.96 |
| 13 | Austin, Tex. | South | 1.93 |
| 14 | Colorado Springs, Colo. | West | 1.76 |
| 15 | Santa Cruz, Calif. | West | 1.73 |
| 16 | Bryan-College Station, Tex. | South | 1.71 |
| 17 | Santa Rosa-Petaluma, Calif. | West | 1.63 |
| 18 | Tampa-Saint Petersburg-Clearwater, Fla. | South | 1.52 |
| 19 | Tucson, Ariz. | West | 1.51 |
| 20 | Provo-Orem, Utah | West | 1.46 |
| 21 | Houston, Tex. | South | 1.44 |
| 22 | Lexington-Fayette, Ky. | South | 1.44 |
| 23 | San Diego, Calif. | West | 1.42 |
| 24 | Gainesville, Fla. | South | 1.36 |

*(continued)*

Northeast or Midwest (tables 1-9 and 1-10). Just as income growth is slightly less concentrated by region than is population growth, it is also somewhat less concentrated in only a few states. Among the 50 MSAs with the fastest-growing total incomes, 9 are in Florida, 7 are in California, and 6 are in Texas. Of the 50 MSAs with the slowest-growing total incomes, 10 are entirely or partly in Ohio, and Pennsylvania, Illinois, and New York have 5 each.

Among the metropolitan areas with rapidly growing populations, there are some obvious contrasts: Las Vegas and Reno, Nevada, are growing in population for very different reasons than are Raleigh-

Table 1-7. *(Continued)*

| Rank | MSA | Region | Growth[a] |
|------|-----|--------|--------|
| 25 | Modesto, Calif. | West | 1.36 |
| 26 | San Jose, Calif. | West | 1.33 |
| 27 | Dallas, Tex. | South | 1.28 |
| 28 | Atlanta, Ga. | South | 1.27 |
| 29 | Sacramento, Calif. | West | 1.26 |
| 30 | Las Cruces, N.Mex. | West | 1.26 |
| 31 | Bremerton, Wash. | West | 1.25 |
| 32 | Vallejo-Fairfield-Napa, Calif. | West | 1.25 |
| 33 | Fort Worth-Arlington, Tex. | South | 1.23 |
| 34 | Boise City, Idaho | West | 1.20 |
| 35 | Santa Barbara-Santa Maria-Lompoc, Calif. | West | 1.19 |
| 36 | McAllen-Edinburg-Mission, Tex. | South | 1.12 |
| 37 | Raleigh-Durham, N.C. | South | 1.08 |
| 38 | Miami-Hialeah, Fla. | South | 1.07 |
| 39 | Laredo, Tex. | South | 1.06 |
| 40 | Columbia, Mo. | Midwest | 1.04 |
| 41 | Tallahassee, Fla. | South | 1.01 |
| 42 | Stockton, Calif. | West | 0.92 |
| 43 | Salt Lake City-Ogden, Utah | West | 0.92 |
| 44 | Athens, Ga. | South | 0.92 |
| 45 | Panama City, Fla. | South | 0.89 |
| 46 | Denver, Colo. | West | 0.89 |
| 47 | Salem, Oreg. | West | 0.89 |
| 48 | El Paso, Tex. | South | 0.88 |
| 49 | Lawrence, Kans. | Midwest | 0.87 |
| 50 | Bakersfield, Calif. | West | 0.86 |

a. Defined as (population in 1990 – population in 1960)/population in 1960.

Durham, North Carolina, or San Jose, California, and their rapid population growth is of a very different kind than that of the retirement communities of West Palm Beach–Boca Raton, Fort Lauderdale, or Sarasota,
Florida. The metropolitan areas with slowly growing populations appear
to have somewhat more in common; they are generally the older heavy-
manufacturing areas and the coal- and steel-producing areas of Pennsylvania, Ohio, and West Virginia.[12]

12. Brezis and Krugman (1997).

Table 1-8. *Fifty Slowest-Growing Metropolitan Areas, Population, 1960–90*

| Rank | MSA | Region | Growth[a] |
|---|---|---|---|
| 1 | Wheeling, W.Va.-Ohio | Midwest | –0.16 |
| 2 | Steubenville-Weirton, Ohio-W.Va. | Midwest | –0.15 |
| 3 | Johnstown, Pa. | Northeast | –0.14 |
| 4 | Duluth, Minn.-Wis. | Midwest | –0.13 |
| 5 | Pittsburgh, Pa. | Northeast | –0.13 |
| 6 | Jersey City, N.J. | Northeast | –0.09 |
| 7 | Charles Town, W.Va. | South | –0.09 |
| 8 | Buffalo, N.Y. | Northeast | –0.09 |
| 9 | Saint Joseph, Mo. | Midwest | –0.08 |
| 10 | Altoona, Pa. | Northeast | –0.05 |
| 11 | Cumberland, Md.-W.Va. | South | –0.05 |
| 12 | Utica-Rome, N.Y. | Northeast | –0.04 |
| 13 | Sioux City, Iowa-Nebr. | Midwest | –0.04 |
| 14 | Cleveland, Ohio | Midwest | –0.04 |
| 15 | Elmira, N.Y. | Northeast | –0.04 |
| 16 | Youngstown-Warren, Ohio | Midwest | –0.03 |
| 17 | New York, N.Y. | Northeast | –0.02 |
| 18 | Pittsfield, Mass. | Northeast | –0.02 |
| 19 | Terre Haute, Ind. | Midwest | –0.01 |
| 20 | Wichita Falls, Tex. | South | –0.01 |
| 21 | Decatur, Ill. | Midwest | –0.01 |
| 22 | Waterloo-Cedar Falls, Iowa | Midwest | 0.02 |
| 23 | Huntington-Ashland, W.Va.-Ky.-Ohio | South | 0.03 |
| 24 | Gadsden, Ala. | South | 0.03 |
| 25 | South Bend-Mishawaka, Ind. | Midwest | 0.04 |

*(continued)*

## Explaining Interregional Shifts

Many explanations have been offered to account for divergent regional experiences. Economists, influenced by international trade theory, emphasized the role of low wages and land prices in inducing the movement of factories from the more expensive locations in the North.[13] But other factors were also adduced to explain the shift of population and firms from the Midwest and Northeast to the South and West.[14] Public policies, tech-

---

13. Borts and Stein (1964).
14. Pack (1980).

Table 1-8. *(Continued)*

| Rank | MSA | Region | Growth[a] |
|------|-----|--------|--------|
| 26 | Pueblo, Colo. | West | 0.04 |
| 27 | Danville, Va. | South | 0.04 |
| 28 | Kankakee, Ill. | Midwest | 0.05 |
| 29 | Newark, N.J. | Northeast | 0.05 |
| 30 | Pine Bluff, Ark. | South | 0.05 |
| 31 | Norfolk-Virginia Beach-Newport News, Va. | South | 0.05 |
| 32 | Gary-Hammond, Ind. | Midwest | 0.05 |
| 33 | Binghamton, N.Y. | Northeast | 0.06 |
| 34 | Great Falls, Mont. | West | 0.06 |
| 35 | Scranton-Wilkes-Barre, Pa. | Northeast | 0.06 |
| 36 | Enid, Okla. | South | 0.07 |
| 37 | Mansfield, Ohio | Midwest | 0.07 |
| 38 | Muncie, Ind. | Midwest | 0.08 |
| 39 | Dubuque, Iowa | Midwest | 0.08 |
| 40 | Detroit, Mich. | Midwest | 0.08 |
| 41 | Peoria, Ill. | Midwest | 0.08 |
| 42 | Williamsport, Pa. | Northeast | 0.09 |
| 43 | Akron, Ohio | Midwest | 0.09 |
| 44 | Canton, Ohio | Midwest | 0.09 |
| 45 | Beaumont-Port Arthur, Tex. | South | 0.09 |
| 46 | Chicago, Ill. | Midwest | 0.10 |
| 47 | Davenport-Rock Island-Moline, Iowa-Ill. | Midwest | 0.10 |
| 48 | Toledo, Ohio | Midwest | 0.10 |
| 49 | Erie, Pa. | Northeast | 0.10 |
| 50 | Lima, Ohio | Midwest | 0.10 |

a. Defined as (population in 1990 – population in 1960)/population in 1960.

nological changes, and market forces all played important roles in the process. Technological changes in manufacturing production, transportation, and communications and more capital-intensive agricultural innovations encouraged a shift from earlier regional economic specialization. The development of air conditioning, the aging of the population, and increases in international competition propelled growth and development in the South and West; lower wages and the absence of unions in the South attracted labor-intensive industries from the Northeast and Midwest. On the policy side, the national highway system, water projects, and continued subsidization of water usage opened up arid areas in California and Arizona to both urban and agricultural use. Defense procurement

Table 1-9. *Fifty Fastest-Growing Metropolitan Areas, Total Income, 1960–90*

| Rank | MSA | Region | Growth[a] |
|------|-----|--------|-----------|
| 1 | Fort Pierce, Fla. | South | 9.22 |
| 2 | West Palm Beach-Boca Raton-Delray Beach, Fla. | South | 8.00 |
| 3 | Las Vegas, Nev. | West | 7.24 |
| 4 | Fort Lauderdale-Hollywood-Pompano Beach, Fla. | South | 6.27 |
| 5 | Seattle, Wash. | West | 6.16 |
| 6 | Fort Collins-Loveland, Colo. | West | 5.69 |
| 7 | Austin, Tex. | South | 5.19 |
| 8 | Boulder-Longmont, Colo. | West | 5.11 |
| 9 | Orlando, Fla. | South | 5.02 |
| 10 | Phoenix, Ariz. | West | 4.65 |
| 11 | Lexington-Fayette, Ky. | South | 4.50 |
| 12 | Scranton-Wilkes-Barre, Pa. | Northeast | 4.45 |
| 13 | Riverside-San Bernardino, Calif. | West | 4.32 |
| 14 | Savannah, Ga. | South | 4.31 |
| 15 | Dayton-Springfield, Ohio | Midwest | 4.26 |
| 16 | Bryan-College Station, Tex. | South | 4.14 |
| 17 | Raleigh-Durham, N.C. | South | 4.06 |
| 18 | Atlanta, Ga. | South | 3.87 |
| 19 | Tampa-Saint Petersburg-Clearwater, Fla. | South | 3.71 |
| 20 | Colorado Springs, Colo. | West | 3.67 |
| 21 | Santa Rosa-Petaluma, Calif. | West | 3.63 |
| 22 | Gainesville, Fla. | South | 3.60 |
| 23 | Tallahassee, Fla. | South | 3.60 |
| 24 | Houston, Tex. | South | 3.25 |
| 25 | Reno, Nev. | West | 3.23 |

*(continued)*

concentrated defense industries in areas with warmer year-round climates and large expanses of open land.[15] The enactment of environmental laws—compliance with which was relatively more difficult in the more industrialized and more densely developed Northeast and Midwest—also resulted in some relocation and start-up of businesses in the South and West.

15. Of course, there were exceptions, such as the production of nuclear submarines in Connecticut, but the quantitative importance of such exceptions in national procurement was small.

**Table 1-9.** *(Continued)*

| Rank | MSA | Region | Growth[a] |
|------|-----|--------|-----------|
| 26 | Vallejo-Fairfield-Napa, Calif. | West | 3.11 |
| 27 | Burlington, Vt. | Northeast | 3.07 |
| 28 | Dallas, Tex. | South | 3.06 |
| 29 | Santa Barbara-Santa Maria-Lompoc, Calif. | West | 3.06 |
| 30 | Fort Worth-Arlington, Tex. | South | 3.03 |
| 31 | Athens, Ga. | West | 3.01 |
| 32 | Modesto, Calif. | West | 3.00 |
| 33 | Tulsa, Okla. | South | 2.97 |
| 34 | Columbia, S.C. | South | 2.86 |
| 35 | Salem, Oreg. | West | 2.80 |
| 36 | Fayetteville, N.C. | South | 2.77 |
| 37 | Charlottesville, Va. | South | 2.77 |
| 38 | Boise City, Idaho | West | 2.76 |
| 39 | Bremerton, Wash. | West | 2.73 |
| 40 | Wilmington, N.C. | South | 2.70 |
| 41 | Lafayette, Ind. | Midwest | 2.66 |
| 42 | Panama City, Fla. | South | 2.62 |
| 43 | Dothan, Ala. | South | 2.60 |
| 44 | McAllen-Edinburg-Mission, Tex. | South | 2.60 |
| 45 | Sacramento, Calif. | West | 2.60 |
| 46 | Washington, D.C. | South | 2.57 |
| 47 | Sarasota, Fla. | South | 2.55 |
| 48 | Charlotte-Gastonia-Rock Hill, N.C.-S.C. | South | 2.54 |
| 49 | Columbia, Mo. | Midwest | 2.52 |
| 50 | Provo-Orem, Utah | West | 2.49 |

a. Defined as (income in 1990 – income in 1960)/income in 1960.

## The Movement from Cities to Suburbs

Market forces as well as public policies have also influenced intraregional shifts. In particular, growing population and industrial bases, technological changes, and increasing incomes are some of the factors that have both spurred and made possible the movement out of central cities to suburbs. As more land was needed to accommodate growth, other factors allowed households and businesses to widen their geographic horizons. Public policies such as subsidization of roads relative to mass transit, subsidies

Table 1-10. *Fifty Slowest-Growing Metropolitan Areas, Total Income, 1960–90*

| Rank | MSA | Region | Growth[a] |
|------|-----|--------|-----------|
| 1 | Steubenville-Weirton, Ohio-W.Va. | Midwest | 0.21 |
| 2 | Wheeling, W.Va.-Ohio | Midwest | 0.26 |
| 3 | Salinas-Seaside-Monterey, Calif. | West | 0.29 |
| 4 | Duluth, Minn.-Wis. | Midwest | 0.34 |
| 5 | Buffalo, N.Y. | Northeast | 0.38 |
| 6 | Youngstown-Warren, Ohio | Midwest | 0.41 |
| 7 | Utica-Rome, N.Y. | Northeast | 0.41 |
| 8 | Cleveland, Ohio | Midwest | 0.42 |
| 9 | Pittsburgh, Pa. | Northeast | 0.44 |
| 10 | Spokane, Wash. | West | 0.45 |
| 11 | Wichita, Kans. | Midwest | 0.45 |
| 12 | Jersey City, N.J. | Northeast | 0.46 |
| 13 | Elmira, N.Y. | Northeast | 0.48 |
| 14 | Waterloo-Cedar Falls, Iowa | Midwest | 0.48 |
| 15 | Johnstown, Pa. | Northeast | 0.48 |
| 16 | Great Falls, Mont. | West | 0.49 |
| 17 | Charles Town, W.Va. | South | 0.51 |
| 18 | Springfield, Mass. | Northeast | 0.51 |
| 19 | Terre Haute, Ind. | Midwest | 0.53 |
| 20 | Altoona, Pa. | Northeast | 0.54 |
| 21 | Mansfield, Ohio | Midwest | 0.55 |
| 22 | Pueblo, Colo. | West | 0.55 |
| 23 | Cumberland, Md.-W.Va. | South | 0.55 |
| 24 | Decatur, Ill. | Midwest | 0.56 |
| 25 | Casper, Wyo. | West | 0.59 |

*(continued)*

for extension of water and sewer infrastructure, and mortgage and tax deductions in the federal income tax are among those that have supported the movement to suburban locations.[16]

In thinking about the dispersal of population and economic activity to the suburbs, it is important to recognize that these shifts have had both

16. On mortgage deductions, see Gyourko and Sinai (2000). It is not accidental that the policies mentioned are largely federal. Most research has found that there is little evidence that state and local governments have much influence on economic development. For many examples, see the papers and discussion in Bradbury, Kodrzycki, and Tannenwald (1997).

Table 1-10.  *(Continued)*

| Rank | MSA | Region | Growth[a] |
|------|-----|--------|--------|
| 26 | Gary-Hammond, Ind. | Midwest | 0.60 |
| 27 | Muncie, Ind. | Midwest | 0.61 |
| 28 | New York, N.Y. | Northeast | 0.61 |
| 29 | Binghamton, N.Y. | Northeast | 0.65 |
| 30 | Davenport-Rock Island-Moline, Iowa-Ill. | Midwest | 0.65 |
| 31 | Chicago, Ill. | Midwest | 0.66 |
| 32 | Jackson, Mich. | Midwest | 0.66 |
| 33 | Milwaukee, Wis. | Midwest | 0.66 |
| 34 | Toledo, Ohio | Midwest | 0.66 |
| 35 | Akron, Ohio | Midwest | 0.67 |
| 36 | Canton, Ohio | Midwest | 0.67 |
| 37 | Williamsport, Pa. | Northeast | 0.68 |
| 38 | Pittsfield, Mass. | Northeast | 0.69 |
| 39 | Enid, Okla. | South | 0.69 |
| 40 | Huntington-Ashland, W.Va.-Ky.-Ohio | South | 0.69 |
| 41 | Beaumont-Port Arthur, Tex. | South | 0.69 |
| 42 | Peoria, Ill. | Midwest | 0.69 |
| 43 | Erie, Pa. | Northeast | 0.74 |
| 44 | Kenosha, Wis. | Midwest | 0.75 |
| 45 | Odessa, Tex. | South | 0.76 |
| 46 | Lima, Ohio | Midwest | 0.77 |
| 47 | Kankakee, Ill. | Midwest | 0.79 |
| 48 | Daytona Beach, Fla. | South | 0.79 |
| 49 | Dubuque, Iowa | Midwest | 0.81 |
| 50 | Topeka, Kans. | Midwest | 0.82 |

a. Defined as (population in 1990 – population in 1960)/population in 1960.

positive and negative effects. The positive impacts were increases in efficiency and consumer satisfaction as firms and households moved to preferred locations. The relatively large cities in the Northeast (average population of 343,460 in 1960), whose populations declined over the period, may have been too large, too dense, and too congested, and therefore their population declines improved the quality of life both for those who left and for those who remained in the cities.[17] Population and employment

17. The central cities of the South and West were much smaller in 1960: their average populations were 146,500 and 194,600, respectively. See Tolley (1974).

relocation to the suburbs increased efficiency, given the negative characteristics of the larger, older cities and the major technical changes of the post–World War II years—the increased ownership of automobiles and land-intensive changes in industrial technology. The policies that are now seen as biased in favor of suburban locations—mortgage interest deductions, property tax deductions, road construction, and infrastructure subsidies more generally—may have been important positive instruments to achieve improvements in quality of life and industrial efficiency.

At the same time, there may have been social costs associated with suburbanization. People were left behind—for various reasons, such as low levels of education or restrictive suburban zoning—who could not take advantage of the new opportunities in the suburbs or in the South and West. The result has been a concentration of poverty and other social ills in the central cities, which has harmed those directly involved and has imposed hardships on other residents.[18] As demonstrated in chapter 3, poverty rates are highly correlated in particular locations from decade to decade, partly because many large cities serve as entry and transformation locations for the poor—immigrants, for example—who are able to take advantage of the cities' opportunities and institutional assistance to increase their human capital and incomes. Having done this, they move on. But new migrants and immigrants continually replace them.[19] Thus both an initial poor population, many of whom are not mobile, and this additional influx of poor persons, many of whom move up the economic ladder and out of the city, put a fiscal burden on the city. As a result, large percentages of city budgets must be devoted to dealing with poverty, leaving little to maintain or improve the efficiency of city services to businesses and nonpoor residents.[20] Accordingly, if federal policies that helped to spur positive goals have also had negative implications, rethinking these policies may now be appropriate.

In sum, both current urban policy recommendations and the many urban and other policies that affect development in urban areas should be viewed in terms of their larger regional context. The development of cities and suburbs may depend on their own characteristics but will be conditioned in major ways by federal policies and by the region in which they are located.

18. Pack (1998).
19. Myers (1999).
20. Pack (1998).

Map 1-1.  *Percent Change in Metropolitan Population in the 1960s*

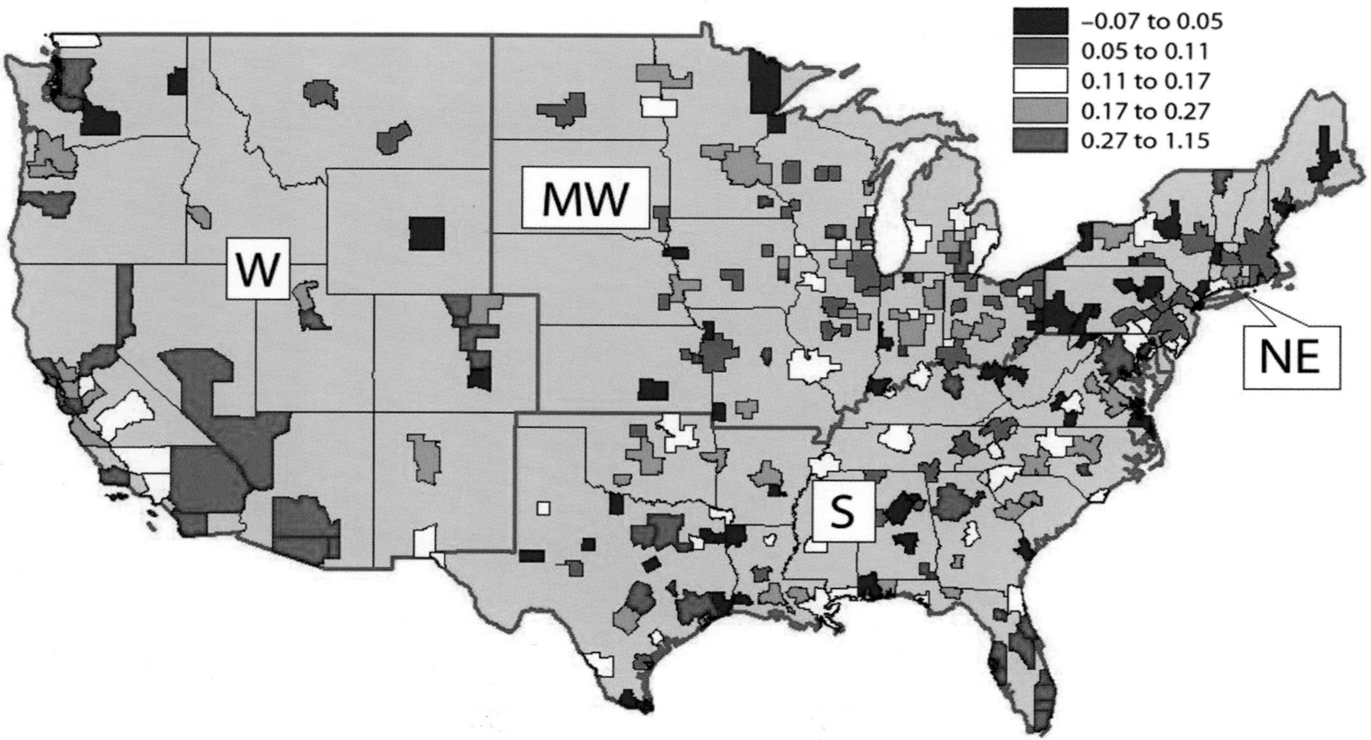

Legend:
- −0.07 to 0.05
- 0.05 to 0.11
- 0.11 to 0.17
- 0.17 to 0.27
- 0.27 to 1.15

NE

S

MW

W

Map 1-2. *Percent Change in Metropolitan Population in the 1970s*

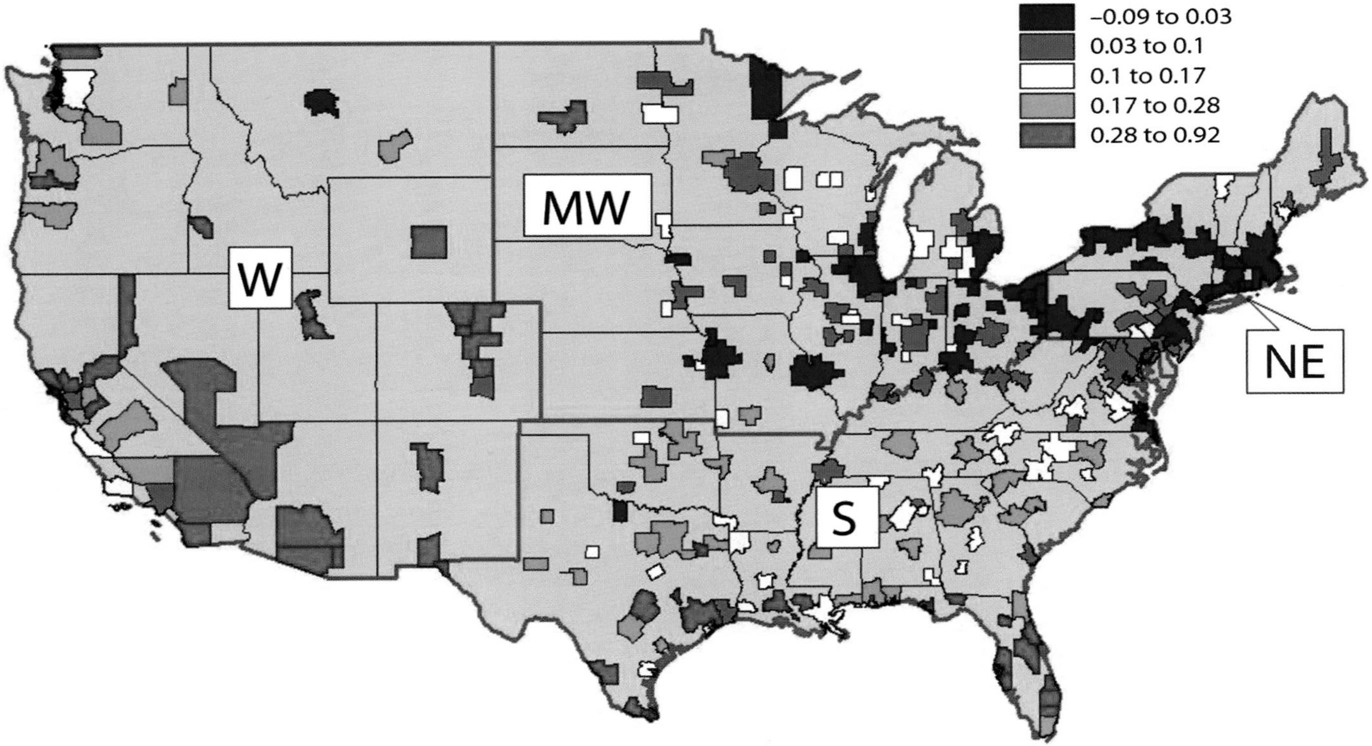

Legend:
- −0.09 to 0.03
- 0.03 to 0.1
- 0.1 to 0.17
- 0.17 to 0.28
- 0.28 to 0.92

Map 1-3. *Percent Change in Metropolitan Population in the 1980s*

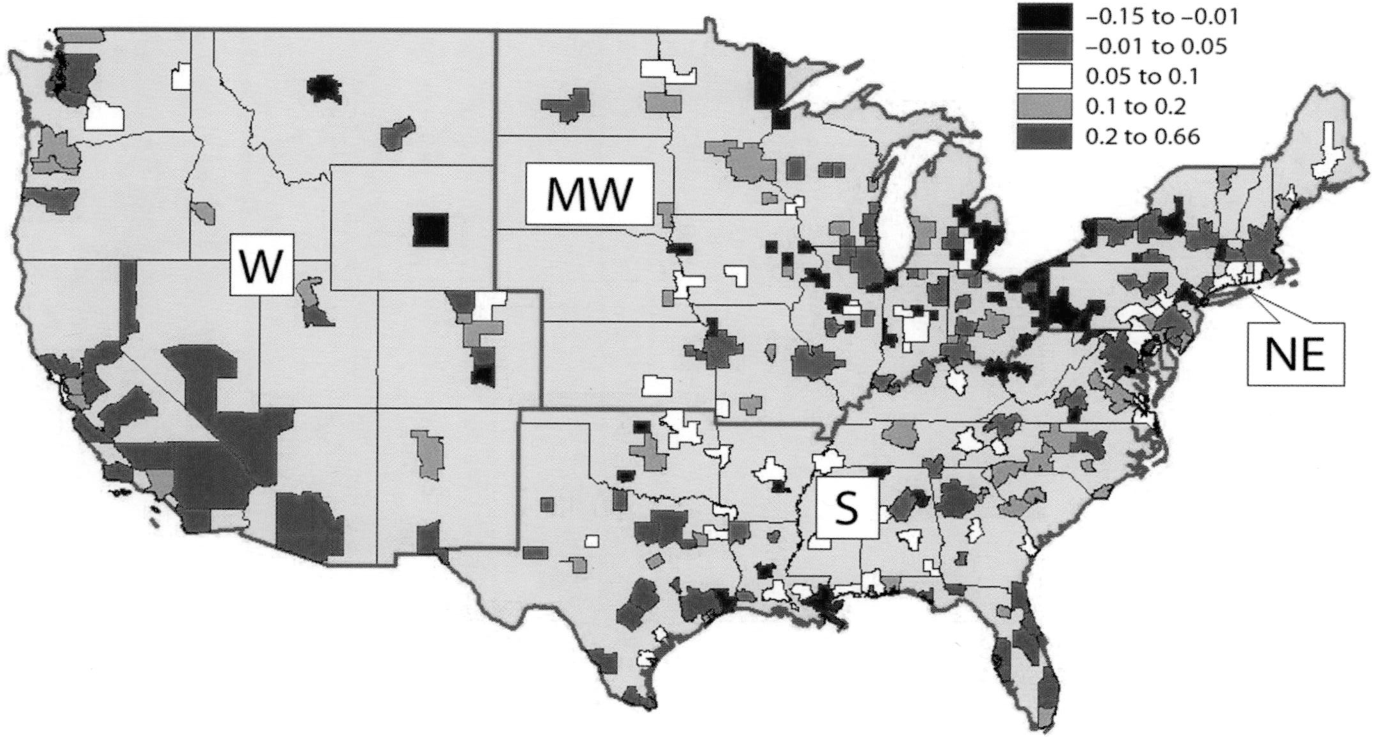

Legend:
- −0.15 to −0.01
- −0.01 to 0.05
- 0.05 to 0.1
- 0.1 to 0.2
- 0.2 to 0.66

Map 1-4. *Percent Change in Suburban Population in the 1960s*

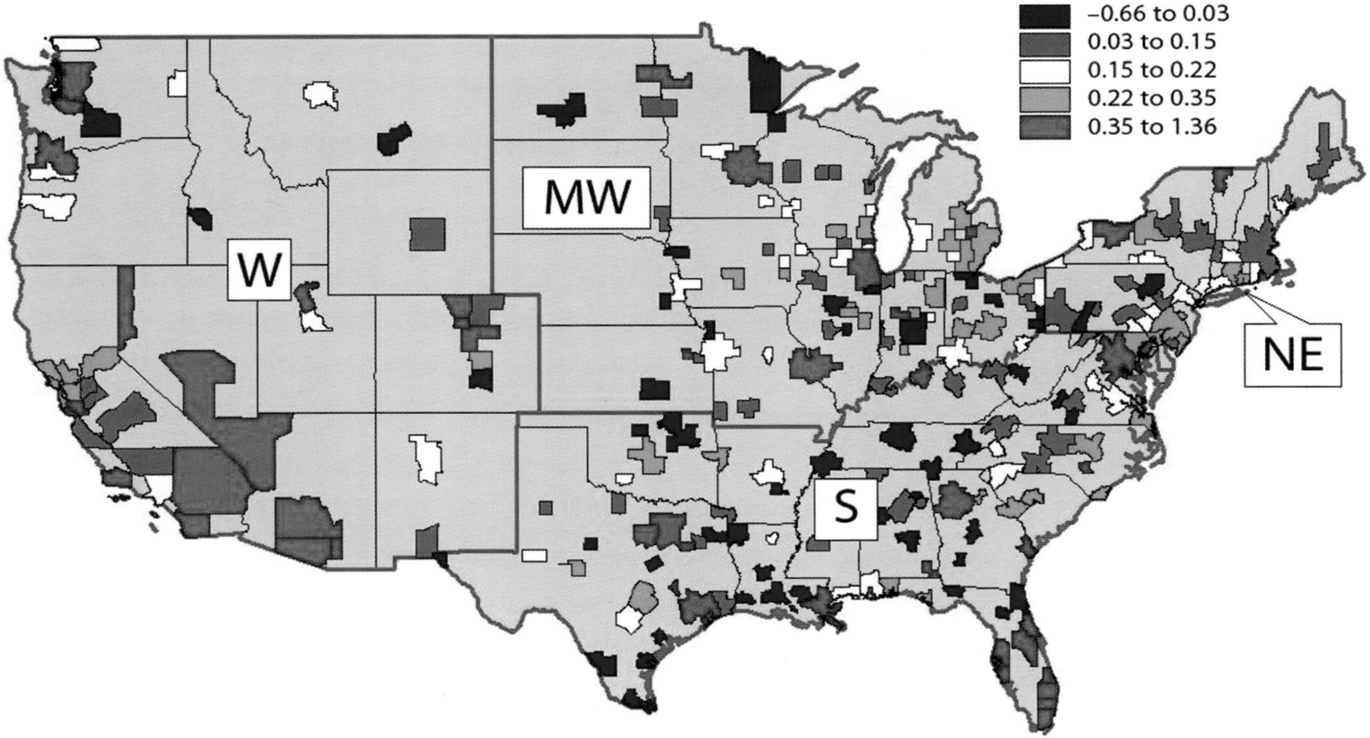

Legend:
- −0.66 to 0.03
- 0.03 to 0.15
- 0.15 to 0.22
- 0.22 to 0.35
- 0.35 to 1.36

Map 1-5. *Percent Change in Suburban Population in the 1970s*

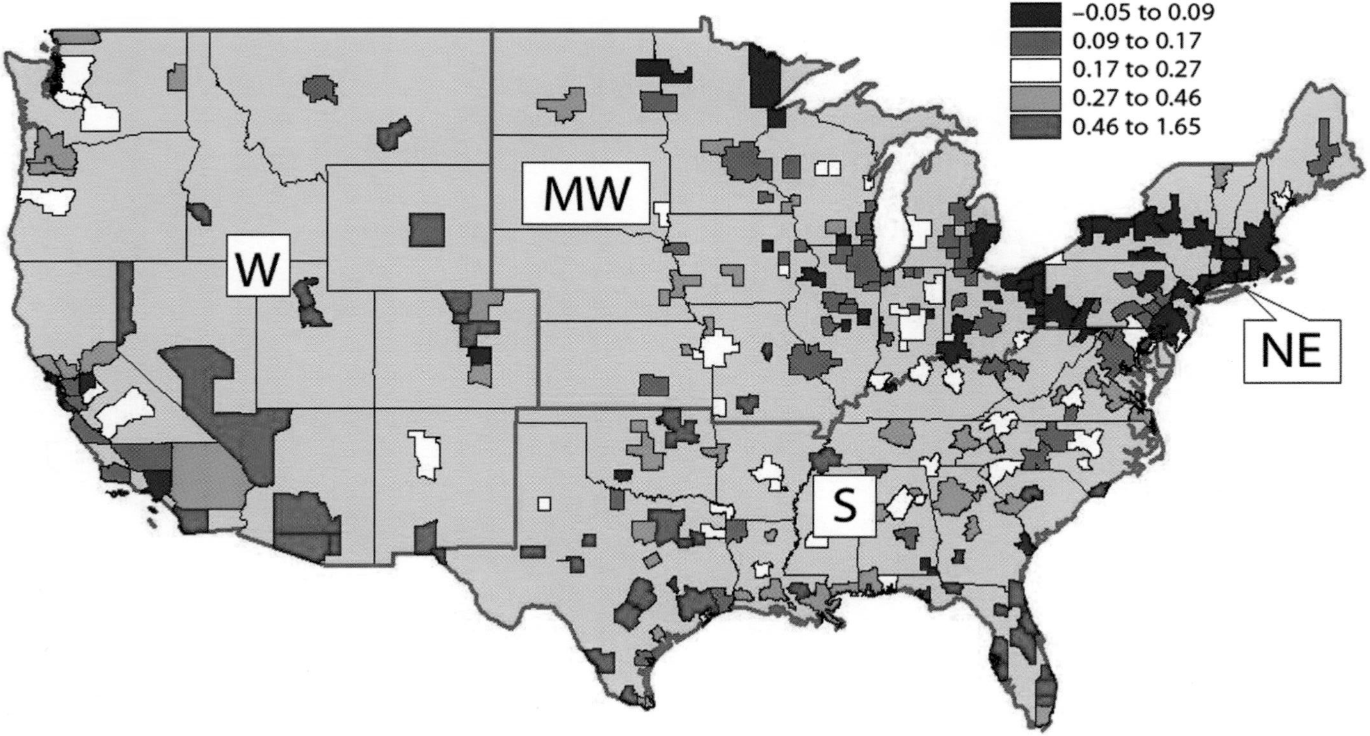

−0.05 to 0.09
0.09 to 0.17
0.17 to 0.27
0.27 to 0.46
0.46 to 1.65

NE

S

MW

W

Map 1-6. *Percent Change in Suburban Population in the 1980s*

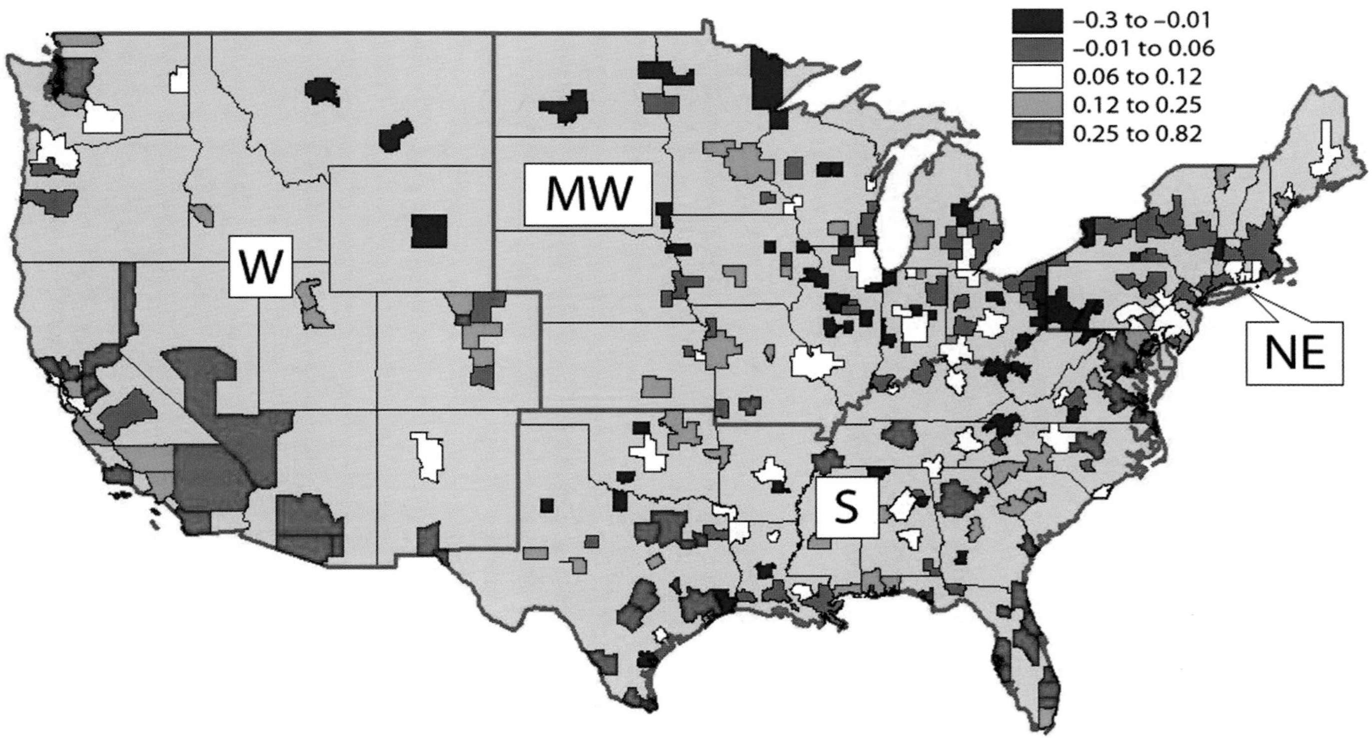

Legend:
- -0.3 to -0.01
- -0.01 to 0.06
- 0.06 to 0.12
- 0.12 to 0.25
- 0.25 to 0.82

Map 1-7. *Percent Change in City Population in the 1960s*

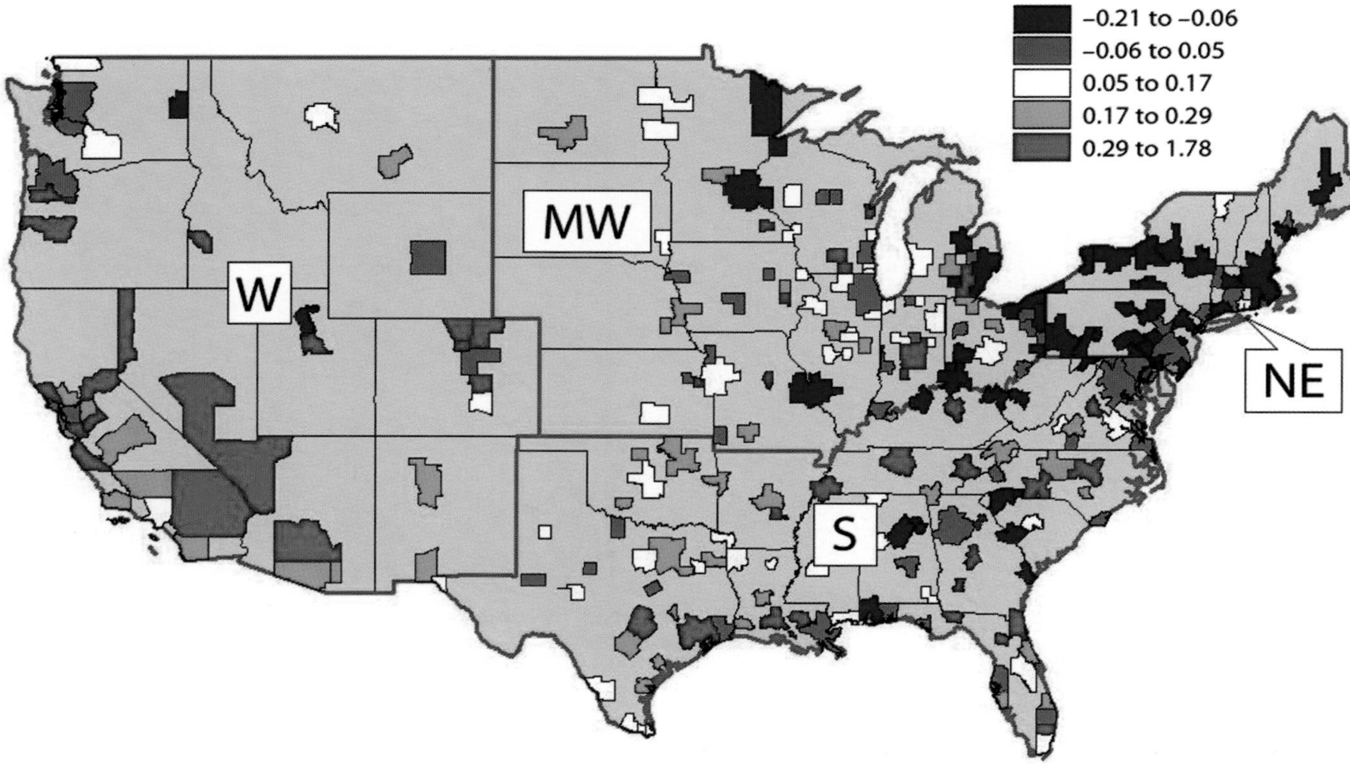

Legend:
- -0.21 to -0.06
- -0.06 to 0.05
- 0.05 to 0.17
- 0.17 to 0.29
- 0.29 to 1.78

Map 1-8. *Percent Change in City Population in the 1970s*

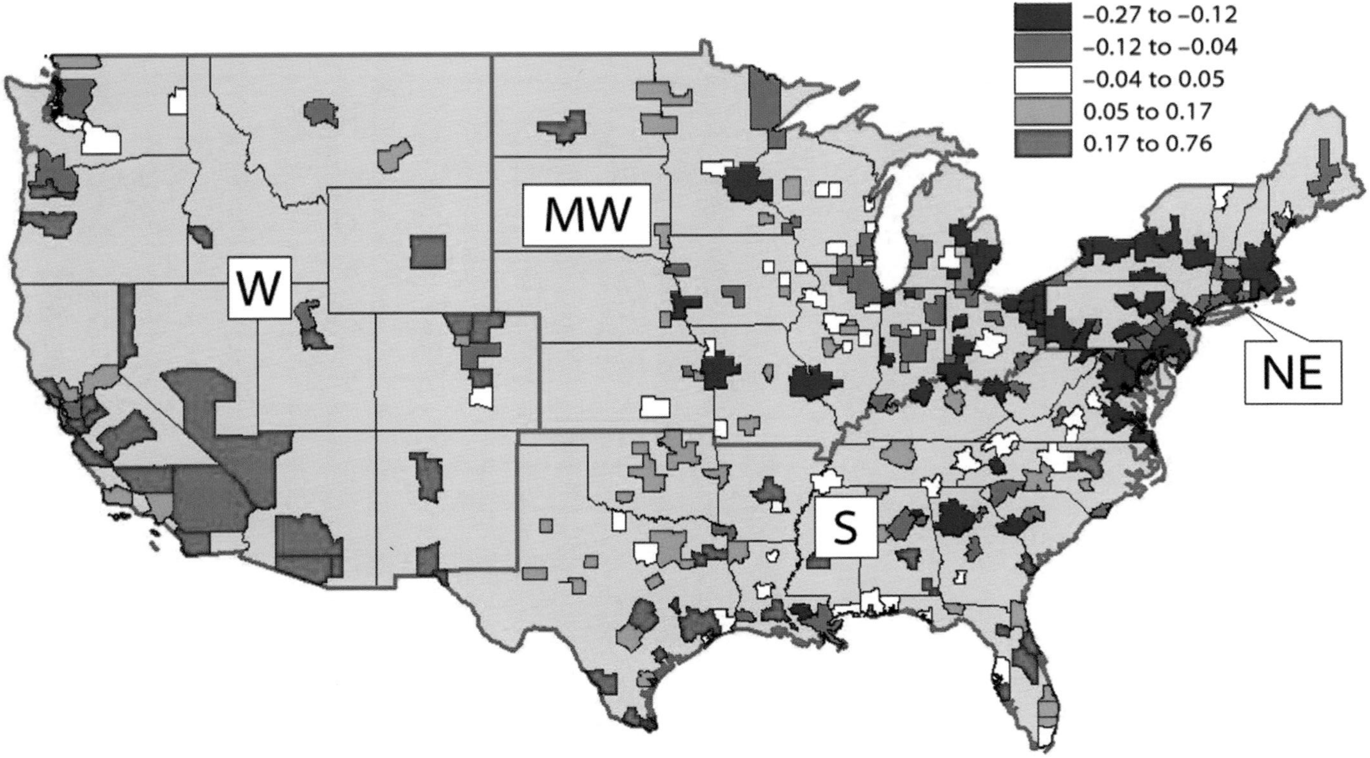

Legend:
- −0.27 to −0.12
- −0.12 to −0.04
- −0.04 to 0.05
- 0.05 to 0.17
- 0.17 to 0.76

Map 1-9. *Percent Change in City Population in the 1980s*

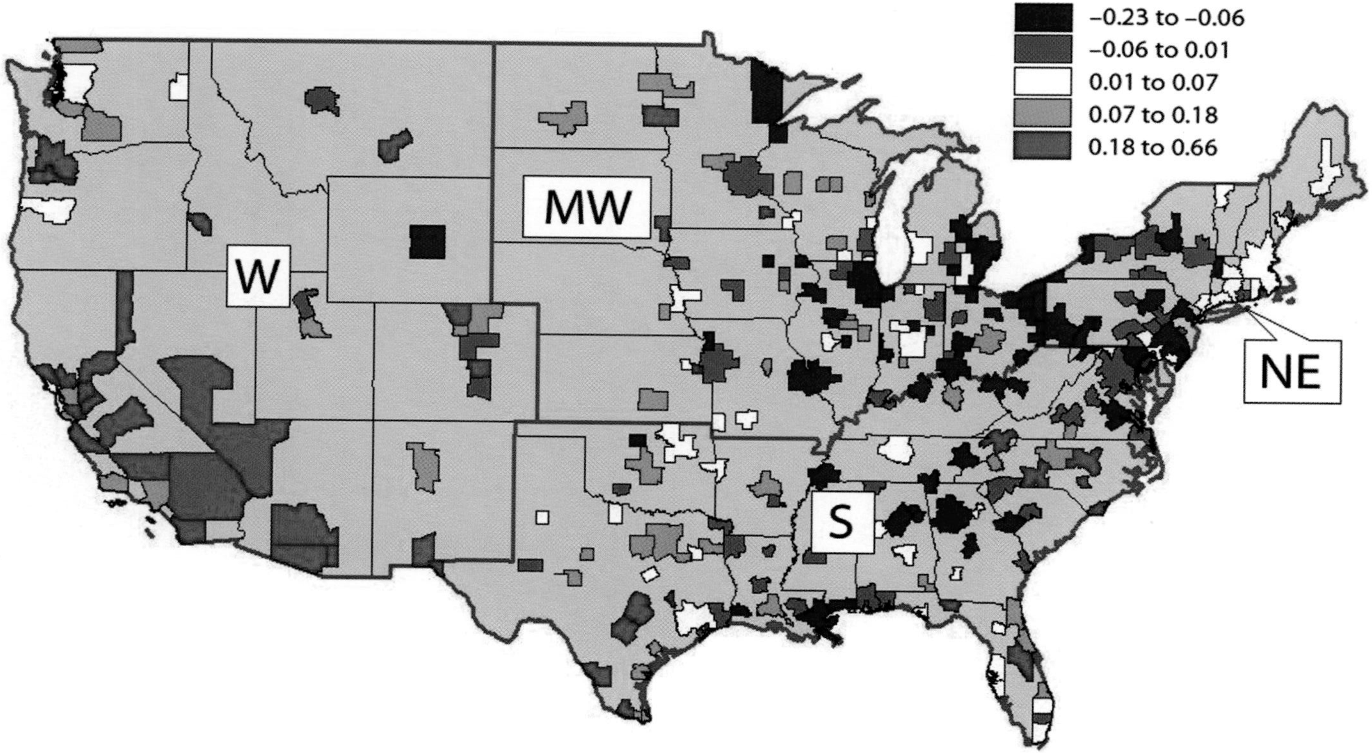

Map 1-10. *Percent Change in Metropolitan Income per Capita in the 1960s*

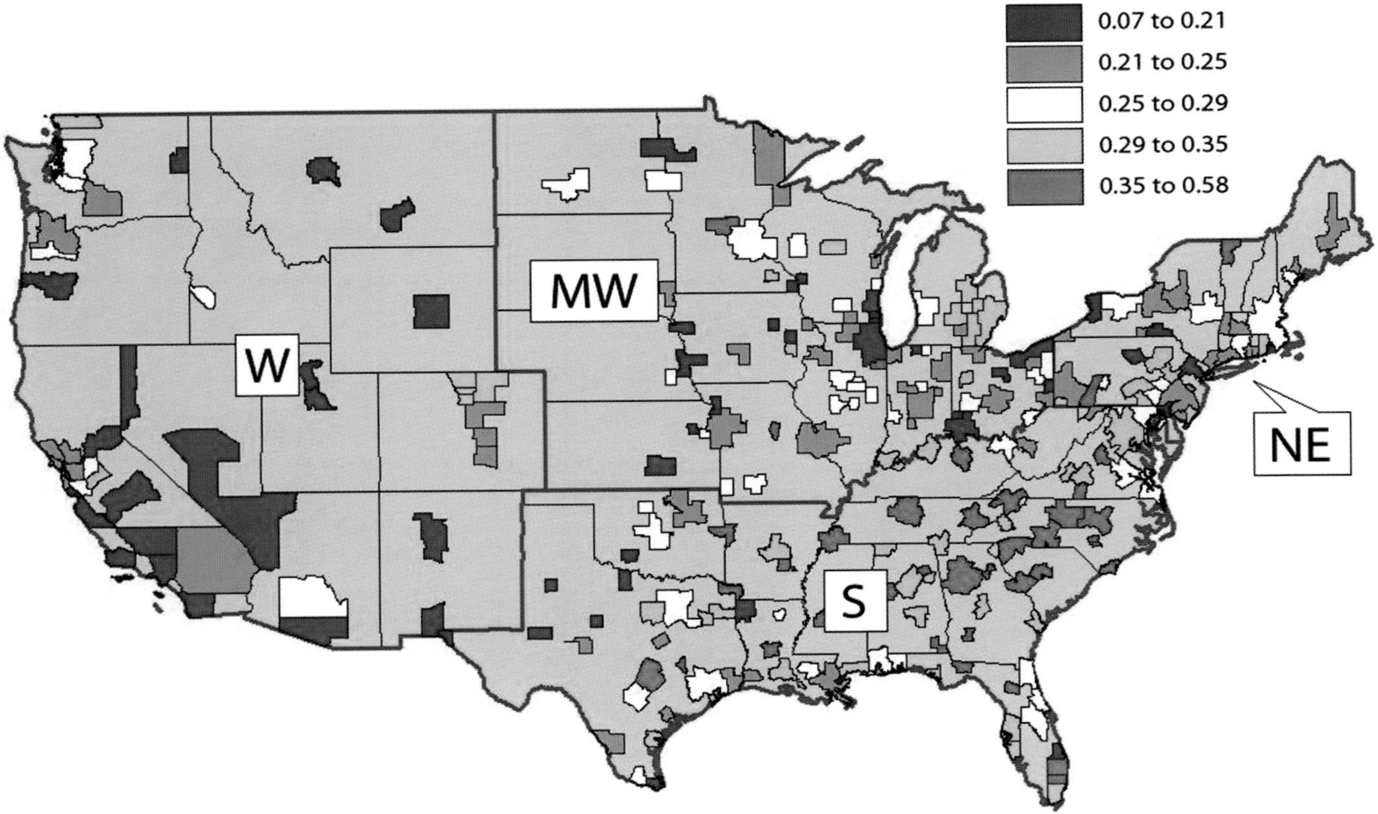

Legend:
- 0.07 to 0.21
- 0.21 to 0.25
- 0.25 to 0.29
- 0.29 to 0.35
- 0.35 to 0.58

NE

S

MW

W

Map 1-11. *Percent Change in Metropolitan Income per Capita in the 1970s*

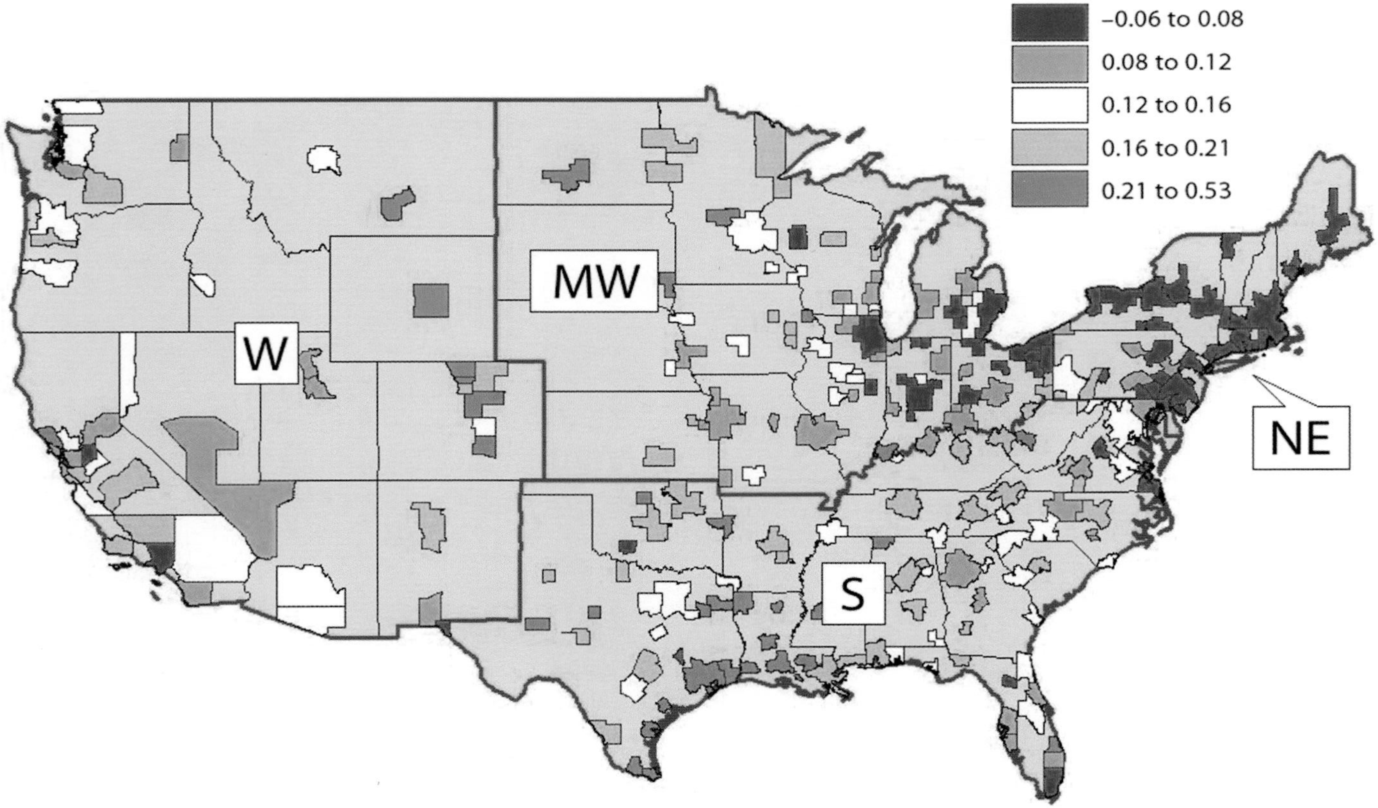

Legend:
- −0.06 to 0.08
- 0.08 to 0.12
- 0.12 to 0.16
- 0.16 to 0.21
- 0.21 to 0.53

Map 1-12.  *Percent Change in Metropolitan Income per Capita in the 1980s*

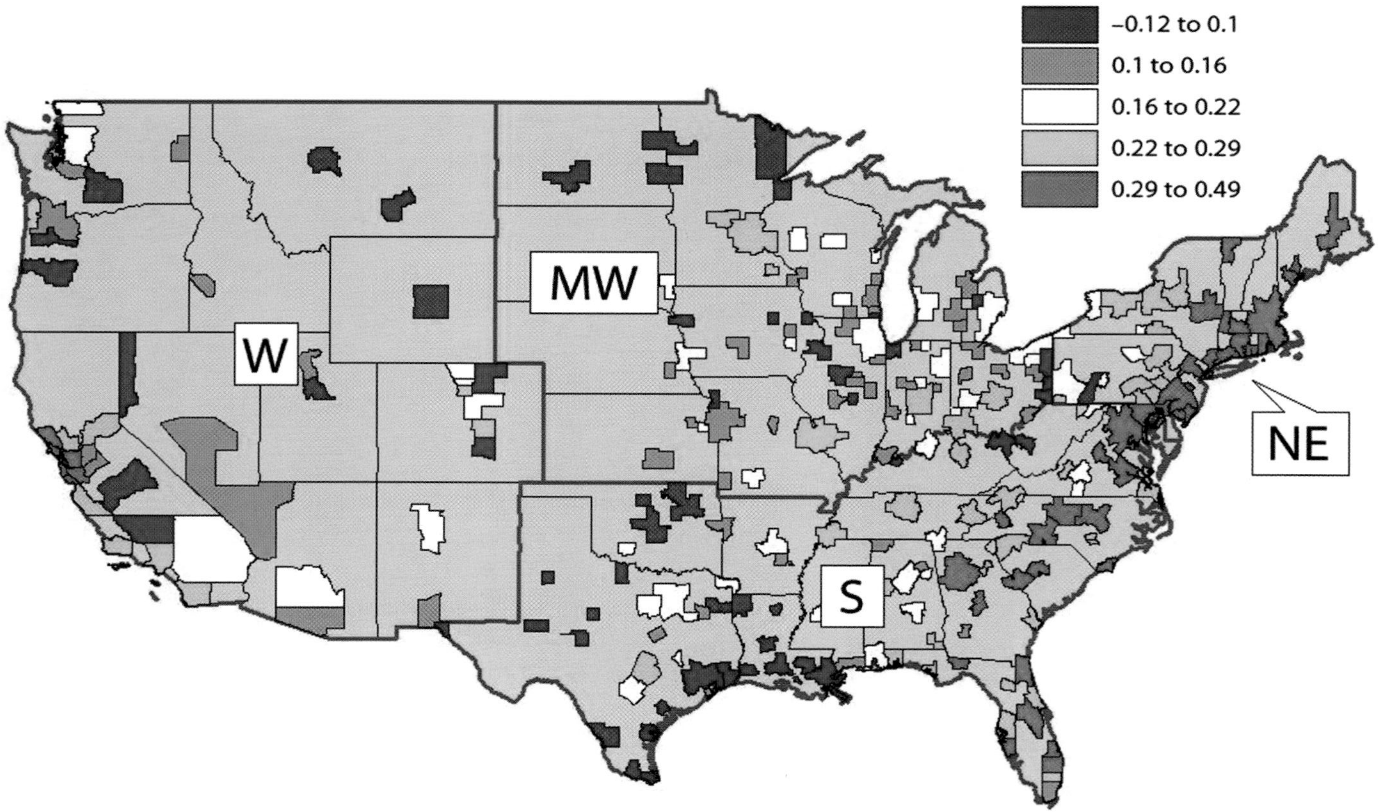

Legend:
- −0.12 to 0.1
- 0.1 to 0.16
- 0.16 to 0.22
- 0.22 to 0.29
- 0.29 to 0.49

NE

S

MW

W

Map 1-13. *Percent Change in Suburban Income per Capita in the 1960s*

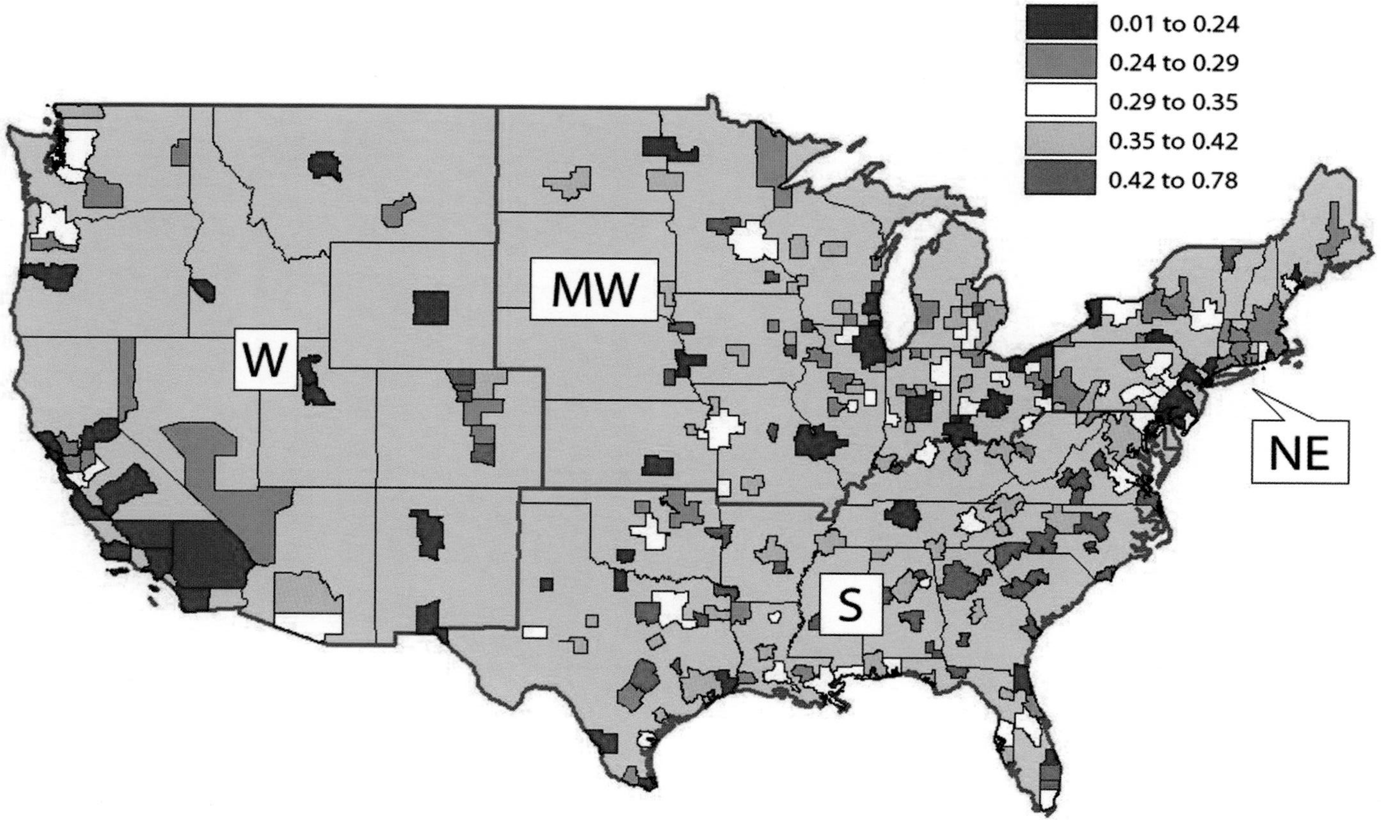

Legend:
- 0.01 to 0.24
- 0.24 to 0.29
- 0.29 to 0.35
- 0.35 to 0.42
- 0.42 to 0.78

NE

S

MW

W

Map 1-14. *Percent Change in Suburban Income per Capita in the 1970s*

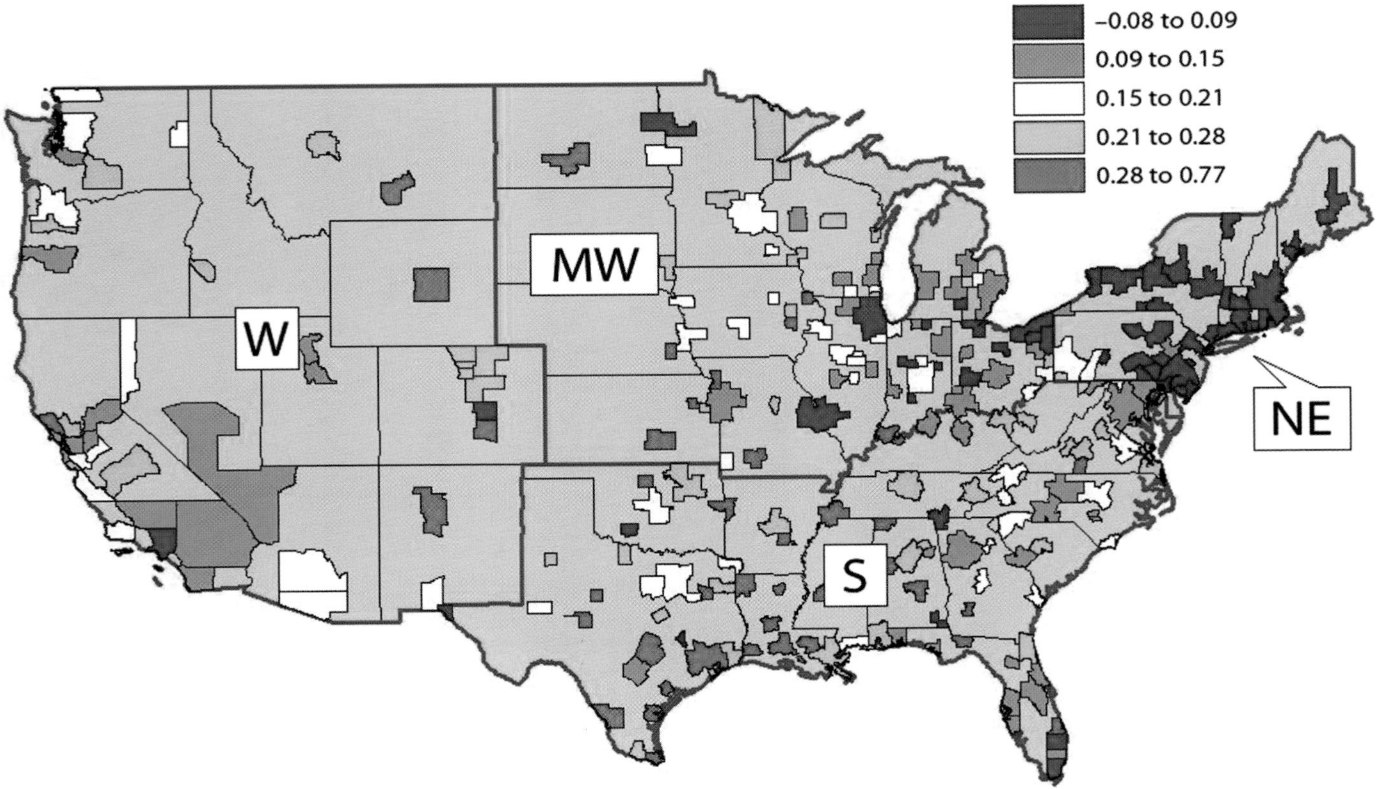

-0.08 to 0.09
0.09 to 0.15
0.15 to 0.21
0.21 to 0.28
0.28 to 0.77

NE

MW

W

S

Map 1-15.  *Percent Change in Suburban Income per Capita in the 1980s*

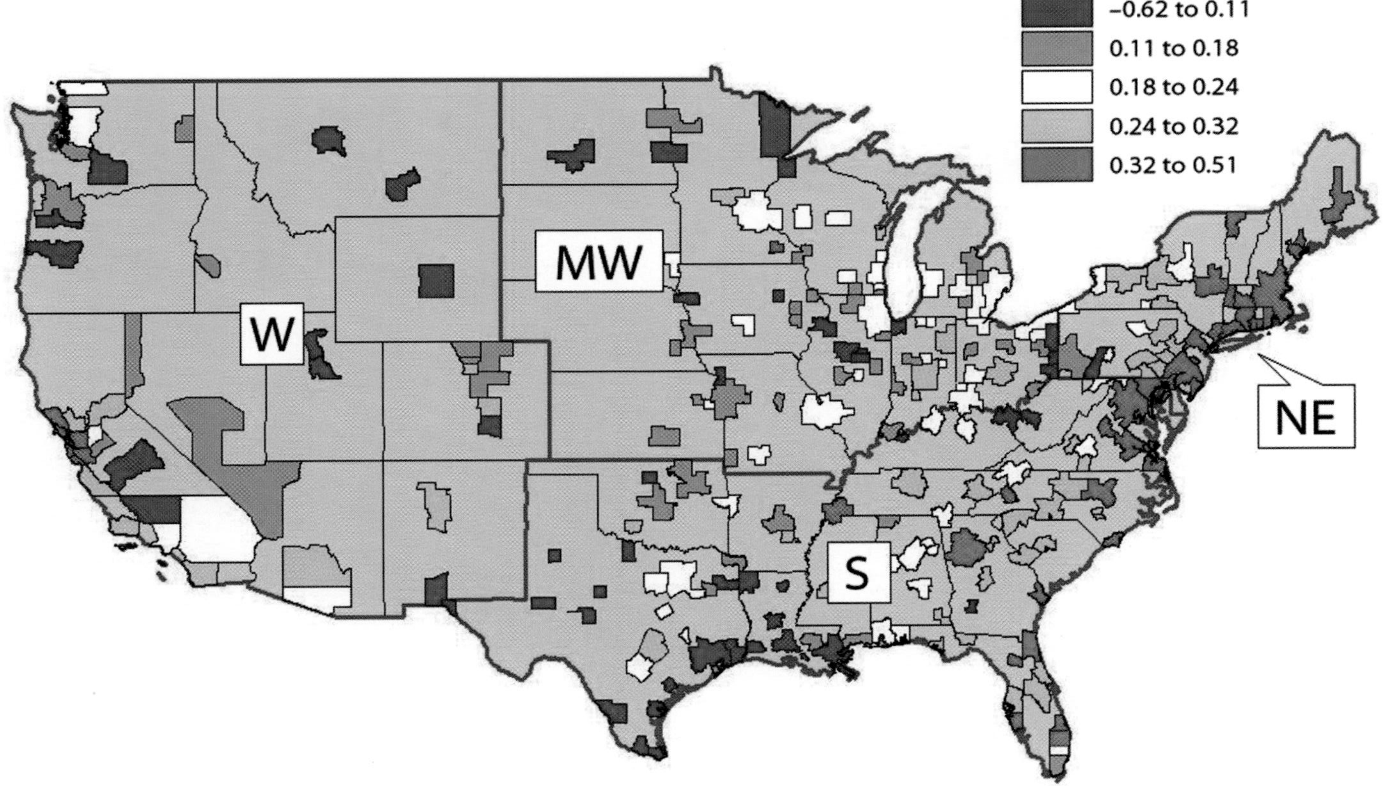

-0.62 to 0.11
0.11 to 0.18
0.18 to 0.24
0.24 to 0.32
0.32 to 0.51

Map 1-16. *Percent Change in City Income per Capita in the 1960s*

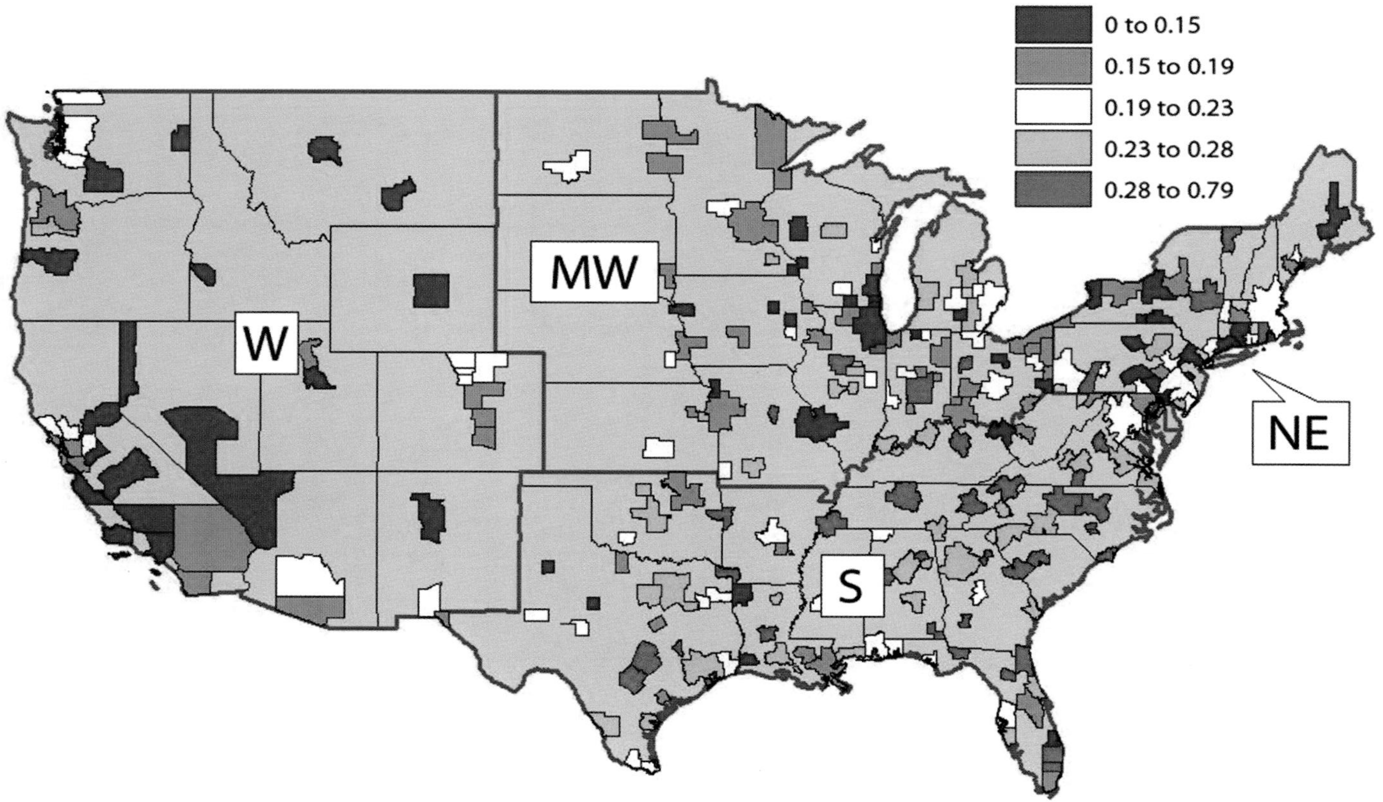

Legend:
- 0 to 0.15
- 0.15 to 0.19
- 0.19 to 0.23
- 0.23 to 0.28
- 0.28 to 0.79

Map 1-17. *Percent Change in City Income per Capita in the 1970s*

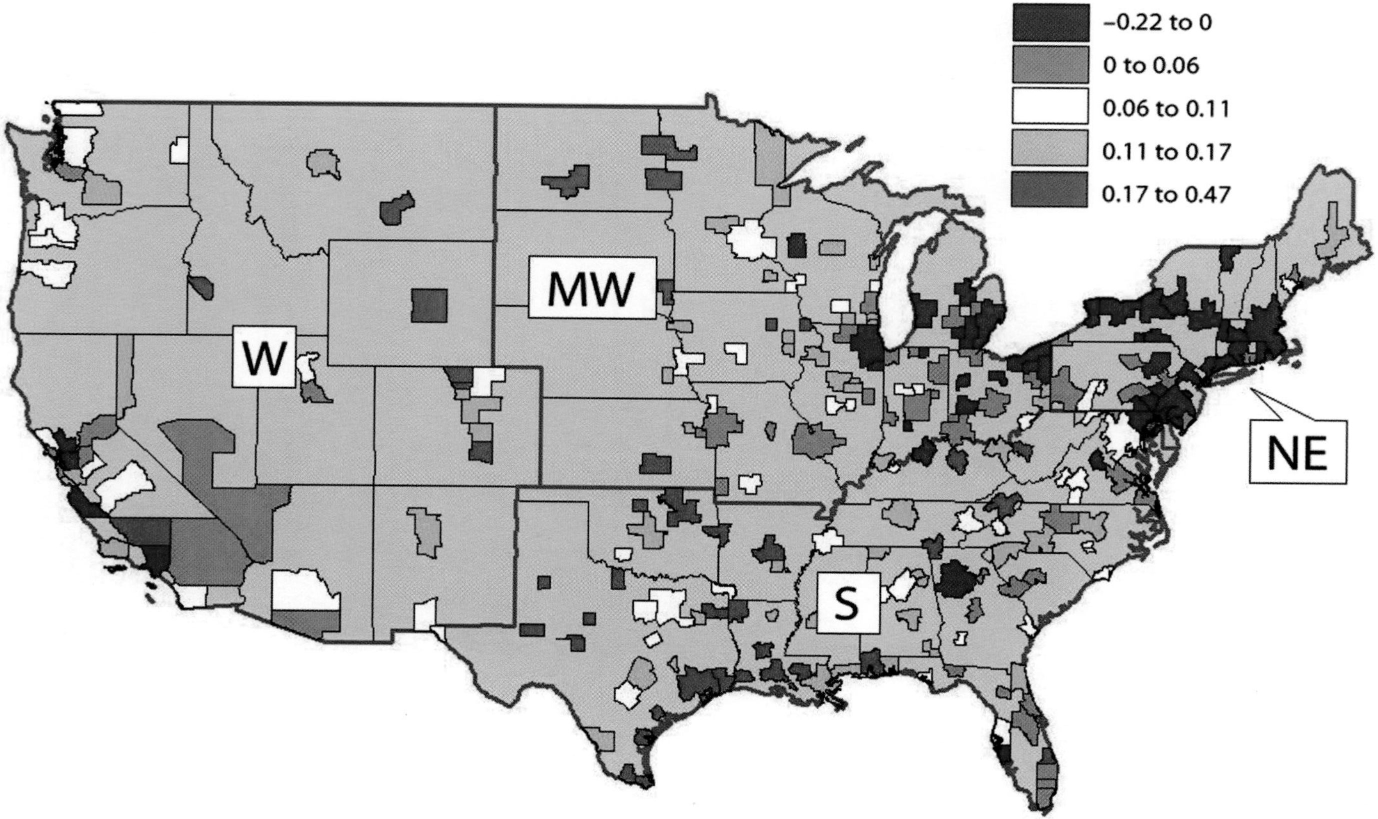

Legend:
- −0.22 to 0
- 0 to 0.06
- 0.06 to 0.11
- 0.11 to 0.17
- 0.17 to 0.47

Map 1-18. *Percent Change in City Income per Capita in the 1980s*

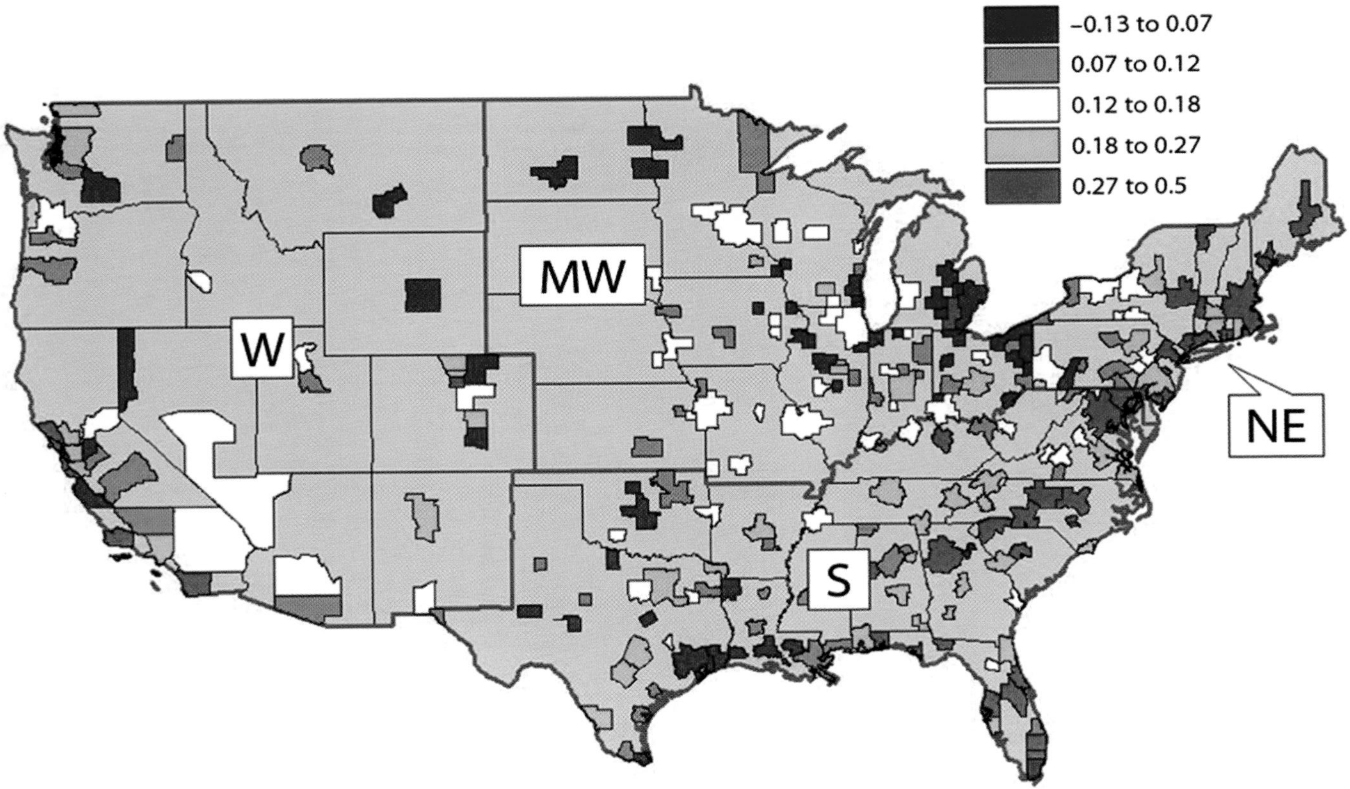

Legend:
- -0.13 to 0.07
- 0.07 to 0.12
- 0.12 to 0.18
- 0.18 to 0.27
- 0.27 to 0.5

NE

S

MW

W

Figure 1-5. *Percentage Change in City and Suburban Population, by Region, 1960s*

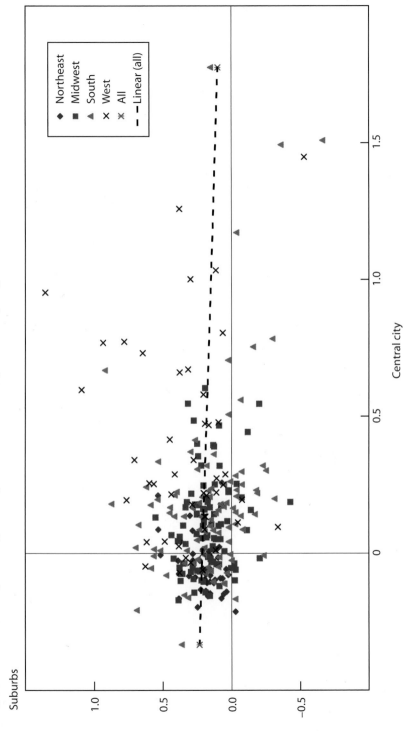

Suburbs

Central city

Northeast
Midwest
South
West
All
Linear (all)

Note: Horizontal axis varies between figures 1-5 and 1-10.

**Figure 1-6.  Percentage Change in City and Suburban Population, by Region, 1970s**

Suburbs

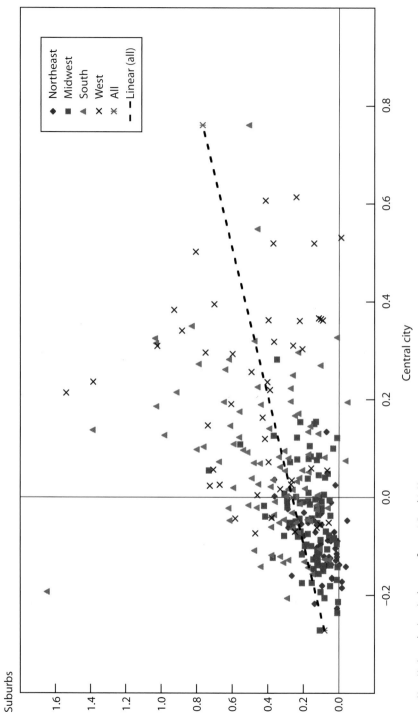

Central city

Note: Horizontal axis varies between figures 1-5 and 1-10.

**Figure 1-7. *Percentage Change in City and Suburban Population, by Region, 1980s***

Suburbs

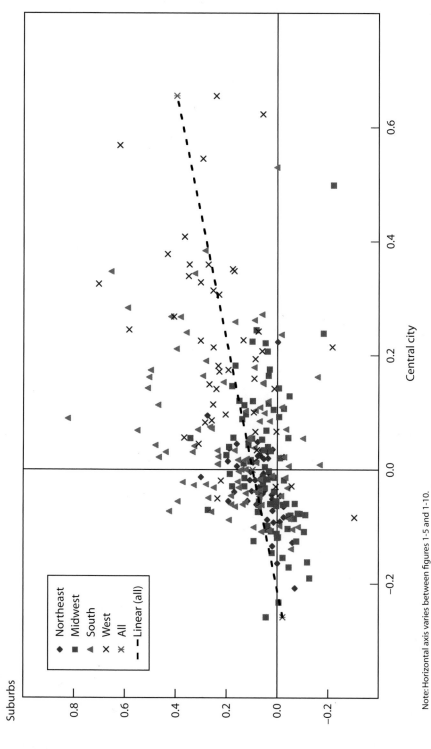

Central city

Note: Horizontal axis varies between figures 1-5 and 1-10.

**Figure 1-8.** *Percentage Change in City and Suburban per Capita Income, by Region, 1960s*

Suburbs

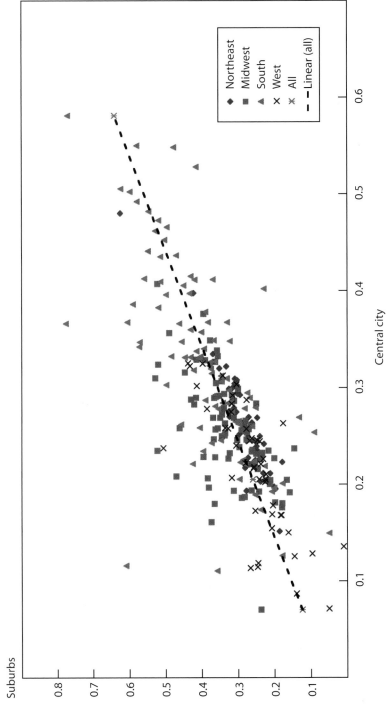

Central city

Note: Horizontal axis varies between figures 1-5 and 1-10.

**Figure 1-9. *Percentage Change in City and Suburban per Capita Income, by Region, 1970s***

Suburbs

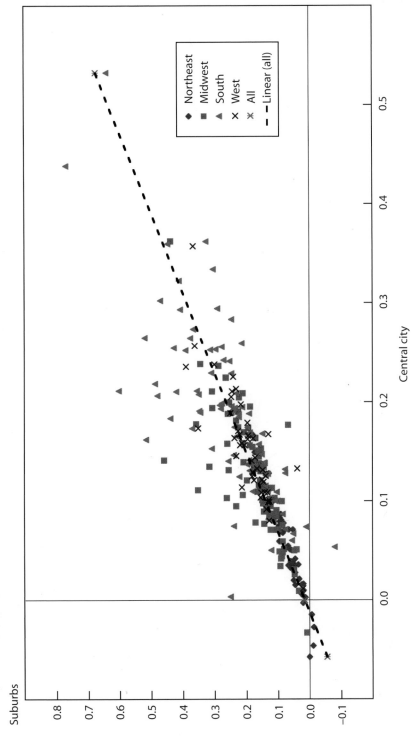

Central city

Note: Horizontal axis varies between figures 1-5 and 1-10.

**Figure 1-10.  Percentage Change in City and Suburban per Capita Income, by Region, 1980s**

Suburbs

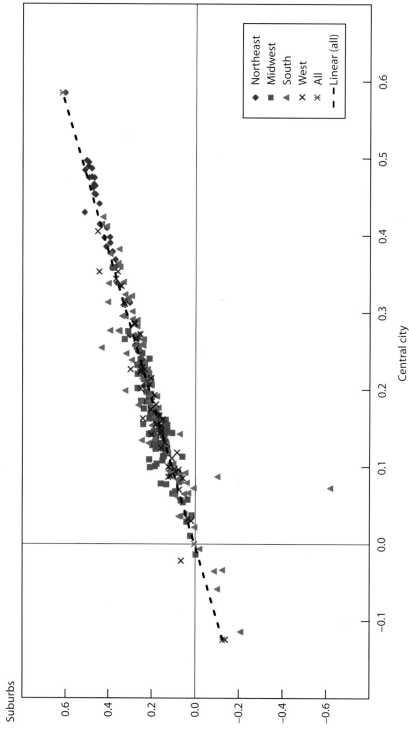

Central city

Northeast
Midwest
South
West
All
Linear (all)

Note: Horizontal axis varies between figures 1-5 and 1-10.

## Intrametropolitan versus Intermetropolitan Orientation: Analysis and Policy Implications

To analyze urban development and formulate a richer set of urban policies, it is necessary to investigate how the interregional differences in
growth rates affect the principal outcomes of concern, that is, the indicators of the well-being of the population: poverty rates, educational attainment, unemployment rates, and per capita income. The intraregional and
interregional perspectives are tied together in the description and analysis of interregional differences and the ways in which they affect intraregional links and the fortunes of metropolitan areas.

### Differing Perspectives: Intrametropolitan

Figures 1-5 through 1-10 (see color plates) provide a way of contrast-
ing the focus on intrametropolitan differences compared with interregional differences and point to much of what requires explanation. They
show the growth in population (figures 1-5 through 1-7) and per capita
income (figures 1-8 through 1-10) of cities and their suburbs within metropolitan areas, by census region and by decade, for the period 1960–90.
Analysts who view the city-suburban link as the critical one for public
policy rely on data and graphs like these that demonstrate the positive
correlations between growth in cities and suburbs within metropolitan
areas (as indicated by the dashed regression line; the only exception to the
positive relationship is that for city and suburban population growth in
the 1960s, when the relationship was insignificantly negative). The correlations are used to support the view that the growth of cities and the
growth of suburbs are complementary.[21]

What can be inferred from the positive correlations between city and
suburban growth rates found in the recent research? The conclusion that
the fates of suburbs and their central cities are intertwined—the "linkage" view—is convincing. The stronger conclusion that healthy suburbs
require healthy cities seems premature. Consider data from a study by the
U.S. Department of Transportation of thirty-nine large metropolitan
areas. The proportion of central-county residents (*note*: not identical to
central city) working in the suburban counties increased between 1980
and 1990 by 2.5 percent, and central-county residents working in the

---

21. This literature is examined in chapter 2.

central county declined by a similar percentage, implying that, nationally, the core city is continuing to lose its importance as a source of employment. In some of the older cities the decline was marked; for example, in Baltimore and Saint Louis, the proportion of central-county residents working in the central county fell by 10 percent in one decade.[22] In addition, the percentage of suburban residents working outside the central county, in other suburban counties, or entirely outside the metropolitan area increased from 16 percent to 20 percent. Individual MSAs had very large shifts; for example, in Washington, D.C., the proportion of suburban residents working in the central county fell from 30 percent in 1980 to 23 percent in 1990; in Baltimore it declined from 29 percent to 20 percent; and in Atlanta it declined from 34 percent to 28 percent. Moreover, these shifts occurred despite a slowdown in the loss of population and an increase in population in some of these older cities. The metropolitan areas that showed large increases in the proportion of suburban residents working in the central county were mainly in the faster-growing regions—in Houston, for example, the proportion increased over the decade from 33 percent to 40 percent. No causality should be inferred.

### Differing Perspectives: Interregional

The regional perspective or intermetropolitan focus can also be seen in these figures. The low population growth rates of the metropolitan areas of the Northeast and Midwest are graphically illustrated in figures 1-5 through 1-7. Many of their cities have declining populations, and their metropolitan areas are relatively tightly clustered. Within these two regions metropolitan areas experience relatively similar low growth (or decline). The South and West commonly have positive and high population growth rates in both cities and suburbs, but there is substantial intraregional variation among their metropolitan areas (maps 1-1 through 1-9). Moreover, contrary to the general pattern, there are many instances of city population growing more rapidly than suburban population in the South and West. Nonetheless, it is still the case that even in these regions, population is generally growing more rapidly in the suburbs than in the cities (figures 1-5 through 1-7).[23] There are two notable

---

22. Rossetti and Eversole (1993, tables 4-8, 4-8A, 4-9, and 4-9A).

23. The regional shifts are most outstanding in figures 1-2 and 1-4, described earlier, which show the average percentage of U.S. metropolitan population growth (figure 1-2) and income growth for cities and suburbs (figure 1-4) by census region and decade.

features of per capita income growth. The most striking is the regional difference between the 1970s, when the Northeastern metropolitan regions were tightly clustered at the lowest end of the per capita income growth scale, and the 1980s, when they shifted to the high end of the distribution (also discussed above in comparing maps 1-2 and 1-3)—a change that is taken into account in the analyses of the effects of growth rates on socioeconomic outcomes in chapter 3 and in chapter 4, in which the determinants of growth are estimated. The other change is the reduction in the variation among the metropolitan areas of the South, particularly in the suburbs (figures 1-6 and 1-7).

In the 1970s and early 1980s, the disparate fortunes of the Northeast and Midwest (the Frost Belt) and the South and West (the Sun Belt) were a source of considerable acrimony and a stimulus to analysis.[24] The implications of the enormous differences in growth rates among regions of the country have received less attention in recent discussions of urban policy despite the fact that the growth differences—those of population in particular—continue unabated. Between 1990 and 1996 (table 1-11), in the West the population of only one city among forty-three declined, and the average change was 10 percent. In the Northeast nearly all cities—thirty-one of thirty-six—experienced continued population declines, and the average change in city population was –4 percent. Even though suburban population growth was, on the average, positive in all regions, the differences were great, ranging from a low 2 percent average expansion in the suburbs of the metropolitan areas of the Northeast to 15 percent in the West. And even though in all regions average metropolitan populations increased, in the Northeast sixteen of thirty-six metropolitan areas had decreasing populations; in the West, only one of forty-three.[25] Census data for the period 1990–99 report the continued migration of population to the South, particularly to the South Atlantic states. The South as

24. This literature is described in chapter 2.
25. Looking only at cities, between 1990 and 1998, Bureau of the Census data show that the five fastest-growing cities with populations of 1 million or more were all in the Sun Belt: three in Texas, one in Arizona, and one in California. Of the twenty-six cities with populations of 500,000 or more, fifteen are in the South or West, and of these six had population growth rates of 10 percent or more over these eight years. Of the eleven cities in the Northeast and Midwest, none had population increases of more than 10 percent over the period; only one grew by more than 5 percent; and in five the population declined. U.S. Census Bureau, "Phoenix and San Antonio Lead Largest Cities in Growth; Small Cities Grow Fastest, Census Bureau Reports." Press Release, June 30, 1999.

**Table 1-11.** *Population Change by Region, 1990–96*

Units as indicated

| Region | Mean percentage change | Number of MSAs declining[a] | Number of MSAs growing[a] |
|---|---|---|---|
| Metropolitan | | | |
| Northeast | 6 | 16 | 20 |
| Midwest | 11 | 11 | 66 |
| South | 18 | 9 | 85 |
| West | 16 | 1 | 42 |
| | | | |
| City | | | |
| Northeast | −4 | 31 | 5 |
| Midwest | 1 | 39 | 38 |
| South | 5 | 28 | 66 |
| West | 10 | 1 | 42 |
| | | | |
| Suburban | | | |
| Northeast | 2 | 14 | 22 |
| Midwest | 7 | 4 | 73 |
| South | 10 | 5 | 89 |
| West | 15 | 2 | 41 |

Source: U.S. Department of Commerce, Bureau of the Census.

a. Number of MSAs in each region: Northeast, 36; Midwest, 77; South, 94; West, 43.

a whole absorbed a net migration of 3.6 million persons; the Northeast and Midwest together lost 3.7 million persons to net migration; and the West gained 100,000 new migrants.[26]

### Policy Implications of the Two Perspectives

In thinking about policy, historical perspective must be added to the discussion. In the 1960s, a period of rapid postwar growth, the country was still playing catch-up in housing. After the depression of the 1930s and the war years of the 1940s, one of the primary consumption items in the vigorous postwar recovery was new housing. Crowded cities contrasted with suburbs with an abundance of vacant land, new infrastructure, and open space. Suburbs were the place to build the new single-

26. U.S. Census Bureau data. David Firestone, "Population Shifts in the Southeast Realign the Politics of the Suburbs," *New York Times*, June 3, 2000, p. A1.

family homes. In comparison, the 1970s were years in which major concern shifted to a "new war between the states" and the far more rapid growth of the states in the South and West than of those in the North and Midwest.[27] Intense regional rivalry, particularly about "unfair" federal taxation and expenditure policies that allegedly discriminated against some regions, became a major policy issue. Despite continuing regional growth differences, the regional consciousness-raising of the 1970s has disappeared. City-suburban disparities now preoccupy the interacting agendas of policymakers and policy analysts.

Notwithstanding this shift in view, the positive relationships between growth in cities and growth in suburbs may still be more closely related to interregional shifts than to intraregional relationships. If households and firms are moving from the North to the South, both the cities and suburbs in the South will be growing more rapidly (or the cities declining less) than those in the North.

INTRAMETROPOLITAN POLICY FOCUS. A concern with intrametropolitan shifts leads to consideration of the important socioeconomic differences between central cities and their suburbs. Although the heterogeneity of suburbs is generally greater than is commonly understood, nevertheless central cities are generally poorer than their suburban neighbors.[28] Cities are not only poorer on average, they also house disproportionate numbers of persons with incomes below the poverty level and exhibit higher levels of unemployment and crime. Finally, cities are home to disproportionate numbers of minority groups and immigrants. Much, if not all, of this increased concentration of poverty is due to the movement out of the cities of middle- and upper-income households, rather than increased numbers of poor households in the cities.[29] This increased concentration of poverty in the central cities characterizes nearly all large metropolitan areas of the United States; whether metropolitan-area poverty rates are low or high, the poverty rates in the cities generally exceed by far those of the suburbs. Associated with this increased poverty concentration are increased tax burdens on the nonpoor who remain in the cities.[30] The overwhelming evidence is that the increased tax burdens

27. Coelen (1978); Haveman and Stanfield (1977); Jusenius and Ledebur (1976); Nourse (1968); Olson (1976); Pack (1980); Perry and Watkins (1977); Peterson (1977); and Weinstein and Firestine (1978).
28. Orfield (1997); Pack and Pack (1977).
29. Pack (1998).
30. Pack (1998); Summers and Jakubowski (1996).

cannot be sustained, as they provide an additional incentive for further movement of the nonpoor out of the cities, higher tax burdens on those remaining, and further movement.[31]

A focus on the linkage between cities and suburbs has produced a policy agenda that emphasizes the provision of incentives for greater intrametropolitan (city-suburb) cooperation. Among the coordinated policies suggested are infrastructure planning and financing, tax base sharing, school finance reform, school district consolidation, and land-use planning (directed against urban sprawl and interjurisdictional competition).[32] Nonetheless, intrametropolitan cooperation is still generally viewed as largely in the interests of cities. There are relatively few examples of significant cooperation, and the potential efficacy of local programs—even if metropolitan area–wide—is unclear.[33]

Skeptical views are often reflected in the news coverage, editorials, and letters to the editor in suburban newspapers. Two citations are typical. A 1995 editorial in the *Doylestown (Pennsylvania) Intelligencer* reflects the strong but quite typical view of most suburban communities that there is little, if any, link between the life, economies, and social development of cities and suburbs within metropolitan areas.[34] A 1995 series of articles in the *Philadelphia Inquirer* illustrated the equally common view that the city's losses are the suburbs' gains.[35]

INTERREGIONAL POLICY FOCUS. To illustrate a major policy issue that arises from interregional growth differences, one can consider metropolitan areas in regions that are not growing or are growing very slowly. If the more rapid growth observed in Phoenix and San Jose is attributable to region-specific factors—climate in the one and the proximity of Stanford University in the other—then promoting city-suburb cooperation in Bridgeport or Milwaukee is hardly likely to transform them into Sun City or Silicon Valley.[36]

31. Bradbury, Downs, and Small (1981); Inman (1992).
32. Carter Center (1997); Katz (1998, 2000); Ledebur and Barnes (1992, 1993); Rusk (1995, 1999); U.S. Department of Housing and Urban Development (1997, 1998). See also Lang and Hornburg (1997).
33. Summers (2000).
34. "We're Not Sold on Regionalism," *Doylestown (Pa.) Intelligencer,* January 29, 1995, p. C2.
35. "Jobs and the Economy: City Losses, Regional Gains," *Philadelphia Inquirer,* 1995.
36. This is not to argue that intrametropolitan cooperation may not be a useful tool for dealing with some intrametropolitan issues, for example, taking advantage of economies of scale in the provision of some public capital and services.

The intrametropolitan policy recommendations and their sources of support and opposition are presented to acknowledge the current thrust of much of urban research and policy. The departure in this book is to demonstrate that these city-suburban linkages cannot be considered apart from the determinants of metropolitan growth differences among regions. As indicated earlier, there is little evidence that state and local policy—coordinated or not—can have much influence on metropolitan growth.[37] Therefore, this analysis is focused on the determinants of regional growth. This undergirds a discussion of the possible role of public-policy intervention in the growth process and a consideration of whether federal policy, in contrast to state or local policy, might be directed toward reducing interregional growth differences as a means of improving the welfare of metropolitan areas.

From this discussion it can be concluded that it is critical to investigate the regional shifts in population and economic activity, the continued differences in growth rates, and their implications for urban development in different regions. The evidence of recent decades suggests that the region in which a metropolitan area is located may have more to do with its prospects than efforts to improve intrametropolitan cooperation. If Buffalo, New York, and its suburbs—with its topography, education, unemployment, and skill levels of 1960—had been scooped up by a giant moving device and deposited in Florida or Arizona, the city and suburbs would have done much better than they did in New York even had they enacted ideal cooperative arrangements. Such a broad statement may be somewhat of an exaggeration, as there were certainly success stories in the older regions. In the chapters that follow, an attempt is made to assess the validity of such views and to assess the importance of metropolitan-area conditions relative to those of the region in determining the vibrancy of a city and its suburbs.

## The Plan of the Book

In chapter 2, the literature on interregional growth differences and city-suburban growth linkages are examined more closely. Recognizing the differences in growth across regions and between decades is critical to the examination in chapter 3 of the relationship between differential

37. Bradbury, Kodrzycki, and Tannenwald (1997); Fisher and Peters (1997); Flynn (1997); Tannenwald (1997); and Wasylenko (1997).

metropolitan growth rates and socioeconomic variables in cities and suburbs; poverty, income inequality, unemployment rates, and educational attainment. If rapid regional growth rates have a positive influence on poverty rates and reduce the income inequality between central cities and their suburbs, then variation in regional growth rates from decade to decade must be explicitly taken into account in the estimation. Also addressed in chapter 3 is the question of whether the most rapidly growing metropolitan areas are characterized by the same types of city-suburban differentiation as older, slowly growing metropolitan areas.

The identification of major differences in growth rates by decade is also essential for the analysis of the determinants of differences in metropolitan growth rates in chapter 4. In light of the variation in the growth rates across decades, any attempt to explain variation in growth rates across metropolitan areas must consider that the factors explaining growth are likely to differ from decade to decade. In chapter 4 the effects of differences in human capital, differences in the structure of employment bases in metropolitan areas across regions, and numerous other factors, such as weather and the presence of research universities, are identified and analyzed.

The findings given in chapters 3 and 4 call for a closer examination in chapter 5 of the faster and more slowly growing metropolitan areas. The chapter examines the major distinguishing characteristics of these places. In addition, chapter 5 tries to go beyond the quantitative analysis of growth rates in chapter 4 to identify the qualitative factors that have played important roles in the growth process in particular places—those that are and those that are not amenable to policy intervention; the systematic and the idiosyncratic; and the replicable and the nonreplicable.

In chapter 6, the findings concerning growth and its relationship to public welfare are brought together to raise questions about the need for a regional policy and, if needed, what the elements of such a policy might be.

## CHAPTER TWO

# Interregional Differences: Characteristics and Explanations

I N CHAPTER I THE differences between viewing urban development from an intrametropolitan perspective and viewing it from an inter-regional perspective were highlighted. The intrametropolitan perspective reveals a strong correlation between growth rates of cities and those of their suburbs. Because of this, many analysts have concluded that it is in the interest of suburbs to cooperate with cities because the future growth of the suburbs depends on continued growth of their central cities. From the interregional perspective, rapid growth in metropolitan areas—both cities and suburbs—is found predominantly in the South and West. In the Northeast and Midwest, by contrast, metropolitan areas have been grow-ing much more slowly, and in many cases city population has actually declined. Indeed, although there is substantial correlation between cities and suburbs within regions, the correlation of city and suburban growth across all regions is higher, indicating the strong regional component behind the overall city-suburb correlations.

This chapter presents an examination of the literature on interregional differences in growth rates in metropolitan areas, cities, and suburbs.[1] One section explores the incorporation of regional considerations into

---

1. In chapter 4, models of differential metropolitan growth rates are estimated, taking into account specific differences among regions that are widely considered important factors propelling growth.

the city-suburb linkage literature. (The major contributions to the intra-metropolitan linkage literature are described in appendix B.)

## Explanations for Interregional Growth Differences

Cities originally grew at transportation nodes—ports, canals, and, later, intersections of rail lines; close to raw materials (for example, iron ore); or as service centers for an agricultural population. Once a city was established, agglomeration economies developed that stemmed from the pooling of labor, the growth of specialty producers, the easier flow of information, and other factors.[2] In recent decades, other forces, including climate and the existence of research universities or research enclaves have propelled regional growth. Some metropolitan areas have prospered, to some extent, on the basis of explicit or implicit policies of the federal government (for example, the subsidization of water for arid areas of the Southwest, the subsidization of highway construction, or the location of defense facilities). Given the initiating force and the ensuing agglomeration economies, a city and its region may encounter natural limits, for example, as the cost of congestion increases.

As indicated in chapter 1, the 1970s were a time when urban discussions were pervasively about the shifts among regions: decline or slow growth in the Northeast and Midwest and rapid growth in the South and West. There were several major explanations for these shifts that could account for the clear regional pattern in the metropolitan linkage found in city and suburban growth rates. The explanations are generally accepted as important in understanding the very large relocations of the post–World War II period.[3] Among the factors that accounted for the regional differences in growth in population and per capita income were the evolution of the industrial structure of the older urban areas, movement by retirees, relative cost differences for labor and land, and federal policies. In addition, the state of the national economy appears to have had important regional implications.

2. These factors have been eloquently analyzed by Marshall (1920).
3. This section draws on Pack (1980). Related studies are Coelen (1978); Haveman and Stanfield (1977); Jusenius and Ledebur (1976); Nourse (1968); Olson (1976); Perry and Watkins (1977); Peterson (1977); and Weinstein and Firestine (1978).

### Economic Maturity or Life-Cycle Models

The maturing of the industrial structure of older urban areas that had a concentration of their employment in slow-growing industries was one of the major hypotheses put forth in the 1970s for the slow growth of the Northeast and Midwest. However, numerous investigators concluded that the sectoral composition of employment in these regions was still favorable. Had their industries grown at the national rates, their growth rates would have been more rapid than they were in fact. A detailed "shift-share" analysis of employment growth in New York State between 1968 and 1973 showed that on the basis of its industrial structure in 1968 and national growth rates over the period, employment might have been expected to increase by just over 13 percent, very similar to the national growth rate of 12.5 percent. In fact, over these five years, employment in New York State grew by only 1 percent.[4] Similar studies for other periods and other places reached similar conclusions; it was not the maturing of the industrial base that accounted for the slow growth rates in the Northeast and Midwest.[5] These analyses were confined to the manufacturing sector only, which limits their value in analyzing the importance of what was then a rapidly changing economic base, which was shifting to a more service-oriented sector and to entirely new types of manufacturing activities. The increasing importance of several factors—the service sector, a more highly educated population, and the growing technology infrastructure—is explored in chapter 4.

### Cost Differences

Other studies sought the reasons for what was seen as a "competitive shift" in regional wage differences: firms set up new plants in low-wage areas, while skilled workers moved to areas where wages were higher. Both factors led to higher per capita income growth in the lower-wage areas, as the demand for workers increased in the low-wage areas and the number of skilled workers increased in the high-wage areas. The inference that it was lower wages that induced firms to move to the South implicitly assumes that differences in labor productivity did not offset the

---

4. Pack (1980).
5. Borts and Stein (1964); Bretzfelder (1973); Perloff and others (1960); Rees (1978).

wage differences. This is consistent with the types of industries that were in the forefront of the earliest waves of moves: generally industries using low-skilled workers—textile production and the manufacture of clothing, food processing—those least likely to experience differences in labor productivity sufficient to offset the wage differentials. These industries were more likely to be responsive to the absence of unionization of the labor force, which introduced into the production process work rules that added to the cost and reduced the flexibility of production alternatives. This was recognized in the *President's National Urban Policy Report*:

> A closer look at the types of manufacturing jobs that central cities have been losing will clarify the problems faced by older industrial cities. A recent study of the largest urban areas showed that cities such as St. Louis, Cleveland, Buffalo, and New York experienced some of their largest employment losses in low-skill industries, such as apparel, textiles, leather goods, and furniture. This simply confirmed a historical tendency of older industrial centers to lose less-skilled, labor-intensive jobs to areas with lower wages. Relocation of mill industries from New England to the Carolinas provides an early example of this dispersion effect. . . . [I]ndustrial cities also suffered major job losses in higher paying basic industries, such as primary metals (steel), fabricated metals (machine tools), and transportation (automobiles). Higher U.S. labor costs, foreign competition, obsolete plants, and increased energy costs are reasons frequently cited for these losses.[6]

The importance of technical changes in transportation and communications in explaining differences in regional economic growth are also cited by several authors.[7]

### National Policies

In the 1970s many analysts attributed differential regional growth to federal revenue and expenditure policies. The principal argument was related to the drag on local economies resulting from the deficit position on federal account of the Northeastern and Midwestern states because their tax payments exceeded the revenues they received from the federal

6. U.S. Department of Housing and Urban Development (1984, pp. 65–68).
7. Olson (1976); Williamson (1977).

government (revenues including income-related transfers, procurement expenditures, and intergovernmental revenues). In the South and West, it was argued, the surplus positions vis-à-vis the federal government stimulated local economies. Given the higher per capita incomes in the Northeast and Midwest (despite their lower rates of growth) and a progressive income tax system combined with transfer programs inversely related to incomes, there is no reason to expect a balance of federal revenues and expenditures across states—quite the contrary. Any analysis of the impact of federal flows is complicated by questions of tax incidence and benefit or expenditure incidence. This was an important issue in the 1960s, when the question of the regional effects of defense expenditures was a heated policy issue. Then, many studies pointed to the difficulty of assuming that the impact of defense expenditures was located in the area of the primary contractor, given the very substantial amount of subcontracting that took place in the defense industry. Nonetheless, it is possible that these flows could have influenced regional growth. An examination of the relationship between state economic growth rates and federal flow-of-funds balances could neither disprove nor demonstrate such a connection.[8] A number of other studies at the time investigated different aspects of the impact of federal revenue and expenditure policies on regional development.[9] "None of these studies tell us, on balance, how much of the recorded past divergence in regional growth patterns can be attributed to differences in overall federal flows of funds. They do, however, appear to sustain the belief that federal expenditure-revenue patterns have differential regional effects; that they have substantially greater positive effects on the states of the South and the West than on those of the Northeast and the Midwest."[10]

### Demographic Change

Another factor in population relocation was the combination of the aging of the population, earlier retirement, and rising incomes that led to substantial movement of retirees to retirement communities in the warmer climates of the South and West: Florida, Georgia, the Carolinas, Arizona, and California. This movement induced the growth of consumer goods and services firms, including health complexes, increasing the

8. Pack (1980). This issue is discussed further in chapter 6.
9. Holmer (1978); Oakland and Chall (1978); Polenske (1969).
10. Pack (1980, pp. 87–88).

demand for labor and the migration of workers seeking expanded opportunities. The influence of this phenomenon is consistent with the concentration of the fastest-growing metropolitan areas in places with warmer climates, identified in chapter 1.

One indicator of the continued importance of these regionally differentiated migration flows has been examined in Adams and Fleeter's analysis of migration patterns.[11] They find that for both 1975–80 and 1985–90, total inmigration to cities and to suburbs was greater in the South and West than in the Northeast and Midwest (supporting both the linkage phenomenon and the regional perspective [see chapter 1]); that migration rates to suburbs exceeded those to cities; and that movement from other metropolitan areas was substantially higher into the South and West than into the Northeast and Midwest (table 2-1). A recent article in the *New York Times* documents continued movement during the 1990s into the Southeast, particularly into the suburbs. During this period, all of the census divisions of the South (the East South Central and West South Central divisions and the South Atlantic states) had positive net domestic migration. The census divisions of the Northeast and Midwest, with one very small exception, experienced net domestic outmigration.[12]

## Regional Distinctions in the City-Suburb Linkage Literature

Although the role of region appears in the intrametropolitan models, its implications are not explained; the focus is on the city-suburb relationship.[13] In analyzing city-suburban linkage, Voith included 28 large metropolitan areas located in the Northeast and Midwest, but metropolitan areas in the South and West were explicitly excluded to avoid the vast differences among regions.[14] Thus, it was not possible to see that the cities and suburbs in the newer regions generally outperformed even suburbs in the Northeast and Midwest. Figures 1-5 through 1-9 (though not figure 1-10, per capita income growth in the 1980s) show this to be the case.

---

11. Adams and Fleeter (1997).
12. David Firestone, "Population Shifts in the Southeast Realign the Politics of the Suburbs," *New York Times*, June 3, 2000, p. A1 (migration table on p. A8).
13. Voith (1992, 1998).
14. Voith (1992).

**Table 2-1.** *Metropolitan Migration Rates, 1975–80 and 1985–90*
Percent (relative to initial population)

| Migration path | 51 Large metro areas | Northeast and Midwest metro areas (N = 29) | South and West metro areas (N = 22) |
|---|---|---|---|
| | | *1975–80* | |
| Into central city | | | |
| Total in-migration | 15.3 | 12.0 | 19.7 |
| Suburb to city | 4.8 | 4.6 | 5.0 |
| Outside to city | 10.5 | 7.4 | 14.7 |
| Into suburbs | | | |
| Total in-migration | 21.2 | 15.7 | 28.3 |
| City to suburb | 8.0 | 6.9 | 9.4 |
| Outside to suburb | 13.2 | 8.8 | 18.9 |
| | | *1985–90* | |
| Into central city | | | |
| Total in-migration | 20.3 | 18.4 | 22.8 |
| Suburb to city | 5.5 | 5.4 | 5.6 |
| Outside to city | 14.8 | 13.0 | 17.2 |
| Into Suburbs | | | |
| Total in-migration | 21.7 | 17.6 | 27.1 |
| City to suburb | 7.7 | 6.3 | 9.4 |
| Outside to suburb | 14.0 | 11.3 | 17.7 |

Source: Adams and Fleeter 1997, tables 1 and 5.

A subsequent study by Voith takes regions into account.[15] The analysis includes 656 counties in 281 metropolitan statistical areas (MSAs) over the period 1960–90 (277 of the 281 MSAs are those considered in chapter 1), in all regions of the country. Using dummy variables for decades and a fixed effects model for regions, Voith finds that suburban income and house value growth are both positively affected by city income growth, but only in the metropolitan areas with cities whose population exceeds 500,000—of which there are only 23. Although the relative importance of region or decade is not indicated, it may be that the very limited linkage finding results from the differences among regions.

15. Voith (1998).

**Table 2-2.** *Population Growth (Equations 2-1 and 2-2)*[a]

Dependent variable: suburban population growth

| Independent variable | 1960s | | 1970s | | 1980s | |
|---|---|---|---|---|---|---|
| | | Constant | | Constant | | Constant |
| | 0.21 | 0.36 | 0.27 | 0.39 | 0.09 | 0.12 |
| | (12.1) | (9.0) | (16.6) | (9.3) | (9.2) | (4.8) |
| City population growth, 1960s | −0.1 | −0.18 | 0.64 | 0.31 | 0.50 | 0.41 |
| | (−1.9) | (−3.3) | (7.0) | (2.9) | (7.8) | (5.6) |
| Northeast | | −0.20 | | −0.27 | | −0.05 |
| | | (−3.6) | | (−4.4) | | (−1.5) |
| Midwest | | −0.17 | | −0.20 | | −0.09 |
| | | (−3.8) | | (−4.1) | | (−2.8) |
| South | | −0.16 | | −0.02 | | 0.03 |
| | | (−3.7) | | (0.4) | | (1.2) |
| Adjusted $R^2$ | 0.24 | 0.24 | 0.16 | 0.27 | 0.19 | 0.28 |

a. Numbers in parentheses are *t* values.

The following simple equations have been estimated to obtain a rough sense of how important regional differences might be:

$$(2\text{-}1) \qquad\qquad y_i^* = \beta_0 + \beta_1 x_i$$

$$(2\text{-}2) \qquad y_i^* = \beta_0 + \beta_1 x_i + \beta_2 d_1 + \beta_3 d_2 + \beta_4 d_3.$$

In these equations, the $y_i^*$ terms are the suburban population or per capita income growth variables, the $x_i$ terms are the population or per capita income variables in the respective central cities, and $d_1$, $d_2$, and $d_3$ are the regional dummy variables, the West being the omitted region.[16] Each equation is estimated separately for the 1960s, 1970s, and 1980s. The results are shown in table 2-2.

For the population growth equations, $\beta_1$ is significant in all of the regression equations. Without the regional dummy variables, the value of $R^2$ is relatively low. Suburbs and cities are linked, but other factors play

16. This is not intended to suggest that suburban values are dependent on city values but rather to estimate the quantitative relationship between the two. An equation allowing for regional variations in both intercepts and slopes was also estimated:

$$y_i^* = \beta_0 + \beta_1 x_i + \beta_2 d_1 + \beta_3 d_2 + \beta_4 d_3 + \beta_5 d_1 x_i + \beta_6 d_2 x_i + \beta_7 d_3 x_i.$$

The slope-region interaction differences are rarely significant and make little difference in other coefficients or in explained variation.

Table 2-3. *Per Capita Income Growth (Equations 2-1 and 2-2)*[a]

Dependent variable: suburban population growth

| | 1960s | | 1970s | | 1980s | |
|---|---|---|---|---|---|---|
| | | *Constant* | | *Constant* | | *Constant* |
| *Independent* | *0.21* | *0.19* | *0.12* | *0.12* | *0.09* | *0.08* |
| *variable* | *(12.1)* | *(9.5)* | *(15.5)* | *(8.0)* | *(8.1)* | *(4.5)* |
| City population | 0.58 | −0.43 | 0.64 | 0.67 | 0.78 | 0.75 |
| growth, 1960s | (7.8) | (5.2) | (7.0) | (10.0) | (7.8) | (5.6) |
| Northeast | | 0.02 | | −0.05 | | 0.08 |
| | | (0.70) | | (−2.1) | | (3.5) |
| Midwest | | 0.05 | | 0 | | 0.03 |
| | | (2.8) | | (0.30) | | (1.4) |
| South | | 0.08 | | 0.04 | | −0.01 |
| | | (4.1) | | (2.2) | | (−0.5) |
| Adjusted $R^2$ | 0.19 | 0.25 | 0.43 | 0.46 | 0.46 | 0.50 |

a. Numbers in parentheses are $t$ values.

a major role. The addition of regional dummy variables decreases the linkage coefficient and increases $R^2$. These linkage coefficients and the signs on the regional dummy variables, which indicate substantially lower population growth in the Northeast and Midwest than in the South and West, quantify what can be seen in figures 1-5 through 1-7.

The per capita income equations also have significant linkage coefficients (table 2-3). However, although many of the regional coefficients are statistically significant, slope coefficients and explanatory power change very little when region is added to the equations. Two important things stand out: the significantly lower intercept for the Northeast in the 1970s and the higher intercept for the Northeast in the 1980s. This major reversal was already clear from the data in chapter 1 and is important in chapters 3 and 4.

Hill, Wolman, and Ford provide interesting evidence concerning the importance of regional differences.[17] They point out that there are numerous exceptions to the general finding that economic growth in cities and suburbs is positively related. As evidence, they cite, for 1990, 27 of 152 metropolitan areas in which the economic performance of the suburban

17. Hill, Wolman, and Ford (1995).

portions of the metropolitan area were "above the mean for all suburban parts of metropolitan areas and central-city performance below the mean for all of the central cities. . . ."[18] Conversely, they find another 27 metropolitan areas where the reverse is the case: the economic performance of the central city portions of the metropolitan area were above the mean for all central city parts of metropolitan areas and suburban performance was below the mean for all of the suburbs. Such outliers can be seen in figures 1-5 through 1-10. The important point about their outliers for this regional discussion is that, of the 27 "unusually healthy center cities," 23 are in the South or West. Of the 27 "unusually healthy suburbs," 23 are in the East or Midwest. Here too there is an important indication that urban development patterns are substantially different in the two sets of regions, providing further support for the importance of looking more closely at both the consequences and the determinants of differences in regional growth rates.

## Regional Distinctions in Other Urban Research

Recognition of the significance of regional distinctions is present in other recent urban research. Regional dummy variables are present in studies as diverse as those seeking to explain the development of cities and metropolitan areas, industrial location, and the incidence of crime. The regional dummy variables are generally included in addition to variables representing specific differences in regional characteristics. For example, in the study by Glaeser, Scheinkman, and Shleifer nearly every equation specification explaining growth in city manufacturing employment, nonmanufacturing employment, city population, or SMSA population contains regional dummy variables whose coefficients are statistically significant and indicate that growth is highest in the Western cities and metropolitan areas.[19] The importance of regional effects also appears in explanations of crime rates across cities. Glaeser and Sacerdote employ regional dummy variables in cross-city regressions of crime rate on city size, other city characteristics, and region.[20] The regional dummy variables are nearly all statistically significant and generally show crime rates higher in the Western region than in the others. Analyzing industrial development,

18. Economic performance is an index number of unspecified economic indicators.
19. Glaeser, Scheinkman, and Shleifer (1995).
20. Glaeser and Sacerdote (1999).

Henderson and colleagues find that since 1970 "relative to the West . . . and South, industries have declined in the Northeast and Midwest, as manufacturing has shifted with regional population and demand shifts."[21]

## Annexation

Another important regional issue concerns annexation, a phenomenon far more common in the South and West than in the Northeast and Midwest. Many claims have been made for the benefits conferred on metropolitan areas by annexation. Because this analysis concentrates on the importance of regional differences in accounting for metropolitan growth differences, the coincidence of region and annexation makes it important to try to separate the effects of annexation from those associated with region.

David Rusk has stimulated the major work in this area.[22] In his book, *Cities Without Suburbs,* he argues that "[the] concept of a city's elasticity is the central idea. . . . The first law of urban dynamics: *only elastic cities grow.*" Elastic cities are low density, and therefore they have room to grow, or they are cities that annex adjacent territory, thereby growing because of annexation either of existing population or of vacant land, which provides room for growth. "Boundary expansion contributed most to municipal elasticity."[23] Because room for growth and annexation have been far more characteristic of the cities and metropolitan areas of the South and West than of the Northeast and Midwest, Rusk's analysis is clearly relevant to the emphasis in this analysis on regional differentiation.

The Rusk argument is primarily about cities relative to their suburbs. Based on data for 320 metropolitan areas, he calculates five categories of elasticity (an index number combining vacant land and annexation of territory by the metropolitan area's cities), ranging from zero elasticity to hyperelasticity. He finds that the greater the elasticity of the city, the greater the increase in population over the four decades 1950–90. Cities with greater elasticity also exhibit lower black and Hispanic segregation indexes in 1990; higher ratios of city to suburban per capita incomes in

---

21. Henderson, Kuncoro, and Turner (1995, p. 1076).
22. Savitch and others (1993) make a similar argument for what they termed "inclusionary" cities—cities that occupy a large proportion of the territory of the metropolitan area.
23. Rusk (1995, p. 10, emphasis in original).

1989; lower school segregation; better bond ratings; greater growth in jobs in the metropolitan areas over the period 1973–88; and greater growth in manufacturing jobs (the two lowest-elasticity groups had decreases in manufacturing jobs from 1973 to 1988), interpreted here as "deindustrialization has hit inelastic areas hard."[24] In addition, the percentage of city population below the poverty line declines with elasticity, although the percentage of the metropolitan area's population below the poverty line increases. The latter is interpreted by Rusk as a regional phenomenon: "Poverty levels have historically been higher in the South and West."[25]

The improvements in the characteristics of the cities may be correct, but there is no evidence presented that the area of the city before annexation exhibits these improvements in health. The positive indicators in elastic cities may be purely the result of arithmetic. For example, adding some suburban population to the denominator (total population) while keeping the city's minority population the same lowers the ratio of minority population in the expanded area but may do nothing to change actual segregation. The same could be said of all the other indicators cited. The one clear change is that the newly enlarged city will generally have a sounder fiscal base after incorporating suburban areas, which will account for the higher city bond rating Rusk cites, and this will be a real benefit to the residents of the original city, at least in the short run. In the longer term, higher-income residents may leave for the suburbs of the new expanded city, just as they did (and do) from the inelastic cities.

The regional concentration of annexations is clear: the highest proportions of annexations occurred in the West and South; many also occurred in the Midwest, but only two in the Northeast (table 2-4). The data in table 2-5 show annexations by decade. However, in many metropolitan areas there were multiple annexations; a city that annexed territory in the 1960s may have done so again in the 1970s or 1980s. Table 2-4 shows the number of metropolitan areas in which annexations occurred during the period (rather than the number of annexations that occurred over the period, as in table 2-5). Table 2-4 also shows the average increase in land area of the central city as a result of these annexations: only 15 percent in the Northeast, 119 percent in the Midwest, 197 percent in the West, and 223 percent in the Southern metropolitan areas.

24. Rusk (1995, p. 68).
25. Rusk (1995, p. 71).

**Table 2-4.** *Number of Central Cities That Annexed Territory between 1960 and 1990 and Average Increase in Land Area*[a]

Units as indicated

| Region | Number of MSAs | Average increase in land area (percent) |
|---|---|---|
| Northeast | 2 of 47 | 15 |
| Midwest | 68 of 87 | 119 |
| South | 83 of 97 | 223 |
| West | 41 of 46 | 197 |
| Total | 176 of 277 | |

Source: See Data Note.
a. Figures include 277 metropolitan areas.

Rusk's conclusions about the beneficial effects of annexation and the analysis on which they are based are briefly described below. Appendix C broadens Rusk's analysis, indicates how the contradictory findings summarized below were reached, and raises some questions about the determinants of annexation.

In table 2-6, growth rates and socioeconomic indicators for metropolitan areas that experienced annexation are compared with those that did not, by region for the period 1960–90. The figures for the 137 metropolitan areas in the South and West include 119 with annexations and only 18 that had no annexations; note that the very small number in the latter

**Table 2-5.** *Number of Annexations by Region and Decade*

| Region | 1960s | 1970s | 1980s |
|---|---|---|---|
| All | 176 (101) | 95 (182) | 109 (168) |
| Northeast | 2 (45) | 0 (47) | 0 (47) |
| Midwest | 64 (23) | 29 (58) | 27 ( 60) |
| South | 71 (26) | 43 (54) | 50 (47) |
| West | 39 (7) | 23 (23) | 32 (14) |

Source: See Data Note.
a. Numbers in parentheses are the number of metropolitan areas in which no annexations occurred (figures include 277 metropolitan areas).

Table 2-6. *Growth Rates and Socioeconomic Indicators, Metropolitan Areas with and without Annexation*

Units as indicated

| Indicator | South and West | | Midwest | |
|---|---|---|---|---|
| | Annexation 1960–90 | No annexation 1960–90 | Annexation 1960–90 | No annexation 1960–90 |
| Number of MSAs[a] | 119 | 18 | 59 | 18 |
| Population growth | | | | |
| 1960–1990, percent | 87 | 57 | 32 | 9 |
| Per capita income | | | | |
| growth, percent | 80 | 76 | 63 | 58 |
| Poverty population, percent | | | | |
| 1990 | 15.5 | 14.5 | 11.7 | 12.9 |
| 1970[b] | 16.8 | 15.4 | 9.7 | 9.8 |
| Ratio 1990/1970 | 0.92 | 0.94 | 1.21 | 1.32 |
| Metropolitan average per capita income | | | | |
| 1990 | $9,929 | $11,298 | $10,238 | $10,472 |
| 1960 | $5,588 | $6,507 | $6,318 | $6,653 |
| Ratio 1990/1960 | 1.77 | 1.74 | 1.62 | 1.57 |
| Unemployment, percent | | | | |
| 1990 | 6.5 | 6.5 | 5.4 | 7.1 |
| 1970[b] | 4.5 | 4.8 | 4.0 | 4.6 |
| Ratio 1990/1970 | 1.44 | 1.35 | 1.35 | 1.54 |
| Population with less than high school education, percent | | | | |
| 1990 | 25 | 25 | 20.1 | 23.2 |
| 1970[b] | 47 | 48 | 42 | 47 |
| Ratio 1990/1970 | 0.53 | 0.52 | 0.48 | 0.49 |

a. This comparison is based on 250 metropolitan areas (instead of 277 MSAs as elsewhere) because the additional socioeconomic variables were available for only 250 metropolitan areas.

b. Unavailable on a consistent geographic basis for 1960.

category limits the validity of the comparisons. (The total of 119 annexations examined in table 2-6 is less than the 124 in table 2-4; see table 2-6, note a.) Rusk's assertions about the metropolitan-wide benefits of annexation receive little support. The percentage changes in the socioeconomic variables are nearly identical in metropolitan areas whose central cities annexed territory and those that did not. The greatest differences are in population growth; the annexing metropolitan areas experienced significantly higher growth rates than those that did not experience annexation. As for the other socioeconomic variables, the measures of the differences in welfare of the population were slight and statistically insignificant.

Looking at the absolute values of each of the variables, it is notable how little initial difference there was between the two groups before annexation—in the base year 1960 (or 1970)—in the socioeconomic indicators in the metropolitan areas that did and those that did not experience annexations. The only substantial difference was in the lower average per capita incomes in the metropolitan areas that subsequently experienced annexation. There were no significant differences in poverty rates, unemployment rates, or proportions of the population with less than a high school education.

In the Midwest, annexations were also frequent (59 of the 77 Midwestern MSAs in the present sample experienced city annexations of territory between 1960 and 1990), but the land areas annexed were relatively small. Nonetheless, the initial picture is very similar to that in the South and West. Initial conditions in the two sets of metropolitan areas are not significantly different. The largest difference between annexing and nonannexing areas is in the population growth rate. The only marginally significant improvements in the socioeconomic measures in the Midwest were in somewhat smaller increases in the percentage of the population in poverty and in the unemployment rate. The differences in other variables are insignificant. The difference in the two sets of MSAs in the Midwest is otherwise the same as in the South and West, namely a higher population growth rate in the metropolitan areas that experienced annexations. But, as might be expected from earlier discussion, the growth rates are much lower in the Midwest. Thus, keeping region constant, a comparison of metropolitan areas in which cities did and did not annex outlying areas does not generally support Rusk's allegations concerning the widespread benefits of annexations for metropolitan areas.

## Conclusion

The principal conclusion of this chapter—supported by the literature and data presented in this chapter and by the discussion and data in chapter 1—is that regional growth differences appear to be the major variable requiring explanation. Both cities and suburbs benefit from vigorous metropolitan-wide growth. In turn, such growth has been highly concentrated regionally, although many factors other than region determined growth, as will be seen in chapter 4.

The literature on intrametropolitan growth linkage (summarized briefly in appendix B) does not entirely ignore the differences among regions, but it sets forth a very different perspective, namely that if cities could increase their growth rates, the entire metropolitan area would benefit.[26] If cities and suburbs in the Northeast and Midwest increased their cooperative efforts to strengthen the central city, the metropolitan areas—both cities and suburbs—would grow more rapidly. There is no explicit indication of whether this would mean that the currently rapidly growing metropolitan areas would have to grow more slowly (that the system is constrained by macroeconomic factors) or whether increased growth in the less rapidly growing metropolitan areas would increase national economic growth rather than reallocate it.

26. These conclusions need not be contradictory. They do, however, point to quite different policy directions.

## CHAPTER THREE

# Socioeconomic Characteristics and Growth

THE PRINCIPAL CONCLUSION to be drawn from chapters 1 and 2 is that the major difference among metropolitan areas—and their cities and suburbs—is the substantial variation in the growth rates of metropolitan areas across regions. It is generally assumed that growth has positive implications for the well-being of the population of growing areas. In *The President's National Urban Policy Report,* the description of the effect of the recession of the early 1980s and subsequent recovery makes this point and the more general point about regional differences:[1]

> While the effects of the recession spread through cities in all regions, the major impacts were in the older cities that specialize in the manufacture of durable goods, such as steel and automobile products. For example, job losses were greater in the North Central regions than in other regions. . . . It is to be expected that different cities will share in economic recovery at different rates. Cities with economies based on growing industries and population and modern plants have in many cases already overcome the effects of recession. . . . Those cities which have been dependent on mature basic industries,

---

1. U.S. Department of Housing and Urban Development (1984).

and which contain much aging and unmodernized plant, will probably lag in their recovery.[2]

Moving forward into the late 1990s, a U.S. Department of Housing and Urban Development report, *Now Is the Time: Places Left Behind in the New Economy*, again emphasizes the differential effects of the national economy—this time an economy characterized not by recession but by a sustained period of expansion.[3]

> [Although] the vast majority of . . . cities are doing quite well and have benefited significantly from the economic recovery of the past six years, . . .
> —Unacceptably high unemployment remains in one in six central cities.
> —Steady population loss affects one in five central cities.
> —Persistently high poverty plagues one in three central cities.[4]

One year later, however, the department's emphasis is somewhat different. The first finding of the report is that "most of America's cities are participating in the New Economy, with high-tech growth driving a new wave of economic prosperity—but at the same time creating both winners and losers."[5] The major point is that vigorous national growth has been widespread rather than concentrated in the 1990s and that this growth has had beneficial effects on socioeconomic measures of well-being in cities.

> —Cities are enjoying new vigor in job growth, drawing closer to suburban growth rates.
> —Business growth in cities is accelerating, and wage growth in cities surpasses that of their surrounding suburbs.
> —Overall, cities had a larger percentage point decline in unemployment rates than suburbs.
> —Incomes are steadily increasing in cities, and poverty has declined.[6]

2. U.S. Department of Housing and Urban Development (1984, pp. 60–63).
3. U.S. Department of Housing and Urban Development (1999).
4. U.S. Department of Housing and Urban Development (1999, pp. 2 and 3).
5. U.S. Department of Housing and Urban Development (2000, p. iv).
6. U.S. Department of Housing and Urban Development (2000, p. iv).

The next area for closer examination is the influence of metropolitan growth rates on the city and suburban socioeconomic variables that measure the well-being of the population, such as poverty rates, levels of per capita income, unemployment rates, educational attainment, and racial segregation. These outcomes are at the heart of the concern about the implications of variations in metropolitan growth performance. Other measures, such as the quality of housing and its availability, infant mortality rates, nutrition levels of children, and out-of-wedlock births are also of great concern. These latter variables, however, are generally perceived to respond less quickly to changes in growth rates and their underlying sources, and thus this analysis concentrates on the more immediate socioeconomic indicators.

A substantial part of local and federal urban policy represents an attempt to stimulate local growth.[7] These policies take numerous forms: tax relief for new firms, direct subsidies, provision of special infrastructure, making land available, and establishing federal urban enterprise zones. They are all based on the belief that rapid growth will result in less poverty, lower unemployment rates, and perhaps less inequality between city and suburb as growth provides increased opportunity throughout a metropolitan area. As shown earlier, metropolitan areas in the South and West—both cities and suburbs—are typically growing more rapidly than those in the Northeast and Midwest. Their tighter labor markets might be expected to be associated with lower poverty and unemployment rates in both cities and suburbs. As a result, less inequality (or greater decreases in inequality) might also be expected in the faster-growing metropolitan areas.[8]

Several of the socioeconomic measures considered here might play two roles, one as a dependent outcome of the growth process and the second as one of its causes. For example, a high poverty rate in 1990 may have been one result of insufficient growth from 1970 to 1990 in a metropolitan area, with residents not being able to find high-income employment. Alternately, an initial high poverty rate in 1970 and the consequent greater tax rates levied on higher-income residents might have discouraged the location of households and firms and thus slowed growth over the ensuing decades.[9]

7. Bartik (1993b).
8. Hill, Wolman, and Ford (1995).
9. Pack (1998).

This chapter thus provides some "explanations" of social indicators. The reduced form results should be thought of as a framework for identifying the proximate factors associated with changes in social indicators rather than as complete explanations of the underlying causal structure. For policymakers, some insight into the determinants of the value of these social indicators is of great interest—what, if anything, can be done in a metropolitan area to ameliorate poverty? For example, consider the impact of growth in per capita income on poverty and city-suburb income differences. Such associations allow statements such as "if per capita income growth can be accelerated by 10 percent, the poverty rate in a metropolitan area may decline by 3 percent." The next step is the identification of mechanisms subject to local influence that could facilitate such changes. Chapter 4 estimates equations that explain growth and would potentially provide policymakers with guidelines about the changes needed to achieve growth in per capita income.

The approach taken in these two chapters does not explicitly take account of the fact that the metropolitan growth rates and the social indicators are determined simultaneously. Without annual data, or at least data more frequent than decadal measures, estimation of a simultaneous equation model that could provide better statistical estimates of the underlying relations is not possible. Yet some guidelines, even tentative ones, are useful to policymakers given their desire to ameliorate social conditions. Thus, fully recognizing the limits imposed by the absence of simultaneous equation estimates, I nonetheless present some single equation estimates that I believe provide useful descriptions of the dependence of social indicators on economic growth (which is further explained in chapter 4).[10]

The sections that follow first provide an overview of the average socioeconomic variables by region for 1970 and 1990. Given that growth rates are highly differentiated across regions, socioeconomic variables—poverty, per capita income and unemployment rates, educational attainment, and racial composition—are expected to differ by metropolitan area. In keeping with the emphasis on regional differences, I begin by

---

10. A full model of the determinants of poverty or unemployment across metropolitan areas would require equations linking, for example, labor market behavior across metropolitan areas to a national econometric model. Such an exercise, although of great importance, is beyond the scope of this volume but is an important next step. Blanchard and Katz (1992) undertake such an effort at the state level.

pointing out some of the substantial variation across regions in the socioeconomic variables. I then turn to the principal concern, the relationship between socioeconomic variables and growth rates, examining the effects of differential growth on the socioeconomic variables across metropolitan areas and analyzing the effect of growth differences for cities and suburbs.

## Socioeconomic Characteristics: Regional Overview and Changes between 1970 and 1990

The basic statistics—averages, standard deviations, coefficients of variation—for these socioeconomic variables are shown in table 3-1, for all the metropolitan areas, and in table 3-2 for individual regions, for cities and for suburbs for 1970 and 1990.[11] Also shown is a measure of city-suburban inequality, namely the ratio of the city average to the suburban average for each of the socioeconomic variables: the closer the ratios are to one, the more similar are the socioeconomic characteristics of cities and suburbs.

Except for the poverty rate and the unemployment rate, all of the socioeconomic indicators improved over the period in both cities and suburbs, although they did not improve by the same magnitudes in the two. (The data are shown in table 3-1, and the differential change in city and suburb may be inferred from the change in the ratio of the city value to the suburb value, also shown in table 3-1.) For the most part, improvements were greater in the suburbs than in the cities. The major difference was that although the overall average poverty rate remained about the same across all the 250 metropolitan areas, the poverty rate rose substantially in the cities, from 15 percent to 19 percent, but fell in the suburbs from about 13 percent to 11 percent. The increase in per capita incomes was greater in the suburbs; in fact, although average per capita incomes were higher in the cities than in their suburbs in 1970, they were lower in 1990. Unemployment rates rose far less in the suburbs than in the central cities, from 4.1 percent to 5.5 percent in the suburbs, but from 4.6 percent to 7.7 percent in the central cities. Education improved in both city and suburb—the proportion of college graduates increasing by more than 70 percent and the proportion of adults without a high school

11. In contrast to earlier analyses of growth rates over the period 1960–90, here a consistent data set is available only for the period 1970–90.

**Table 3-1.** *Socioeconomic Variables and Basic Statistics, Metropolitan Areas, Central Cities, and Suburbs, 1970 and 1990*[a]

Units as indicated

| Variable | Metropolitan areas | | Central cities | | Suburbs | |
|---|---|---|---|---|---|---|
| | 1970 | 1990 | 1970 | 1990 | 1970 | 1990 |
| Poverty rate | | | | | | |
| Mean | 13.50 | 13.60 | 15.30 | 19.10 | 12.80 | 10.90 |
| SD[b] | 6.10 | 5.10 | 5.70 | 6.00 | 7.10 | 6.00 |
| CV[b] | 0.5 | 0.4 | 0.4 | 0.3 | 0.6 | 0.5 |
| City/suburb | 1.2 | 1.7 | | | | |
| Per capita income | | | | | | |
| Mean | $7,629 | 10,339 | 7,741 | 9,679 | 7,431 | 10,588 |
| SD | 1,139 | 1,769 | 1,050 | 1,632 | 1,434 | 2,226 |
| CV | 0.1 | 0.2 | 0.1 | 0.2 | 0.2 | 0.2 |
| City/suburb | 1.0 | 0.9 | | | | |
| Unemployment rate | | | | | | |
| Mean | 4.31 | 6.20 | 4.63 | 7.67 | 4.05 | 5.53 |
| SD | 1.35 | 1.73 | 1.40 | 2.66 | 1.51 | 1.90 |
| CV | 0.3 | 0.3 | 0.3 | 0.3 | 0.4 | 0.3 |
| City/suburb | 1.1 | 1.4 | | | | |
| Percent college graduates | | | | | | |
| Mean | 11.12 | 19.89 | 12.28 | 21.28 | 9.87 | 18.48 |
| SD | 4.23 | 6.28 | 6.35 | 8.85 | 4.06 | 6.41 |
| CV | 0.4 | 0.3 | 0.5 | 0.4 | 0.4 | 0.3 |
| City/suburb | 1.2 | 1.2 | | | | |
| Percent with less than high school education | | | | | | |
| Mean | 46.06 | 23.67 | 45.82 | 25.78 | 47.01 | 23.18 |
| SD | 6.28 | 8.42 | 10.16 | 8.38 | 9.47 | 7.61 |
| CV | 0.1 | 0.4 | 0.2 | 0.3 | 0.2 | 0.3 |
| City/suburb | 1.0 | 1.1 | | | | |
| Percent non-Hispanic white | | | | | | |
| Mean | 82.65[c] | 80.18 | 73.63[c] | 69.30 | 87.45[c] | 85.47 |
| SD | 14.58 | 15.83 | 18.86 | 20.48 | 13.55 | 15.22 |
| CV | 0.2 | 0.2 | 0.3 | 0.3 | 0.2 | 0.2 |
| City/suburb | 0.8 | 0.8 | | | | |

a. Based on 250 MSAs.
b. SD is standard deviation; CV is the coefficient of variation.
c. 1980 data.

education falling by nearly 50 percent. Discussed below is the perhaps surprising fact—given the other socioeconomic data—that the percentage of college graduates in the central cities exceeds that in the suburbs in both decades.

The very substantial regional differences in the socioeconomic variables are shown in table 3-2.[12] Considering only the 1990 socioeconomic data for the various regions (table 3-2), the South generally has less favorable indicators than other regions, although in some instances the differences are small. It has the highest poverty rates and lowest per capita incomes; the highest unemployment rates; the lowest proportion of college graduates; and the largest proportion of persons with less than a high school education. No other region can be so uniformly characterized. In 1990 the West had the highest rates of educational attainment—the greatest proportions of college graduates and lowest proportions of adults with less than a high school education—but the Northeast had the lowest poverty rate and highest per capita income. The Midwest had a higher poverty rate than the Northeast but the lowest unemployment rate of all the regions.

The changes that took place between 1970 and 1990 (table 3-2) provide a somewhat different perspective, particularly for the South. In important dimensions, conditions in the South showed the greatest improvement, considerably narrowing the gap with respect to other regions. Metropolitan poverty rates fell in the South but increased in all the other regions. Per capita incomes increased in all regions, but the increase was greatest by far in the metropolitan areas of the South.[13] Despite still having the highest poverty rate and lowest per capita income in 1990, the South had the greatest improvement on both these variables over the period 1970–90.[14] Unemployment was a major exception to this pattern. It increased in all regions but increased most in the South and

12. Although the standard deviations show substantial overlap in the distributions, the distributions are quite different; in the South in 1990, the mean poverty rate plus or minus one standard deviation yields a range of 10.3 percent to 22.7 percent in the average poverty rates of metropolitan areas, compared with 7.6 percent to 13 percent in the Northeast.

13. In chapter 6, we will take up the question of regional convergence, pointing to the change from convergence that was characteristic of the period before 1980 and some divergence in per capita income that occurred during the 1980s as a result of a large, unusually high growth in per capita incomes in the Northeast.

14. Bishop, Formby, and Thistle (1994) examine income distributions within and across regions for the 1970s and find that "while the South was converging to the average distribution of the rest of the nation in the 1970s, the income distributions of the . . . regions . . .

**Table 3-2. Socioeconomic Variables and Basic Statistics, Metropolitan Areas, Central Cities, and Suburbs, by Region, 1970 and 1990[a]**

Units as indicated

| Variable | Metropolitan areas | | | | Central cities | | | | Suburbs | | | |
|---|---|---|---|---|---|---|---|---|---|---|---|---|
| | NE | MW | S | W | NE | MW | S | W | NE | MW | S | W |
| **Poverty rate** | | | | | | | | | | | | |
| *1970* | | | | | | | | | | | | |
| Mean | 9.7 | 9.8 | 18.7 | 12.1 | 14.3 | 11.5 | 19.9 | 12.9 | 8.1 | 8.7 | 18.3 | 11.8 |
| SD[b] | 1.8 | 2.1 | 6.7 | 3.3 | 3.1 | 2.7 | 6.2 | 2.6 | 2.1 | 3.2 | 7.8 | 4.9 |
| CV[b] | 0.2 | 0.2 | 0.4 | 0.3 | 0.2 | 0.2 | 0.3 | 0.2 | 0.3 | 0.4 | 0.4 | 0.4 |
| City/suburb | 1.8 | 1.3 | 1.1 | 1.1 | | | | | | | | |
| *1990* | | | | | | | | | | | | |
| Mean | 10.3 | 12.0 | 16.5 | 12.8 | 19.8 | 17.9 | 21.3 | 15.7 | 7.7 | 8.4 | 14.2 | 11.1 |
| SD | 2.7 | 2.8 | 6.2 | 4.0 | 4.4 | 6.1 | 6.2 | 4.4 | 2.6 | 2.9 | 7.5 | 4.5 |
| CV | 0.3 | 0.2 | 0.4 | 0.3 | 0.2 | 0.3 | 0.3 | 0.3 | 0.3 | 0.3 | 0.5 | 0.4 |
| City/suburb | 2.6 | 2.1 | 1.5 | 1.4 | | | | | | | | |
| Percent change, 1970–90 | 1.1 | 22.4 | -11.8 | 5.8 | | | | | | | | |
| **Per capita income** | | | | | | | | | | | | |
| *1970* | | | | | | | | | | | | |
| Mean | $8,092 | 7,990 | 6,092 | 8,097 | 7,559 | 8,055 | 7,246 | 8,417 | 8,346 | 7,821 | 6,597 | 7,788 |
| SD | 943 | 780 | 1,131 | 1,147 | 1,403 | 701 | 1,144 | 1,024 | 1,269 | 1,111 | 1,317 | 1,449 |
| CV | 0.1 | 0.1 | 0.2 | 0.1 | 0.2 | 0.1 | 0.2 | 0.1 | 0.2 | 0.1 | 0.2 | 0.2 |
| City/suburb | 0.9 | 1.0 | 1.1 | 1.1 | | | | | | | | |
| *1990* | | | | | | | | | | | | |
| Mean | $11,222 | 10,293 | 9,755 | 10,958 | 9,222 | 9,472 | 9,565 | 10,860 | 11,887 | 10,733 | 9,761 | 11,046 |
| SD | 1,800 | 1,065 | 1,840 | 2,113 | 1,403 | 1,428 | 1,666 | 1,832 | 2,350 | 1,428 | 2,233 | 2,609 |
| CV | 0.2 | 0.1 | 0.2 | 0.2 | 0.2 | 0.2 | 0.2 | 0.2 | 0.2 | 0.1 | 0.2 | 0.2 |
| City/suburb | 0.8 | 0.9 | 1.0 | 1.0 | | | | | | | | |
| Percent change, 1970–90 | 38.7 | 28.8 | 60.1 | 35.3 | | | | | | | | |

**Unemployment rate**

| | | | | | | | 1970 | | | | | |
|---|---|---|---|---|---|---|---|---|---|---|---|---|
| Mean | 3.9 | 4.2 | 3.9 | 6.0 | 4.6 | 4.5 | 4.0 | 6.2 | 3.7 | 3.8 | 3.6 | 5.7 |
| SD | 1.0 | 1.0 | 1.1 | 1.5 | 1.2 | 1.2 | 1.1 | 1.4 | 1.0 | 1.2 | 1.3 | 1.7 |
| CV | 0.2 | 0.2 | 0.3 | 0.2 | 0.3 | 0.3 | 0.3 | 0.2 | 0.3 | 0.3 | 0.4 | 0.3 |
| City/suburb | 1.2 | 1.2 | 1.1 | 1.1 | | | | | | | | |

| | | | | | | | 1990 | | | | | |
|---|---|---|---|---|---|---|---|---|---|---|---|---|
| Mean | 6.1 | 5.8 | 6.5 | 6.3 | 8.9 | 7.6 | 7.7 | 6.8 | 5.3 | 4.9 | 5.9 | 6.1 |
| SD | 1.3 | 1.6 | 2.0 | 1.6 | 2.0 | 3.6 | 2.2 | 1.7 | 1.3 | 1.5 | 2.2 | 1.9 |
| CV | 0.2 | 0.3 | 0.3 | 0.3 | 0.2 | 0.5 | 0.3 | 0.2 | 0.2 | 0.3 | 0.4 | 0.3 |
| City/suburb | 1.7 | 1.6 | 1.3 | 1.1 | | | | | | | | |
| Percent change, 1970–90 | 56.4 | 38.1 | 66.7 | 5.0 | | | | | | | | |

**Percent college graduates**

| | | | | | | | 1970 | | | | | |
|---|---|---|---|---|---|---|---|---|---|---|---|---|
| Mean | 9.7 | 11.2 | 10.6 | 13.4 | 8.0 | 12.5 | 12.4 | 15.2 | 10.5 | 9.5 | 9.1 | 11.8 |
| SD | 2.9 | 5.3 | 3.3 | 6.7 | 3.1 | 8.5 | 4.6 | 5.5 | 3.7 | 3.7 | 4.2 | 4.0 |
| CV | 0.3 | 0.5 | 0.3 | 0.5 | 0.4 | 0.7 | 0.4 | 0.4 | 0.4 | 0.4 | 0.5 | 0.3 |
| City/suburb | 0.8 | 1.3 | 1.4 | 1.3 | | | | | | | | |

| | | | | | | | 1990 | | | | | |
|---|---|---|---|---|---|---|---|---|---|---|---|---|
| Mean | 19.6 | 19.6 | 19.1 | 22.4 | 17.0 | 20.7 | 21.6 | 25.2 | 20.5 | 18.1 | 17.2 | 20.4 |
| SD | 5.6 | 6.9 | 5.7 | 6.4 | 7.0 | 10.8 | 6.8 | 9.0 | 6.5 | 5.3 | 6.7 | 6.8 |
| CV | 0.3 | 0.4 | 0.3 | 0.3 | 0.4 | 0.5 | 0.3 | 0.4 | 0.3 | 0.3 | 0.4 | 0.3 |
| City/suburb | 0.8 | 1.1 | 1.3 | 1.2 | | | | | | | | |
| Percent change, 1970–90 | 102.1 | 75.0 | 80.2 | 67.2 | | | | | | | | |

**Percent with less than high school education**

| | | | | | | | 1970 | | | | | |
|---|---|---|---|---|---|---|---|---|---|---|---|---|
| Mean | 48.3 | 43.4 | 51.4 | 37.3 | 53.9 | 43.7 | 49.2 | 35.5 | 45.8 | 43.9 | 53.7 | 39.1 |
| SD | 6.4 | 7.0 | 6.6 | 6.5 | 8.3 | 10.3 | 7.4 | 6.6 | 7.0 | 6.9 | 8.1 | 8.7 |
| CV | 0.1 | 0.2 | 0.1 | 0.1 | 0.2 | 0.2 | 0.2 | 0.2 | 0.2 | 0.2 | 0.2 | 0.2 |
| City/suburb | 1.2 | 1.0 | 0.9 | 0.9 | | | | | | | | |

*(continued)*

**Table 3-2. (Continued)**

Units as indicated

| Variable | Metropolitan areas | | | | Central cities | | | | Suburbs | | | |
|---|---|---|---|---|---|---|---|---|---|---|---|---|
| | NE | MW | S | W | NE | MW | S | W | NE | MW | S | W |
| | | | | | *1990* | | | | *1990* | | | |
| Mean | 24.4 | 20.8 | 27.5 | 19.8 | 31.3 | 23.3 | 28.5 | 19.7 | 22.5 | 19.8 | 27.7 | 20.1 |
| SD | 4.7 | 4.6 | 6.6 | 6.6 | 7.5 | 1.9 | 7.4 | 6.8 | 4.9 | 4.1 | 8.4 | 7.8 |
| CV | 0.2 | 0.2 | 0.2 | 0.3 | 0.2 | 0.1 | 0.3 | 0.3 | 0.2 | 0.2 | 0.3 | 0.4 |
| City/suburb | 1.4 | 1.2 | 1.0 | 1.0 | | | | | | | | |
| Percent change, 1970–90 | −49.5 | −52.1 | −46.5 | −46.9 | | | | | | | | |
| **Percent non-Hispanic white** | | | | | *1980*c | | | | | | | |
| Mean | 90.0 | 91.5 | 73.7 | 80.1 | 76.0 | 83.3 | 63.4 | 76.8 | 94.2 | 96.2 | 80.4 | 81.8 |
| SD | 10.7 | 6.0 | 15.8 | 13.1 | 19.6 | 15.6 | 17.5 | 15.7 | 7.4 | 2.8 | 15.4 | 13.4 |
| CV | 0.1 | 0.1 | 0.2 | 0.2 | 0.3 | 0.2 | 0.3 | 0.2 | 0.1 | 0.0 | 0.2 | 0.2 |
| City/suburb | 0.8 | 0.9 | 0.8 | 0.9 | | | | | | | | |
| | | | | | *1990* | | | | | | | |
| Mean | 87.2 | 90.0 | 71.7 | 75.2 | 69.4 | 80.1 | 59.8 | 70.8 | 92.0 | 95.3 | 78.6 | 77.6 |
| SD | 12.8 | 6.3 | 16.9 | 15.5 | 22.6 | 14.3 | 18.6 | 18.4 | 9.4 | 3.5 | 17.3 | 15.4 |
| CV | 0.1 | 0.1 | 0.2 | 0.2 | 0.3 | 0.2 | 0.3 | 0.3 | 0.1 | 0.0 | 0.2 | 0.2 |
| City/suburb | 0.8 | 0.8 | 0.8 | 0.9 | | | | | | | | |
| Percent change, 1980–90 | −3.1 | −1.7 | −2.7 | −6.1 | | | | | | | | |

a. Based on 250 MSAs.

b. SD is standard deviation; CV is the coefficient of variation.

c. A consistent data set for this racial variable is available only for 1980 and 1990.

**Figure 3-1.** *Average Metropolitan Poverty Rate, by Decade and Region, 1970s–90s*

Percent

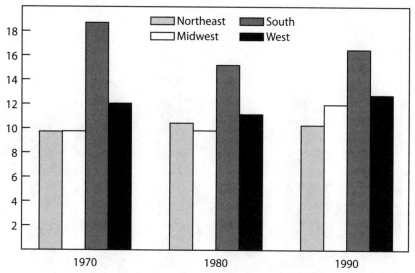

Northeast. On educational attainment, there was improvement every-where—increased proportions of college graduates and smaller percent-ages of persons without high school education. (The regional differences and changes over time can also be seen in figures 3-1 through 3-5.)

### Poverty Rates

A comparison of cities and suburbs in 1990 (tables 3-1 and 3-2) gen-erally indicates that suburbs look better on most of the socioeconomic variables than do cities, but the cities and suburbs of the West and South are generally more similar to each other than those of the Northeast and Midwest.[15] The greatest differences between cities and suburbs and

---

[of] the Non-South [Northeast, Midwest, and West] were diverging from each other" (p. 234). The figures for average per capita incomes by region in chapter 6 (see figure 6-1) show the substantial relative increase in the South during the 1970s. The divergence in the other regions may be said to be indicated by a somewhat greater difference in their average per capita incomes, although this came about almost entirely due to the very large relative decrease in average per capita incomes in the Northeast—from about 5 percent above national average in 1970 to about 2 percent below average in 1980.

15. This may be an arithmetic artifact of the more frequent annexations in the South and West or of the higher rates of growth in these regions. See the discussion in chapter 2.

**Figure 3-2.** *Average Metropolitan Unemployment Rate, by Decade and Region, 1970s–90s*

Percent

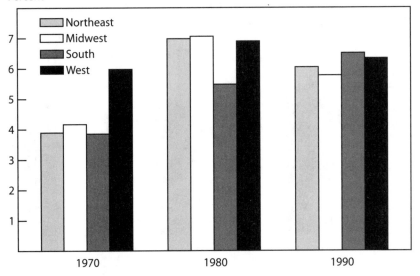

**Figure 3-3.** *Average Metropolitan Education Attainment: Percentage College Graduates, by Decade and Region (Population Age 25 or Older), 1970s–90s*

Percent

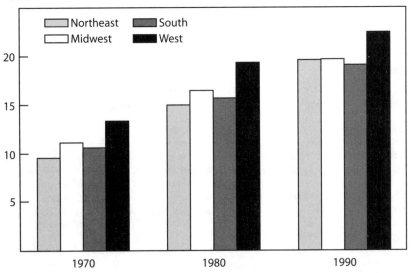

**Figure 3-4.** *Average Metropolitan Education Attainment: Less than High School Education, by Decade and Region (Population Age 25 or Older), 1970s–90s*

Percent

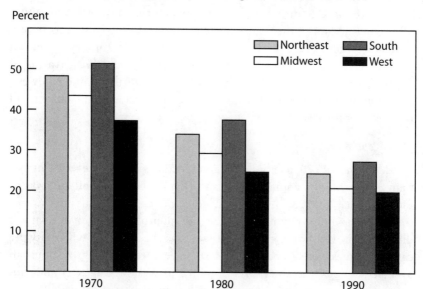

**Figure 3-5.** *Average Metropolitan Immigrant Percentage of Population, by Decade and Region, 1970s–90s*

Percent

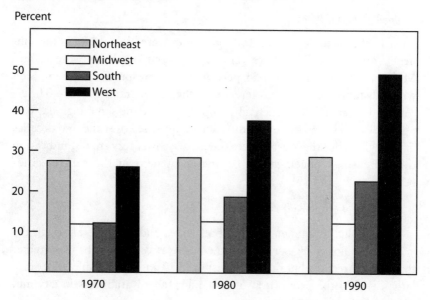

among regions are found in the city-suburb poverty rates. In 1990 average poverty rates in the cities of the Northeast and Midwest metropolitan areas were more than twice those in the suburbs, but they were about 50 percent greater in the South and West (table 3-2). These ratios represent large increases over their 1970 values. In 1970, city-suburban poverty rates were about the same in the South and West (ratios of approximately 1) but were greater than 1 in the Northeast and Midwest. Thus the poor population became more concentrated in the cities in all regions over the two decades.

### Per Capita Incomes

Although in 1970, average per capita incomes in the cities were higher than in the suburbs with the sole exception of the metropolitan areas of the Northeast (table 3-2), in 1990 average per capita incomes in the central cities of all four regions fell below the suburban averages. The largest differences in 1990 were in the Northeast and the Midwest, where city per capita incomes were 78 percent and 88 percent, respectively, of suburban average per capita incomes. In the South and West, average city and suburban per capita incomes were about the same—the ratios were 0.98—although the ratio of city to suburb per capita income had declined since 1970. Thus in 1990, average per capita incomes that were lower in cities than in suburbs were largely characteristic of the Northeast and Midwest.

### Unemployment Rates

In 1990, unemployment rates in the cities were higher than in the suburbs (table 3-2). They were very much higher in the Northeast and Midwest—68 percent and 55 percent higher, respectively—compared with substantially smaller differences in the South and the West—31 percent and 11 percent, respectively. Approximately the same regional pattern prevailed in 1970, but the differences increased over the two decades in all regions but the West (where the increase was very small), indicating the increasing concentration of unemployment in the central cities between 1970 and 1990.

### Educational Attainment

Educational attainment rose in both cities and suburbs, although the average ratio of college graduates in cities relative to suburbs was greater than 1 in all regions but the Northeast in 1970 and 1990 (table 3-2). Similarly, in 1970 the proportion of non–high school graduates in city and suburb was about the same in all regions but the Northeast, where the city proportion exceeded that in the suburbs. By 1990, there were fewer non–high school graduates everywhere, but the city-suburb ratio increased in all regions. In the South and West the increases were small, but in the Northeast and Midwest the city-suburb ratio of non–high school graduates increased to substantially greater than 1, another indication of the deterioration of cities relative to suburbs in the Northeast and Midwest.

### Race

Race is by far the most polarized of the socioeconomic characteristics. The average metropolitan non-Hispanic white population was 83 percent of the total in 1980 and 80 percent of the total in 1990. The differences between cities and suburbs are great and have increased over time. Whereas the average minority population in the cities in 1980 was nearly 26 percent, it had increased to 31 percent in 1990. In the suburbs, the racial minority proportion was much lower than in the cities and changed very little over the decade, rising from about 13 to only 15 percent (table 3-1). (These data are available only for 1980 and 1990.)

This extreme picture of racial separation shows the least variation across regions. Although the Northeast and Midwest have substantially lower ratios of minority population than do the South and West, the city-suburban ratios hardly differ—0.8 or 0.9 in each of the regions in both 1980 and 1990.[16]

### In Sum: Regional and City Suburban Differences

From the foregoing discussion, it appears that many of the conventional assumptions about city-suburban socioeconomic differences are largely a phenomenon of the Northeast and to some extent of the Midwest. Only relatively recently have the cities of the South and West exhibited notably inferior socioeconomic characteristics relative to their suburbs, although city and suburb are still more similar in these regions than in the Northeast and Midwest. Moreover, even though the South, in

16. It is well known that the distribution of population, by race and ethnicity, associated with large numbers of immigrants concentrated in a small number of states and metropolitan areas, is an important factor in intrametropolitan and interregional development patterns. Having carried out substantial analysis of racial and ethnic characteristics as both independent and dependent variables throughout the analysis, it is clear that to do this subject justice requires a separate volume.

both 1970 and 1990, lagged behind other regions in most socioeconomic measures of well-being, its metropolitan statistical areas (MSAs) experienced by far the greatest improvements over the period on many of the important socioeconomic indicators—poverty rate decreases and per capita income increases in particular.

## Poverty, Income Inequality, and Unemployment Rates: Growth and Region

The generally higher poverty and unemployment rates and lower per capita incomes in cities than in suburbs, and their regional variation, are a major concern of urban analysts and policymakers. It is thus important to establish, even proximately, the determinants of these differences across metropolitan regions in both the cities and the suburbs.

Given the identification of major growth differences among census regions and the differences of both city and suburban growth rates by region, this analysis concentrates on the implication of these growth differences for changes in poverty and unemployment rates over time as well as changes in income inequality between cities and suburbs. An important question is whether once differences in growth rates are taken into account, region has any residual influence on the socioeconomic variables.

In chapter 4 it is shown that growth across metropolitan areas in income per capita and population depends on many variables, among them some of the welfare measures, such as education. While recognizing the need for a simultaneous equation system estimation of the underlying relations, this is not possible given the data available. Thus, I proceed in two stages. In this chapter, the relation between the various socioeconomic indicators and per capita income and population growth are considered, without assuming that the magnitudes found would not change were more appropriate data available to allow system estimation. Rather, it can be assumed that the qualitative properties would hold and that the exercise allows some rough, stylized facts to be inferred. In chapter 4, the determinants of the growth in per capita income and population are considered. Judicious utilization of both sets of results allows some insights into metropolitan growth patterns and provides the basis for policy analysis provided in chapter 6.

The equations estimated are:

(3-1) $$y_i = \beta_0 + \beta_1 x_1 + \beta_2 x_2 + \beta_3 y_b$$

(3-2)        $y_i = \beta_0 + \beta_1 x_1 + \beta_2 x_2 + \beta_3 y_b + \beta_4 d_1 + \beta_5 d_2 + \beta_6 d_3 ,$

where $y_i$ is the change in the poverty rate, the unemployment rate, or the ratio of city to suburban poverty rates or per capita incomes in the 1970s or 1980s,[17] $x_1$ is the growth in metropolitan per capita income in the 1970s or 1980s, $x_2$ is the population growth rate in the 1970s or 1980s,[18] $y_b$ is the level of poverty, unemployment, city-suburb poverty ratio, or per capita income ratio in the base period, 1970 or 1980, and the $d$s are the regional dummy variables.

Estimates of these equations permit the identification of some of the patterns of association but do not provide precise indications of causality. Rather they can be viewed as offering guidelines for the likely evolution of welfare indicators if a metropolitan area could achieve higher growth in income per capita or population (both analyzed in chapter 4). Whether it is possible for a metropolitan area to affect its own growth or for state or federal governments to do so is considered in chapters 5 and 6. Moreover, it is important to remember the national constraint, namely, that not all metropolitan areas can improve their performance unless the national economy experiences an increase in its growth rates. Nevertheless, for poorly performing metropolitan areas, even small improvements in their share of national growth, if feasible, could have a significant positive effect on their social indicators.

Population enters the equations as an indicator of labor force changes, as indicated above. However, population reflects three independent components, namely, retirees, new immigrants, and inmigration of labor force members from other parts of the country. As retiree relocation has become a substantial source of population relocation to "retirement magnet areas," MSAs in the Northeast and Midwest tend to lose population, and the South and West tend to gain.[19] Two-thirds of the thirty counties with the greatest percentage changes in elderly population between 1980 and 1997 were "in traditional Florida or South Atlantic 'retiree

17. Given the very different patterns in regional per capita income growth in the two decades (described in chapter 1), equations 3-1 and 3-2 have been estimated separately for the 1970s and the 1980s.

18. The correlation coefficients between growth in per capita income and population for the 1960–90 period and for each of the decades are not high: only .30 for the entire period. Although the correlation was higher for the Northeast and Midwest for the entire period, the correlations by decade were much lower. This is discussed in chapter 4.

19. Frey (1999).

magnets,'"[20] and an additional three were in the Southwest (Arizona and Texas). This would be consistent with the earlier identification of the fifty metropolitan areas with the most rapidly growing populations. Since relocating retirees are unlikely to be part of the poverty population, poverty rates in the areas they leave are likely to rise and conversely to decline in the areas to which they move. Although retirement migration is very important for some of these magnet areas, retirement migration tends to be a relatively small part of total population relocation.[21]

Another important component of population change is immigration. More than 8.5 million immigrants moved to the United States in the 1980s, and about half as many came in the 1970s. The location of the immigrant population is highly concentrated. Fifty percent of all immigrants and 54 percent of immigrants who arrived in the United States in the 1980s settled in four (consolidated) MSAs: Los Angeles–Anaheim–Riverside (24 percent); New York–Northern New Jersey–Long Island (17 percent); San Francisco–Oakland–San Jose (7 percent), and the Miami–Fort Lauderdale area (6 percent).[22] In each of these areas the cumulative immigration, defined as total foreign-born population, was exceptionally high. In Miami–Fort Lauderdale, 34 percent of the population in 1990 was foreign born; in Los Angeles–Anaheim–Riverside, 27 percent; in San Francisco–Oakland–San Jose and New York–Northern New Jersey–Long Island, 20 percent.[23] Although immigrants tend not to remain poor, the places with large recent immigrant populations are likely to experience an increase in poverty rates due to low levels of education of immigrants in many places and to rapid shifts in labor supply that may also increase unemployment rates.[24] Given the concentration of immigration, particularly in the West and South, such effects are most likely to show up in MSAs in those regions.

The third major source of population change comes from the response to economic opportunity. Behind this movement, related to the variations in the growth of regional economies, are differential expansions and declines of existing firms, interregional relocation of firms, and differences in productivity growth rates across MSAs (see chapter 4). If the poor are the least mobile sector of the population, the combination of

20. Frey (1999, p. 26).
21. Frey (1999, p. 19).
22. Daniel (1994).
23. Daniel (1994).
24. Chiswick and Sullivan (1995); Jasso and Rosenzweig (1990); Myers (1999).

sluggish mobility of the least-skilled workers and slower growth of the demand for labor in the more slowly growing regions would be expected to increase the unemployment rates in the areas that are losing population (the unemployed or marginally employed remain where they are, but firms decline or leave these areas, as do more highly skilled workers). In growing areas, the unemployment rates would be expected to fall or remain relatively unchanged as the demand for labor increases and supply responds more slowly.

As it has not been possible to disaggregate the streams of population growth and decline among retirees, immigrants, or labor force migrants, the focus on the total population change may confound interpretation of the coefficients. On the whole, rapid growth of population is expected to be associated with reduced poverty rates. The results presented provide an indication of the association of population growth and some key social variables, but the precise interpretation requires data on each source of population growth for all MSAs, and these data are not currently available.

The inclusion in equations 3-1 and 3-2 of the value of each dependent variable at the beginning of the decade allows for a persistence effect. Despite the high mobility of the U.S. population, poverty is known to vary little over time in some areas—the Appalachian region being the best-known long-term example. This persistence may result from numerous factors: limited human capital of the poor, their attachment to community institutions, and their dependence on friends and relatives may result in the initial poverty population not moving to MSAs offering greater opportunity. The poor may also be held in place by the availability of low-cost housing, income maintenance programs, the social climate, and their accumulated skills in dealing with the local bureaucracy. Some of these factors may also lead potential migrants to locate in the area. New immigrants, generally poor, may be attracted to locations in which earlier immigrants, even if poor, have congregated. Persistence does not necessarily mean the same individuals remain at low income levels. Rather, the location may attract or absorb low-income residents, many of whom may be new residents who, for some of the reasons indicated above, reside in the metropolitan area as their point of entry into the larger society.[25]

The correlations, or persistence, in the values of the levels of socio-economic variables between decades are shown in table 3-3 for all the metropolitan areas and for each of the four census regions. The evidence

25. Myers (1999).

**Table 3-3.** *Correlations of Socioeconomic Variables between Decades: Cities, Suburbs, and Metropolitan Areas, 1970 and 1980, 1980 and 1990*

| Region | 1970–80 | 1980–90 | Region | 1970–80 | 1980–90 |
|---|---|---|---|---|---|
| *Poverty* | | | *Per capita income* | | |
| All | | | All | | |
| Cities | 0.80 | 0.85 | Cities | 0.78 | 0.81 |
| Suburbs | 0.88 | 0.86 | Suburbs | 0.88 | 0.86 |
| Metropolitan areas | 0.91 | 0.89 | Metropolitan areas | 0.89 | 0.82 |
| Northeast | | | Northeast | | |
| Cities | 0.84 | 0.71 | Cities | 0.75 | 0.73 |
| Suburbs | 0.88 | 0.85 | Suburbs | 0.96 | 0.93 |
| Metropolitan areas | 0.77 | 0.79 | Metropolitan areas | 0.92 | 0.97 |
| Midwest | | | Midwest | | |
| Cities | 0.82 | 0.92 | Cities | 0.69 | 0.87 |
| Suburbs | 0.78 | 0.78 | Suburbs | 0.87 | 0.91 |
| Metropolitan areas | 0.69 | 0.83 | Metropolitan areas | 0.83 | 0.86 |
| South | | | South | | |
| Cities | 0.82 | 0.82 | Cities | 0.83 | 0.83 |
| Suburbs | 0.83 | 0.81 | Suburbs | 0.85 | 0.80 |
| Metropolitan areas | 0.90 | 0.89 | Metropolitan areas | 0.91 | 0.84 |
| West | | | West | | |
| Cities | 0.83 | 0.87 | Cities | 0.84 | 0.84 |
| Suburbs | 0.89 | 0.91 | Suburbs | 0.94 | 0.93 |
| Metropolitan areas | 0.87 | 0.87 | Metropolitan areas | 0.93 | 0.89 |
| *Unemployment* | | | *Income inequality, ratio of city to suburb* | | |
| All | | | *per capita income, metropolitan areas* | | |
| Cities | 0.47 | 0.67 | All | 0.85 | 0.86 |
| Suburbs | 0.62 | 0.44 | Northeast | 0.94 | 0.97 |
| Metropolitan areas | 0.53 | 0.47 | Midwest | 0.87 | 0.99 |
| Northeast | | | South | 0.78 | 0.74 |
| Cities | 0.35 | 0.80 | West | 0.88 | 0.96 |
| Suburbs | 0.35 | 0.63 | | | |
| Metropolitan areas | 0.33 | 0.61 | | | |
| Midwest | | | | | |
| Cities | 0.56 | 0.71 | | | |
| Suburbs | 0.68 | 0.53 | | | |
| Metropolitan areas | 0.56 | 0.52 | | | |
| South | | | | | |
| Cities | 0.53 | 0.52 | | | |
| Suburbs | 0.66 | 0.36 | | | |
| Metropolitan areas | 0.62 | 0.46 | | | |
| West | | | | | |
| Cities | 0.38 | 0.69 | | | |
| Suburbs | 0.66 | 0.54 | | | |
| Metropolitan areas | 0.58 | 0.47 | | | |

*(continued)*

**Table 3-3.** *(Continued)*

| Region | 1970–80 | 1980–90 | Region | 1970–80 | 1980–90 |
|---|---|---|---|---|---|
| *College graduates* | | | *Non-Hispanic whites* | | |
| All | | | All | | |
| Cities | 0.97 | 0.98 | Cities | n.a. | 0.99 |
| Suburbs | 0.94 | 0.95 | Suburbs | n.a. | 0.98 |
| Metropolitan areas | 0.97 | 0.97 | Metropolitan areas | n.a. | 0.99 |
| Northeast | | | Northeast | | |
| Cities | 0.96 | 0.97 | Cities | n.a. | 0.99 |
| Suburbs | 0.98 | 0.98 | Suburbs | n.a. | 0.99 |
| Metropolitan areas | 0.97 | 0.97 | Metropolitan areas | n.a. | 0.99 |
| Midwest | | | Midwest | | |
| Cities | 0.98 | 0.99 | Cities | n.a. | 0.99 |
| Suburbs | 0.94 | 0.98 | Suburbs | n.a. | 0.96 |
| Metropolitan areas | 0.98 | 0.99 | Metropolitan areas | n.a. | 0.99 |
| South | | | South | | |
| Cities | 0.96 | 0.98 | Cities | n.a. | 0.99 |
| Suburbs | 0.93 | 0.91 | Suburbs | n.a. | 0.98 |
| Metropolitan areas | 0.97 | 0.98 | Metropolitan areas | n.a. | 0.99 |
| West | | | West | | |
| Cities | 0.94 | 0.97 | Cities | n.a. | 0.98 |
| Suburbs | 0.91 | 0.98 | Suburbs | n.a. | 0.98 |
| Metropolitan areas | 0.95 | 0.98 | Metropolitan areas | n.a. | 0.98 |
| *Non–high school graduates* | | | | | |
| All | | | | | |
| Cities | 0.96 | 0.95 | | | |
| Suburbs | 0.94 | 0.88 | | | |
| Metropolitan areas | 0.96 | 0.87 | | | |
| Northeast | | | | | |
| Cities | 0.97 | 0.96 | | | |
| Suburbs | 0.97 | 0.98 | | | |
| Metropolitan areas | 0.97 | 0.97 | | | |
| Midwest | | | | | |
| Cities | 0.97 | 0.98 | | | |
| Suburbs | 0.94 | 0.97 | | | |
| Metropolitan areas | 0.97 | 0.98 | | | |
| South | | | | | |
| Cities | 0.92 | 0.91 | | | |
| Suburbs | 0.89 | 0.77 | | | |
| Metropolitan areas | 0.93 | 0.92 | | | |
| West | | | | | |
| Cities | 0.90 | 0.94 | | | |
| Suburbs | 0.94 | 0.96 | | | |
| Metropolitan areas | 0.94 | 0.96 | | | |

n.a. indicates data not available.

for persistence in poverty rates is clear: overall and within regions, poverty rates in metropolitan areas, in cities, and in suburbs are extremely highly correlated from decade to decade—generally between 0.8 and 0.9. The correlations in per capita incomes from decade to decade—for metropolitan areas, their central cities, and suburbs—are as high or higher, as is the persistence of city-suburban inequality. The persistence of unemployment rates is generally lower than for poverty rates or per capita incomes.

Despite the high correlation in socioeconomic variables from period to period, the present analysis estimates changes in the values of these variables. As observed earlier (table 3-2), the South has the highest poverty rates throughout the period, but it was the only region in which metropolitan-area poverty rates declined between 1970 and 1990. Therefore, it is not inconsistent to observe high correlations in levels from decade to decade and convergence on the margin—greater decreases in poverty rates, for example, in places with the highest initial poverty rates.

### Poverty

Average city poverty rates rose in both decades; by about 7.5 percent in the 1970s and by 21 percent in the 1980s. In the suburbs, in contrast, poverty rates fell by nearly 14 percent, and then they rose by only about 6 percent in the 1980s. Clearly in both periods, suburbs were doing much better with respect to poverty than the cities. The estimated equations, 3-1 and 3-2, are shown in table 3-4. The coefficients on initial poverty rates are all negative, indicating smaller increases or greater decreases in poverty rates in places with relatively high initial poverty rates in both cities and suburbs, on average, in both decades. All of the coefficients on base period poverty rates are statistically significant when regions are not included (equation 3-1), with the exception of the suburban coefficient for the 1980s.[26] When the region dummy variables are introduced, the significance of the initial poverty rate largely disappears. In the suburban equation for the 1970s and the cities for the 1980s, the initial poverty rate remains significant.

The coefficient of per capita income growth rates suggests that poverty rates are highly responsive to metropolitan growth in both cities and

26. Madden (2000) estimates the "major factors in growth in metropolitan poverty and income inequality" (table 9.1, p. 155) and finds a similar relationship for 1990. The dependent variable in her analysis is the 1990 metropolitan-area poverty rate, and the effect of the 1980 rate is negative and statistically significant, albeit small.

**Table 3-4.** *Percentage Change in Poverty Rates, Cities and Suburbs, 1970s and 1980s*[a]

| | Equation | | | |
|---|---|---|---|---|
| | Cities | | Suburbs | |
| Independent variable | 3-1 | 3-2 | 3-1 | 3-2 |
| | | 1970s | | |
| Constant | 40.30 | 24.79 | 13.81 | 20.14 |
| | (13.38) | (5.62) | (7.16) | (5.87) |
| Poverty rate, 1970 | −0.60 | −0.15 | −0.67 | −0.58 |
| | (−3.31) | (−0.67) | (−4.36) | (−3.33) |
| Growth in metropolitan per capita income, 1970–80 | −158.00 | −141.80 | −132.48 | −133.74 |
| | (−11.88) | (−10.03) | (−10.09) | (−9.53) |
| Growth in metropolitan population, 1970–80 | −8.78 | 5.23 | −3.31 | −11.65 |
| | (−1.38) | (0.86) | (−0.59) | (−1.77) |
| Northeast | | 10.11 | | −6.72 |
| | | (2.42) | | (−1.79) |
| Midwest | | 11.59 | | −7.70 |
| | | (3.45) | | (−2.53) |
| South | | −3.22 | | −6.69 |
| | | (−0.98) | | (−2.39) |
| Adjusted $R^2$ | 0.47 | 0.51 | 0.52 | 0.53 |
| | | 1980s | | |
| Constant | 55.19 | 49.90 | 39.88 | 43.84 |
| | (18.70) | (14.27) | (10.11) | (8.46) |
| Poverty rate, 1980 | −0.48 | −0.40 | −0.28 | −0.53 |
| | (−2.68) | (−2.09) | (−0.98) | (−1.60) |
| Growth in metropolitan per capita income, 1980–90 | −121.56 | −142.95 | −160.16 | −186.03 |
| | (−14.19) | (−14.33) | (−13.82) | (−13.04) |
| Growth in metropolitan population, 1980–90 | −26.25 | −4.99 | 3.87 | 13.95 |
| | (−3.95) | (−0.62) | (0.40) | (1.21) |
| Northeast | | 15.46 | | 12.87 |
| | | (3.84) | | (2.29) |
| Midwest | | 8.94 | | −1.91 |
| | | (3.02) | | (−0.45) |
| South | | 2.74 | | 3.66 |
| | | (0.98) | | (0.93) |
| Adjusted $R^2$ | 0.57 | 0.60 | 0.46 | 0.47 |

a. Numbers in parentheses are *t* values.

suburbs, in both decades, in the equations that do and do not include regional dummy variables. Growth in per capita income was associated with a substantial reduction in poverty rates. Places with initially high poverty rates but high growth rates experienced notable decreases in poverty rates.[27] But per capita income growth, as is emphasized in chapter 4, is not a variable over which metropolitan areas can easily exercise control. Most of the major determinants are outside the policy ability of local authorities.[28]

In contrast to the effect of per capita income growth, the coefficient on population growth, although more often negative than positive, is statistically insignificant in all specifications but one. Only in the equation for the cities in the 1980s that excludes regional intercept variables is the coefficient negative and statistically significant. When this equation is compared with its counterpart that includes regional dummy variables, it is clear that this difference is the result of the statistically significant differences between the Northeast and Midwest compared with the South and West. Thus population growth is rarely associated with changes in poverty rates, and where it is its effects are small.

Despite the significance of per capita income growth rates, and the association of these growth rates with region, there are still some differences among regions that show up in the form of statistically significant coefficients on the regional intercept variables. Nonetheless, the addition of the regional intercept variables barely affects the size or significance of the other coefficients nor the explained variation in changes in poverty rates. Cities in the Northeast and Midwest have larger increases in poverty rates than those in the South and West. The smaller decreases in suburban poverty rates in the 1970s are consistent with the fact that many Western cities have lower poverty rates than their suburban areas. In the 1980s, the experience of the Northeastern cities and suburbs was about the same—both had greater increases in poverty rates than in the West.

In sum, per capita income growth was associated with reduced poverty rates in both cities and suburbs in both the 1970s and the 1980s. An increase in average metropolitan per capita income growth in the 1970s of one standard deviation would have been associated (other things being equal) with a reduction in poverty rates in cities by about 22 percent com-

27. Madden (2000) finds that increases in median per capita income reduce 1990 poverty rates very substantially.
28. Bradbury, Kodrzycki, and Tannenwald (1997).

pared with an actual increase of about 8 percent.[29] In the suburbs, where poverty rates fell by nearly 14 percent in the 1970s, with higher growth (one standard deviation greater than average), it would have fallen still further, by about 32 percent. In the 1980s, when poverty rates rose in cities by 21 percent and in suburbs by about 6 percent, had metropolitan per capita income growth rates been higher by one standard deviation, the changes would have been a decrease of poverty rates in the cities of about 6 percent and in the suburbs a decrease of about 29 percent. Despite the fact that poverty rates are quite persistent from decade to decade, in both cities and suburbs, it is also the case that there is a tendency toward convergence. The greater the initial poverty rate, the greater the incidence of decreases or smaller increases in the poverty rate in the subsequent decade in both cities and suburbs. This may indicate that the poor are responding to economic opportunities by moving to regions of more rapid growth.

As noted earlier, a full understanding of the mechanisms that give rise to these phenomena requires much more complex models. What is relevant is that metropolitan per capita income growth, whatever its source, is associated with a decrease in poverty, quite apart from national and local efforts at redistribution. Not only is the status of the lowest income groups (those with incomes below the poverty level) improved but insofar as there are negative externalities from a concentration of poverty, the metropolitan area as a whole is better off.

### Income Disparities

Urban policy discussions have been increasingly concerned with growing disparities between average per capita incomes in cities and suburbs. The data provide evidence of these differences but also show that more rapid metropolitan per capita income growth is associated with per capita income growth in both cities and suburbs. Estimates of equations 3-1 and 3-2, where $y_i$ measures the ratio of per capita incomes in city and suburbs—in either 1990 or 1980 (table 3-5)—shows yet again that the major factor explaining the city-suburb income inequality ratio is persistence. In the 1970s, neither the growth of per capita income nor that of population had any significant impact on the income ratio in 1980. In contrast, in the

29. Neither this calculation nor the ones that follow are meant to suggest that average growth rates can be increased. The point is rather that where growth rates are higher, socioeconomic conditions improve relative to what they would have been had growth rates been lower.

**Table 3-5.** *Income Inequality: per Capita Income City/Suburb, 1990 and 1980*[a]

| Independent variable | Equation 3-1 | Equation 3-2 | Independent variable | Equation 3-1 | Equation 3-2 |
|---|---|---|---|---|---|
| *1990* | | | *1980* | | |
| Constant | −0.03 (−0.56) | −0.01 (−0.15) | Constant | 0.12 (3.42) | 0.13 (3.19) |
| City/suburb per capita income, 1980 | 1.02 (23.88) | 0.99 (22.93) | City/suburb per capita income, 1970 | 0.79 (22.23) | 0.79 (21.70) |
| Growth in metropolitan per capita income, 1980s | −0.18 (−2.91) | −0.26 (−3.66) | Growth in metropolitan per capita income, 1970s | 0.04 (0.51) | 0.05 (0.57) |
| Growth in metropolitan population, 1980s | 0.14 (3.00) | 0.15 (2.62) | Growth in metropolitan population, 1970s | 0.04 (1.28) | 0.03 (0.74) |
| Northeast | | 0.04 (1.43) | Northeast | | −0.01 (−0.58) |
| Midwest | | −0.01 (−0.35) | Midwest | | −0.01 (−0.75) |
| South | | 0.04 (2.24) | South | | −0.01 (−0.95) |
| Adjusted $R^2$ | 0.75 | 0.76 | Adjusted $R^2$ | 0.73 | 0.73 |

a. Numbers in parentheses are *t* values.

1980s, each had a small influence. The higher the rate of growth in metropolitan per capita income, the greater the inequality and the lower city relative to suburban per capita income.[30] As in the case of poverty inequality, population growth had a small influence in the other direction; the greater the increase in metropolitan population, the higher city to suburban per capita income. What shows up most clearly, however, is the persistence of inequality in per capita incomes between cities and suburbs. In 1990, the coefficient of the ratio of city to suburb per capita income in the previous decade was 1; in 1980, it was about 0.8.

### Unemployment

Average unemployment rates rose substantially in both cities and suburbs during the 1970s, reflecting nationwide trends. In the 1980s, however, average unemployment rates rose in the cities (nearly 14 percent) but fell in the suburbs (nearly 22 percent). Just as in the case of the poverty equations, the results of estimating equations 3-1 and 3-2 (table 3-6) indicate

---

30. See Hill, Wolman, and Ford (1995) for a contrary argument.

Table 3-6. *Percentage Change in Unemployment Rates, Cities and Suburbs, 1970s and 1980s*[a]

| | Equation | | | |
| | Cities | | Suburbs | |
| Independent variable | 3-1 | 3-2 | 3-1 | 3-2 |
|---|---|---|---|---|
| *1970s* | | | | |
| Constant | 156.98 (13.75) | 100.74 (4.89) | 143.70 (18.66) | 136.05 (9.69) |
| Unemployment rate, 1970 | −11.85 (−5.66) | −7.91 (−3.10) | −13.74 (−8.22) | −13.73 (−7.09) |
| Growth in metropolitan per capita income, 1970–80 | −207.93 (−5.39) | −183.75 (−4.29) | −143.37 (−4.36) | −136.96 (−3.67) |
| Growth in metropolitan population, 1970–80 | −75.39 (−4.10) | −28.60 (−1.27) | −56.05 (−3.60) | −38.67 (−2.08) |
| Northeast | | 43.55 (3.17) | | 2.19 (0.19) |
| Midwest | | 38.00 (3.24) | | 14.35 (1.51) |
| South | | 23.81 (2.22) | | −2.34 (−0.27) |
| Adjusted $R^2$ | 0.29 | 0.31 | 0.36 | 0.37 |
| *1980s* | | | | |
| Constant | 79.22 (11.14) | 54.42 (6.90) | 108.32 (9.75) | 95.14 (6.87) |
| Unemployment rate, 1980 | −6.23 (−7.80) | −4.61 (−6.58) | −13.02 (−9.04) | −11.21 (−7.91) |
| Growth in metropolitan per capita income, 1980–90 | −111.15 (−5.53) | −192.54 (−9.30) | −192.98 (−7.21) | −274.50 (−9.03) |
| Growth in metropolitan population, 1980–90 | 10.56 (0.62) | 46.18 (2.66) | 78.26 (3.57) | 99.00 (9.94) |
| Northeast | | 49.42 (5.94) | | 47.23 (3.83) |
| Midwest | | 6.08 (0.98) | | −7.79 (−0.84) |
| South | | 43.35 (7.71) | | 30.68 (3.57) |
| Adjusted $R^2$ | 0.30 | 0.51 | 0.35 | 0.45 |

a. Numbers in parentheses are *t* values.

that for both cities and suburbs, in both decades, metropolitan per capita income growth is associated with declining, or more slowly increasing, unemployment rates. The substantial negative coefficient indicates that the greater the growth rate the smaller the increase or the greater the decrease in the unemployment rate. The effect of the growth in population is different for the unemployment rates than for the poverty rates. In the 1980s, when immigration was very substantial, all of the coefficients are positive and generally significant—population growth was associated with growing unemployment rates. In the 1970s, when immigration was about half that in the 1980s, the coefficients are negative, indicating that the population increases were associated with smaller unemployment rate increases—population growth may have consisted of relatively more retirees and fewer labor force members, with retirees generating additional demand for labor without providing an offsetting supply.

Just as in the case of the poverty equations, the coefficients in the unemployment equations indicate that in cities and suburbs, higher initial unemployment rates were associated with smaller increases in the unemployment rates in both cities and suburbs, on average, in both decades.

Although accounting for initial values and for variations in growth rates does not eliminate the influence of regions, an increase in metropolitan per capita income growth in the 1970s of one standard deviation would have been associated (other things being equal) with a reduction in the increase in the average unemployment rate over the decade in cities from 60 percent to 45 percent: the average city unemployment rate would have been 6.2 percent, rather than 6.9 percent. In the suburbs, where unemployment rates rose by a similar percentage (59 percent), a similar increase in metropolitan per capita income growth would have reduced the average increase in unemployment rates to 47 percent in the 1970s. In the 1980s, when unemployment rates rose in cities by 14 percent, on average, an increase in metropolitan per capita income growth rates by one standard deviation would have actually resulted in a 7 percent decline in unemployment rates. In the suburbs, where unemployment rates declined over the decade, the decrease would have been even greater— 52 percent compared with an actual decrease of 22 percent.

Although unemployment rates, like poverty rates, are quite persistent from decade to decade in both cities and suburbs, there is also evidence of convergence: the greater the initial unemployment rate, the greater the decrease or smaller the increase in the unemployment rate in the subsequent decade in both cities and suburbs. And in both cities and suburbs, the marginal impact of high growth rates on reducing unemployment is large.

As indicated above, despite the significance of growth rates and the association of growth rates with region, there are still some differences among regions that show up in the form of statistically significant coefficients on the regional intercept variables that increase the explained variation of the changes in unemployment rates in the 1980s but not in the 1970s.

## Educational Attainment: Growth and Region

Education is often viewed as a measure of the quality of life offered by a region—college attendance or SAT scores are frequently cited as an indication of the robustness of an area. This may reflect the income elasticity of demand of population and firms for better school systems and the ability of school districts to meet such demands. But the achievements of a local school system are only one part of a more complex interaction between education and growth. An economically dynamic area might attract more highly educated persons, and it might provide an incentive for those in the local labor force to seek more education to respond to employment opportunities opened up by rapid growth.[31] Conversely, slow growth may reduce opportunities and discourage local students from completing high school. A major difference between college graduates and adults without a completed high school education is the far greater mobility of the former. The college graduates are highly mobile, often locating away from the areas in which they grew up or in the areas in which they were educated. Not only will the observed educational attainment of the area's population respond to opportunity, there may be reverse causality as well. High education levels may lead to high rates of growth of productivity and per capita income, as higher-productivity firms from outside the area are attracted or local residents establish new firms—the Silicon Valley story. Here the analysis focuses on the response of educational attainment of the population to income growth. Chapter 4 contains an analysis of the effect of education on income.

To determine the relationship of growth with educational attainment of the population, equations 3-1 and 3-2 have again been estimated for cities

31. A substantial body of literature links growth and industrial location patterns to the education of the labor force. See Glaeser, Scheinkman, and Shleifer (1995). This relationship is explored in chapter 4.

and suburbs. In this case $y_i$ is either the change in the proportion of college graduates or non–high school graduates between 1970 and 1980 or between 1980 and 1990. As before, the $y_b$ terms are the base year variables, either the 1970 or the 1980 proportion of college graduates or non–high school graduates. The estimated equations are shown in tables 3-7 and 3-8. The explained variation for college graduates is somewhat higher in the 1980s equations than in the 1970s for cities, and the individual coefficients more consistent with expectations. The constants indicate the nationwide trend in MSAs: increasing proportions of college graduates and decreasing proportions of those without a high school education. The results also indicate convergence across MSAs in the proportion of college graduates but divergence at the lower end of educational achievement. This would be consistent with the differential mobility patterns described above. The growth in per capita income is associated with increasing proportions of college-educated population in the suburbs in both decades and in the cities only in the 1980s. The importance of the large, positive, and statistically significant association of growth in per capita income and the percentage increase in the college-educated population accounts in large part for the increase in explanatory power of the city equation, from 0.19 in the 1970s to 0.32 in the 1980s. Higher per capita income growth is associated with decreasing proportions of persons at the lower end of the educational attainment range only in the 1980s; in the 1970s its coefficients, although negative, are not statistically significant.

The Northeast metropolitan areas experienced unusually rapid average growth in per capita income in the 1980s, 32 percent. In the South, the increase was only 19 percent (about the same as the average metropolitan growth rates in the Midwest and West in the 1980s). The percentage change in the proportion of college graduates in Southern cities was 16 percent in the 1980s compared with 36 percent in the Northeast. Of the 20 percentage point difference, 8 percentage points—or 40 percent of the difference—is associated with the higher average per capita income growth rate in the Northeastern cities. In the suburbs the percentage point difference in the increase in the average proportion of college graduates is 15, of which more than 60 percent is accounted for by the effect of differences in metropolitan per capita income growth rates. Thus, differences in growth rates of per capita income are major factors associated with increased educational attainment of the population.

The interpretation of the association of the growth in per capita income and higher education is suggestive. Given the high mobility rates of

Table 3-7. *Percentage Change in College Graduates, Cities and Suburbs, 1970s and 1980s*[a]

| | Equation | | | |
| | Cities | | Suburbs | |
| Independent variable | 3-1 | 3-2 | 3-1 | 3-2 |
|---|---|---|---|---|
| | *1970s* | | | |
| Constant | 62.09 | 59.28 | 80.67 | 69.84 |
| | (23.94) | (13.96) | (15.86) | (9.57) |
| Percent college graduates, 1970 | -0.89 | -0.79 | -2.91 | -2.81 |
| | (-5.46) | (-4.77) | (-7.99) | (-7.66) |
| Growth in metropolitan per capita income, 1970s | -5.61 | 13.92 | 42.73 | 54.81 |
| | (-0.43) | (0.97) | (2.20) | (2.56) |
| Growth in metropolitan population, 1970s | -15.63 | -13.73 | 5.76 | 19.73 |
| | (-1.95) | (-1.82) | (0.51) | (1.91) |
| Northeast | | 7.99 | | 9.70 |
| | | (1.88) | | (1.63) |
| Midwest | | -3.95 | | 11.29 |
| | | (-1.16) | | (2.33) |
| South | | -2.65 | | 2.72 |
| | | (-0.91) | | (0.66) |
| Adjusted $R^2$ | 0.15 | 0.19 | 0.27 | 0.28 |
| | *1980s* | | | |
| Constant | 17.06 | 15.45 | 22.11 | 21.53 |
| | (9.31) | (6.11) | (10.97) | (7.84) |
| Percent college graduates, 1980 | -0.35 | -0.31 | -0.62 | -0.65 |
| | (-4.34) | (-3.68) | (-4.65) | (-4.61) |
| Growth in metropolitan per capita income, 1980s | 57.39 | 51.25 | 62.18 | 68.27 |
| | (9.98) | (7.09) | (9.93) | (8.65) |
| Growth in metropolitan population, 1980s | 10.83 | -8.02 | -22.99 | -24.80 |
| | (-2.26) | (-1.37) | (-4.69) | (-4.09) |
| Northeast | | 4.20 | | -2.85 |
| | | (1.39) | | (-0.94) |
| Midwest | | 1.06 | | 0.79 |
| | | (0.49) | | (0.36) |
| South | | 2.38 | | 0.18 |
| | | (1.23) | | (0.09) |
| Adjusted $R^2$ | 0.32 | 0.32 | 0.30 | 0.30 |

a. Numbers in parentheses are *t* values.

the educated population, it is unlikely that the growth in per capita income is capturing a high income elasticity of demand for education among initial residents in a given metropolitan area. Rather, it probably indicates the responsiveness of the educated labor force to economic opportunity. For metropolitan areas, as well as their cities and suburbs,

**Table 3-8.** *Percentage Change in Non–High School Graduates, Cities and Suburbs, 1970s and 1980s*[a]

| | Equation | | | |
|---|---|---|---|---|
| | Cities | | Suburbs | |
| Independent variable | 3-1 | 3-2 | 3-1 | 3-2 |
| | 1970s | | | |
| Constant | −49.65 | −47.24 | −48.35 | −43.84 |
| | (−23.88) | (−19.66) | (−26.35) | (−20.54) |
| Percent less than high school graduates, 1970 | 0.48 | 0.43 | 0.38 | 0.31 |
| | (12.32) | (9.50) | (9.37) | (6.67) |
| Growth in metropolitan per capita income, 1970s | −0.21 | −6.63 | −10.23 | −9.63 |
| | (−0.04) | (−1.22) | (−2.03) | (−1.79) |
| Growth in metropolitan population, 1970s | 2.30 | 0.06 | −3.16 | −7.96 |
| | (0.95) | (0.02) | (−1.40) | (−3.04) |
| Northeast | | −0.74 | | −0.55 |
| | | (−0.44) | | (−0.35) |
| Midwest | | 0.09 | | −3.48 |
| | | (0.07) | | (−2.80) |
| South | | 2.45 | | 0.91 |
| | | (1.98) | | (0.75) |
| Adjusted $R^2$ | 0.39 | 0.41 | 0.27 | 0.32 |
| | 1980s | | | |
| Constant | −32.62 | −28.79 | −29.86 | −26.67 |
| | (−17.56) | (−14.59) | (−10.60) | (−7.99) |
| Percent less than high school graduates, 1980 | 0.30 | 0.40 | 0.15 | 0.20 |
| | (5.90) | (7.28) | (2.06) | (2.22) |
| Growth in metropolitan per capita income, 1980s | −17.50 | −17.29 | −26.90 | −32.32 |
| | (−3.98) | (−3.50) | (−4.62) | (−4.45) |
| Growth in metropolitan population, 1980s | 18.68 | 12.21 | 21.90 | 19.73 |
| | (5.16) | (3.00) | (4.66) | (3.44) |
| Northeast | | −5.86 | | 0.15 |
| | | (−2.70) | | (0.05) |
| Midwest | | −8.47 | | −5.75 |
| | | (−5.56) | | (−2.71) |
| South | | −8.26 | | −4.90 |
| | | (−5.55) | | (−2.21) |
| Adjusted. $R^2$ | 0.16 | 0.27 | 0.12 | 0.16 |

a. Numbers in parentheses are *t* values.

the presence of a highly educated populace may confer externalities: more participation in government, more thoughtful voting patterns, the setting of higher standards for publicly provided services, and a greater tax base. As seen in chapter 4, the presence of college graduates at the beginning of a period also contributes to the subsequent decade's growth in per capita income, particularly in the 1980s. Together the two results (and again it must be remembered that a simultaneous equation system has not been estimated) imply that the presence of college graduates may lead to growth in per capita income, the latter in turn attracting more college graduates—a positive reinforcement mechanism. If this interpretation is correct, it still presents the problem for policymakers of how to attract the initial group of graduates who may help initiate growth.

The effect of population growth varies. Its greatest consistency is its association with increasing proportions (or smaller decreases) of persons without a high school degree in both cities and suburbs in the 1980s. No such association is found in the 1970s, with the exception of a statistically significant negative coefficient in the suburban equation that includes regions—indicating smaller proportions of persons with less than a high school education. As for college graduates, the population growth variable is significant only in the suburbs in the 1980s and is associated with smaller increases in the proportion of adults with a college education. Here, too, it is expected that the differences in the components of the population increase variable—retirees, immigrants, labor force—at different times and places could explain the lack of consistency across time and between cities and suburbs.

After taking into account base year variables and growth in per capita income and population, the addition of the regional variables has little effect. Only in the city equations for non–high school graduates in the 1980s are all the regional coefficients significant, and does the adjusted $R^2$ increase when the regions are added to the equation. The addition of region makes virtually no difference in the equations for college graduates. Finally, the explained variation of the equations shows no consistent pattern: it is substantially greater in the city equations for college graduates in the 1980s than in the 1970s; the opposite is true for those with less than a high school education; it is the same for college graduates in the suburbs in both decades but substantially lower for non–high school graduates in the 1980s. The increase in explanatory power for college graduates in the cities in the 1980s appears to be attributable to the significance of the per capita income growth in that decade. The decrease in explanatory power for persons with less than a high school education is puzzling, given the greater numbers of explanatory variables that become statistically significant in the 1980s.

In sum, in the 1980s, educational attainment in both cities and suburbs appears to have benefited from per capita income growth; in the 1970s, this was the case only for the suburbs. In contrast, population growth appears to have been associated with an increase in the proportion of persons with less than a high school education in both cities and suburbs in the 1980s, due perhaps to the arrival of new immigrants, but with a small decrease in the proportion in the suburbs in the 1970s.

One of the more interesting differences between the equations for college graduates and non–high school graduates is that there is convergence in the proportion of college graduates in both cities and suburbs in both decades, but the opposite tendency is observed for those at the lower end of the educational attainment distribution. The cities and suburbs with lower proportions of college graduates in the previous decade (other things being equal) had larger increases in their proportions of college graduates over the next decade, and the cities and suburbs with higher proportions of non–high school graduates in the previous decade (other things being equal) had smaller decreases in their proportions of non–high school graduates over the next decade. Per capita income growth had generally beneficial effects on both educational groups in cities and in suburbs, but the effect of population growth on educational attainment varies over space and time. After taking these factors into account, residual regional effects on the proportions of college graduates are generally insignificant. The residual regional effects on the proportions of non–high school graduates are more variable: generally insignificant in the 1970s and negative, indicating smaller decreases in this category in other regions compared with the West, in both cities and suburbs.

## Racial Segregation and Growth

Growth might also be expected to have an effect on the ability of minority populations to leave city residences for the suburbs. However, in this case the reduced form equations are inadequate for even beginning to explore the effect of growth, compared with other variables, on residential segregation. A great variety of social and economic characteristics of the population, as well as the spatial distribution of employment and of the housing stock, influence both the desire of minority populations to leave the central cities and their ability to do so.

In addition, immigration of minority populations—Asian, Hispanic, Dominican (all counted as minority)—may so confound the analysis as to make any computation, without highly detailed data on immigration, difficult to interpret. With substantial immigration of minority populations and, in general, their initial location concentrated largely in central cities, interpreting the effects of growth on segregation without detailed data on immigrants by place of residence, compared with older residents by place of residence, can distort the interpretation of residential patterns and of segregation of minority groups. The differences in settlement patterns of minority and immigrant populations in cities and suburbs in the West pose an additional challenge to interpretation, particularly, compared with the Northeast and Midwest. New immigrants are generally more concentrated in the central cities in the latter than in the former. For these reasons, although versions of equations 3-1 and 3-2 have been estimated, there is insufficient reason to attach any significance to them.[32]

## Conclusions

This chapter has presented an analysis of the ways in which the socio-economic variables differ among regions, across metropolitan areas, and between cities and suburbs and has tried to identify the source(s) of these variations. The chapter has been particularly concerned with whether the large differences in growth rates across regions and among metropolitan areas are related to changes in these variables: poverty rates, income inequality, unemployment rates, educational attainment, and segregation in cities and suburbs. Given the very great difference in per capita income growth patterns in the 1970s and 1980s, it was important to analyze each of the decades separately. The estimates also show the persistence of socioeconomic characteristics over long periods of time, as indicated by the correlation coefficients shown in table 3-3. In each case a central concern is whether, after taking the differences in regional growth rates and initial conditions into account, there is any residual regional effect.

The socioeconomic contrasts between cities and suburbs, over time and across regions, are substantial. Cities and suburbs were more differentiated with respect to the economic variables—poverty rates, per capita

---

32. Estimates of equations 3-1 and 3-2 (only for the 1980s), where the dependent variable is the percentage change in the proportion of the non-Hispanic white population living in the central city relative to that in the suburbs, provide almost no explanatory power—adjusted $R^2$ of 0.04. Although both growth variables, population and per capita income, are statistically significant, given the previous comments about difficulties of measurement and of interpretation, particularly of changing populations and the very low explained variation of this equation, it would be foolish to have any confidence in inferences drawn from these coefficients. Neither constant, base period ratio, nor regional dummy variables are even marginally significant.

income, and unemployment rates—in 1990 than they had been in 1970. In 1970 the average city to suburb ratio for poverty rates was 1.2; for per capita incomes, 1.0; and for unemployment rates, 1.1. By 1990 the poverty ratio had increased to 1.7 and the unemployment ratio to 1.4; per capita incomes in the cities had fallen to 90 percent of those in the suburbs. The population of the cities was less well off by these economic indicators in both decades, and the gap had widened over the two decades.

In contrast, the ratio between average city and suburban educational achievement variables indicates a higher percentage of college graduates in cities (a city-suburb ratio of 1.2) and was unchanged between 1970 and 1990. The average percentage of non–high school graduates in cities and suburbs was similar in 1970 (a ratio of approximately 1.0) and increased slightly by 1990 (to 1.1).

Regional variations in socioeconomic characteristics of city and suburb are notable. Population characteristics of cities and suburbs in the metropolitan areas of the South and the West are quite similar, compared with the Northeast and Midwest. For the most part, cities in the Northeast and Midwest have greater concentrations of poverty than their suburbs, lower per capita incomes, higher unemployment rates, smaller proportions of college graduates, larger proportions of persons with less than a high school education, and higher proportions of minority population; in the metropolitan areas of the South and West, the differences between city and suburb are narrower.

Although, as indicated in several places, causality is difficult to identify in the interaction between growth rates and improvements in socioeconomic conditions, it appears from the reduced form equations that for most of the socioeconomic variables, growth in per capita income is associated with improvement in both cities and suburbs: reduced poverty rates, increased per capita income,[33] and increased proportion of the population with a high school education.

Per capita income growth, however, does not appear to reduce income inequality between central city and suburbs; indeed in the 1980s it has a more positive effect on per capita income in suburbs than cities, thereby increasing income inequality.

---

33. As we have noted, higher per capita incomes may indicate higher wages resulting from compensating differentials for negative features of an MSA. The association with high levels of growth makes this less likely.

Do population growth and per capita income growth have similar effects on socioeconomic characteristics?

In contrast to the generally positive relation between per capita income growth and socioeconomic variables, population growth is generally insignificant. It has no significant relationship to per capita incomes in cities or suburbs in the 1970s or the 1980s; its effect on poverty is generally insignificant, and it has mixed effects on educational attainment. Only in the 1980s does population growth appear to be positively associated with educational attainment in both cities and suburbs, in particular with a decrease in persons with less than a high school education.

City-suburban income inequality also appears to be unaffected by population growth in the 1970s, but in the 1980s higher population growth decreases inequality, increasing the ratio of city to suburban per capita incomes. This may be related to differences in the sources of population growth—more workers moving in response to economic opportunity relative to retirees or immigrants.

Persistence effects are substantial. With the exception of the unemployment rates, decade-to-decade correlation coefficients are rarely below 0.8 for any of the other variables—be they metropolitan areas, cities, or suburbs—across all regions. The positive but relatively low decade-to-decade correlations among the unemployment rates are explained by the lack of correlation in the state of the economy from decade to decade. The greatest persistence is found in minority composition from decade to decade. This persistence is difficult to interpret for the many reasons described above.

Despite persistence, there are substantial changes on the margin, as indicated by the regression coefficients on base period values and growth rates. Convergence is more frequent than divergence. For example, the higher the poverty rate in 1970 and 1980, the smaller the increase in the poverty rate over the following decade; the higher the per capita income in 1970 or 1980, the smaller the increase in per capita income in the subsequent decade; the lower the proportion of college graduates in the base period, the greater the increase in the proportion of college graduates in the subsequent decade.

After taking growth and persistence into account, are there still unexplained regional differences? Despite the important explanatory power of differences in growth rates and the major differences in the growth rates of different regions of the country, and after taking into account persistence or path-dependence effects, there are still some residual regional influences on many of these variables. Thus, chapter 4 presents a more extended analysis of the determinants of growth and of regional growth differentials.

What can be concluded from the facts and associations presented in this chapter? Despite high persistence of critical variables, growth in per capita income is generally associated with improving social indicators. The decline in poverty as per capita income increases may reflect changes in wage rates, or unemployment rates, or labor force participation rates for households. The reduced forms estimated do not permit any decomposition of this type. Despite their proximate nature and the absence of a simultaneous equation model that would allow greater precision about the determinants of the indicators, the strong relation between growth in per capita income and the various indicators would probably remain in a more complex model. Increased metropolitan-wide per capita income would be expected to improve the welfare of the residents of both cities and suburbs, although the strength of these effects might diverge in a fully articulated model from those shown in this chapter. To determine these effects, two types of knowledge are necessary, namely, identifying the variables associated with per capita income growth and ascertaining which, if any, of them is amenable to policy influences. Chapters 4 and 5 address these issues.

## CHAPTER FOUR

# Estimating Growth

THE PRECEDING CHAPTERS have contained arguments that a major issue in understanding urban development is the difference in growth rates of metropolitan areas. Robust growth in a metropolitan statistical area (MSA) is usually shared by both city and suburb, and slow growth affects both. The determinants of the growth of MSAs or cities have been the subject of many studies. A large body of literature attempts to identify the source of business investment, which in turn is an important determinant of job growth. Despite considerable ingenuity, the results of these extensive empirical investigations have been inconclusive. Although variables such as proximity to transportation axes and airports, the size of the regional market, the level and composition of local taxes and expenditures, and the quality of life explain some part of the location decisions of business firms, the explanatory value of these variables is limited and is not robust, as the empirical results differ significantly among various studies.[1] Gambling laws (Las Vegas, Nevada), warm weather (San Diego, California), an exceptional university engineering or computer science program (San Jose, California), quick access to outdoor recreation (Portland, Oregon, and Seattle, Washington) all play a part in the location decisions of firms. Although there is a systematic economic component, there are also many idiosyncratic factors.

1. Wasylenko (1997).

The relative decline or rise of regions may also have sources that reflect national trends. Regions heavily dependent on manufacturing in the post–World War II period faced an inevitable decline in their manufacturing activity given the lower income elasticity of demand for manufactured goods compared with services, a decline hastened by the increasing openness of the economy to lower-cost imports. MSAs with a heavy concentration of clothing, textile, and steel producers suffered a decline relative to those specialized in software and financial services. Although declining industrial activity might have been offset by compensating growth in other sectors, as occurred in financial services in the Boston and New York areas in the 1980s, in many MSAs such a transformation did not occur.

In examining the factors associated with different rates of growth across MSAs, the discussion in this chapter considers the entire period 1970–90, as well as the two component decades. The factors conducive to growth changed over the twenty-year period. Both periods exhibited quite idiosyncratic behavior at the national level that inevitably had a counterpart at the level of the MSAs, whose economic activity constitutes the bulk of nationwide gross domestic product (GDP). As changes in the national economy are frequently cited as being important, some of the major changes are briefly outlined here.

The 1970s and early 1980s were characterized by historically high and variable inflation rates (figure 4-1), partly generated by rising energy costs, partly by tight labor markets in the late 1960s and early 1970s, which led to higher nominal wages. The perception that both wage levels and energy prices were lower in the South and the West led firms to seek lower-cost production locations in both regions, to the disadvantage of the Northeast and Midwest. The rapid decline in inflation rates in the 1980s enabled firms to concentrate on improved productivity that does not necessarily have a regional bias. There was also a continuously increasing penetration of the U.S. market by imports (figure 4-2). Although some of the increased imports represented the impact of higher oil prices, there was a large growth in manufactured imports. Combined with the relatively low income elasticity of demand for manufactured products (compared with services), this led to a rapid shift in the structure of production away from manufacturing toward services (figure 4-3). One summary measure of the atypical behavior of the economy in the 1970s was the Dow Jones stock average, which had come close to reaching 1,000 in 1968 but was below 800 in the summer of 1982 when the

**Figure 4-1.** *Inflation, Gross Domestic Product Deflator*

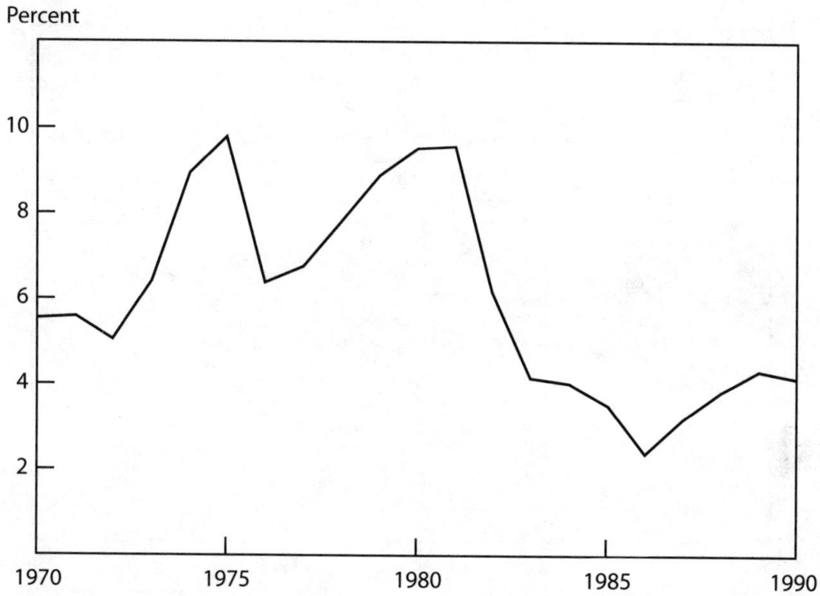

Percent

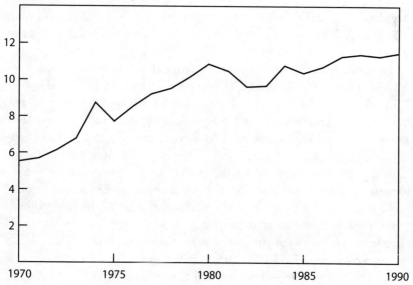

**Figure 4-2.** *Imports of Goods and Services*

Percent of gross domestic product

**Figure 4-3.** *Sectoral Shares of Gross Domestic Product*[a]

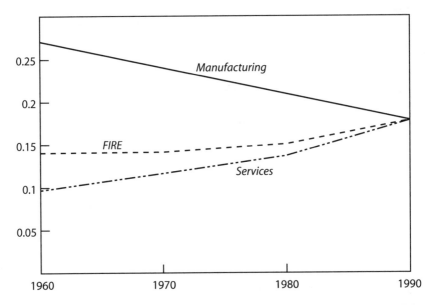

a. The three sectors sum to less than 100 percent of gross domestic product. Services do not include whole-sale and retail trade. Other sectors excluded from the figure are agriculture; forestry and fishing; mining and construction; and transportation and public utilities.

sustained bull market began. Given that the GDP price deflator had risen threefold in this period, the real value of the Dow Jones average was less than a quarter of its 1968 level.

These shifts in the structure of the national economy had major consequences for MSAs. In the 1970s, the concern by both firms and households about energy prices reinforced the existing movement of households to warmer climates. Few MSAs in the Northeast and Midwest were able to maintain high population or income growth, as noted in chapter 1. Moreover, the changing sectoral mix of production favored metropolitan areas that possessed attributes that made them attractive venues for firms and households. In the 1980s the impact of financial deregulation combined with the shifting U.S. comparative advantage toward high technology (in both manufacturing and services). One of the goals of this chapter is to identify the initial factors that allowed some MSAs to thrive in this rapidly changing environment while many experienced absolute or relative decline in both population and per capita income.

Figures 4-1 through 4-3 suggest that it is unlikely that the forces propelling growth were identical over the two decades. Not only was inflation very different, but there were also substantial increases in the finance, insurance, and real estate and the service sectors in the 1980s, although the decline in manufacturing was fairly continuous. A still more disaggregated view would show the greater growth of the high value-added sectors in the 1980s. Although the regressions in this chapter to explain growth rates across MSAs report results for the two decades as well as the component decades, the economy-wide changes suggest that greater insights are to be obtained from results for the separate decades.

In the face of idiosyncratic features such as gambling laws and inherited characteristics such as dependence on manufacturing, the fates of MSAs might be viewed as being outside their control. Much of the recent literature that attempts to explain growth patterns relies on the initial values of critical variables such as the share of manufacturing in total employment and some measure of education.[2] I utilize similar analysis but recognize that such specifications—although useful for obtaining an understanding of past growth patterns—do not readily yield insights about positive policy measures that regions should undertake. They suggest that the past growth of regions from which both cities and suburbs benefited (or lost) was largely due to initial conditions that could not have been altered significantly by policymakers. Chapter 6 includes an analysis of potential policy measures that have been suggested to improve regional growth prospects.

The absence of definitive results on the sources of growth has resulted, not surprisingly, in widely varying policies by the public sector to accelerate growth in a city or state, occasionally in a coordinated regional effort. Subsidies and tax benefits to sports complexes, performing art centers, convention centers, industry incubators, and research and development consortia are all pursued in one jurisdiction or another. In the case of subsidized convention centers and tax benefits to attract firms, there is a nationwide zero-sum game. All MSAs cannot increase their share of convention visitors or total investment. These policy questions are considered in detail in chapter 6.

Despite the problematic nature of quantitatively determining the sources of MSA or city growth, it is an important exercise, because it helps to focus attention on a number of critical dimensions of MSA

---

2. Glaeser, Scheinkman, and Shleifer (1995).

growth that ultimately affect the intertwined fate of cities and suburbs. Although explanations of the past are, as mutual fund advertisements proclaim, no guarantee of future performance, they help to structure the question of the desirability and feasibility of specific growth-enhancing public policies. Assuming that no public officials are likely to be as prescient as Bugsy Siegel was in assessing the potential growth rate of Las Vegas, some systematic evidence is a necessary base for future discussions. This chapter considers the determinants of the growth of MSAs, whereas in chapter 6 an attempt is made to evaluate policy proposals in light of the empirical results.

## Quantitative Models of the Growth of MSAs

In explaining MSA growth patterns, the first task is to choose the relevant measure of growth. The well-being of an MSA is, in my view, best captured by the level of per capita income and its growth. In earlier chapters it was shown that variables reflecting social welfare, such as unemployment and poverty rates, are improved by per capita income growth. Although per capita income may reflect compensating differentials for negative characteristics of an area, its association with positive socioeconomic changes suggests otherwise, namely that it more closely reflects productivity differentials.

Population growth is often viewed as the growth variable to be explained, although it is not closely related to the growth of private living standards and social welfare. Population loss will reduce the vibrancy of an MSA; lead to loss of tax revenue and public expenditures that enhance the business environment and the quality of life; and may set in motion further losses as both businesses and households view the area as undesirable. The simple correlation coefficients between population and per capita income growth for 1960–90 and for each of the individual decades are shown in table 4-1. They are not highly correlated. Over the entire period, the correlation between the growth rates in per capita income and population was .30. The correlations for each decade were .18 in the 1960s, .35 in the 1970s, and .30 in the 1980s for all. They were higher for the Northeast and Midwest for the entire period, but even in these regions the correlation in most decades was much lower.

Presented below is an attempt to explain both population growth and per capita income growth—the former is the conventional measure of the growth of MSAs, and the latter captures the quality of the growth. The

Table 4-1. *Correlation between Population and per Capita Income Growth Rates, MSAs*

| Region | 1960–90 | 1960–70 | 1970–80 | 1980–90 |
|---|---|---|---|---|
| All | .30 | .18 | .35 | .30 |
| Northeast | .71 | .34 | .44 | .50 |
| Midwest | .57 | .29 | .37 | .65 |
| South | .38 | .43 | .05 | .48 |
| West[a] | .42 | .07 | .30 | .42 |

a. Excludes one extreme outlying observation in the West.

two explanation are related but are not necessarily identical. For example, labor inmigration, a large component of population growth, may respond positively to high wages and negatively to poverty rates due to the fiscal or social negative externalities attributed to the poor.[3] Wages, the major determinant of per capita income, may exhibit a different pattern. Potential migrants are attracted by higher wages but may require a compensating differential if the MSA has undesirable characteristics such as congestion or a high unemployment rate.[4] Thus per capita income levels might be expected to have a positive relation to initial poverty rates, wages being increased beyond a pure productivity-based differential. Growth in per capita income could thus be positively associated with initial poverty rates or other indicators of low values of quality-of-life indicators, whereas the labor inflow effect would be negative.

3. Pack (1998).

4. One relevant study estimates the effect of "environmental goods" in an earnings equation covering 237 MSAs. The environmental goods include crime rates, local government services, the number of television and radio stations, air pollution, and climate (average January temperature). Two slightly different specifications of the equations are estimated for male earnings and for female earnings. Although the author concludes that "the results confirm the hypothesis that a tradeoff exists between the quantity and the quality of environmental goods, earnings levels, and house values," the earnings equations are substantially at variance with the author's expectations. The crime rate comes closest to supporting the hypothesis that negative characteristics of a location are associated with higher earnings. Air pollution results are nearly as consistent, although they have the correct sign and are statistically significant in only two of the specifications, one for males and one for females. The climate effect is puzzling: negative and significant, as anticipated, for males but for females, positive in both equations and statistically significant in only one. Local government services are statistically insignificant in all specifications and have the correct sign in only one; television and radio stations have the wrong sign in the two equations in which their coefficients are statistically significant. See Izraeli (1987). Other studies of the relation between wages and quality of life are Greenwood and Hunt (1989) and Greenwood and others (1991).

### Growth in per Capita Income

Why should growth rates of per capita income differ by region? If there is no migration, the growth rate of income per worker, assuming a Cobb-Douglas production function for expositional simplicity, is

$$(4\text{-}1) \qquad (Y/L)^* = A^* + \alpha(K/L)^*,$$

where $Y$ is metropolitan value added, $L$ is the metropolitan labor force, $A$ is the level of productivity, $K$ is the MSA capital stock, and $\alpha$ is the elasticity of output with respect to capital. An asterisk denotes growth rates. If the ratio of labor force growth to population growth is similar among regions, equation 4-1 describes the growth rate of per capita income.

What accounts for different values of $A$ and $A^*$ across regions? Levels of $A$ may vary due to localized knowledge and to agglomeration economies. If knowledge is localized in the Route 128 area near Boston, firms may move there to gain access to and more effectively absorb the knowledge. Location at a distance is likely to be second best to frequent face-to-face interaction.[5] Insofar as knowledge is geographically concentrated, firms in the region may obtain a temporary advantage in $A$. A considerable body of literature provides support for the view that knowledge is localized.[6] Does such a level effect translate into a growth effect, namely, higher values of $A^*$? There is some literature on differential values of $A^*$ across states, but these have not been related to initial levels of $A$.[7] Sustained differences in both $A$ and $A^*$ are not likely, given the importance of knowledge that is not formally written out or codified in manuals and blueprints but is embodied in mobile individuals or groups of workers. Such knowledge is often readily available to nearby firms but not to distant ones.[8]

The other source of differences in $A$ (but not necessarily $A^*$) is agglomeration economies stemming from a higher-quality set of inputs. Firms may locate in an MSA that is dense with firms and workers with whom they can interact. Firms benefit from access to a large pool of workers with specific skills and from fast access to specialized intermediate and

5. For a description of this process in Silicon Valley, California, and the Route 128 hub near Boston, see Saxenian (1994).

6. Audretsch (1998); Audretsch and Feldman (1996); Jaffe, Trajtenberg, and Henderson (1993).

7. Beeson (1987).

8. Saxenian (1994).

capital goods that are only slowly available from other regions. Better workers may locate in a "thick" industrial area to reduce the risk of unemployment should demand for their skills decrease in one or two industries.[9] This group of features, collectively known as Marshall-Arrow-Romer agglomeration economies, or MAR in recent literature, could account for a high value of $A$. It could translate into high values of $A^*$ if a large, interacting set of enterprises attracts new firms and their investment and leads to still greater specialization and the influx of skilled workers. Without additional firms and workers entering, agglomeration is best thought of as explaining the level of $A$ in a given MSA rather than $A^*$.

To explain growth in wages, a major part of per capita income, requires some measures of the determinants of $A^*$. As stated above, some of the growth of wages may also be a compensating differential, necessary to offset any decline in the quality of life.

### Growth in Population

Over a decade, labor force growth, a primary determinant of population growth, will respond to the wage rate, which in turn depends on the growth in labor's marginal product, itself a function of $A^*$ and $(K/L)^*$. Given the lack of internal obstacles to capital movement, investment and thus $K^*$ will respond to $A^*$. If returns to investment are high but saving is low in Albuquerque, saving done by residents of Boston will be channeled by the financial system to New Mexico. But as suggested above, other determinants not captured by the neoclassical model such as gambling laws and weather will also affect investment and the generation of high-paying jobs. Most recent models view the basic determinant of the growth of the labor force to be the value of $A^*$ and avoid explicitly modeling the location of investment. Yet there is abundant anecdotal evidence, some of it discussed in chapter 5, of the influence of quality-of-life factors.

Inmigration from other parts of the United States and migration from abroad may also respond to the number of jobs as well as wage levels. In the migration decision, it is not only the wages that are relevant but also the probability of obtaining employment that pays these wages.[10]

---

9. These real external economies were discussed by Marshall (1890) and elaborated by Arrow (1962) and Romer (1986). For discussions see Quigley (1998) and David and Rosenbloom (1990).

10. For formal models of this process see Todaro (1969) and Sjaastad (1962).

Migration may occur in response to differences in income per capita and the probability of obtaining a job, assuming that the present discounted value (PDV) of gains in income to migrants exceeds the PDV of costs of moving. In addition, potential migrants will consider not only increases in income but also any loss in the quality of life, whether due to pollution, cost of living, or congestion. Thus, most of the research on the determinants of city or MSA population growth considers two sets of variables that affect labor-force decisions. The characteristics that increase $A^*$, and ultimately wage levels, induce growth in the labor force through inmigration; those that decrease the quality of life ($Q$) retard such growth.

Population growth will, in addition, be affected by inmigration of non–labor force members such as retirees. Some MSAs have received large inflows of retirees, whose movement is less likely to be explained by potential gains in wages than by climate, and perhaps also the presence of cultural institutions and the availability of medical care.

The considerations outlined above imply a similar model to explain both income per capita and population, namely,

(4-2) $$L^* = f(A^*, Q)$$

(4-3) $$(Y/L)^* = g(A^*, Q).$$

Many empirical exercises have been implemented to explain the cross-regional growth of population and per capita income, with the typical estimating equations having the following form:

(4-4) $$L^* \text{ or } (Y/L)^* = b_0 + b_1 X_A + b_2 X_B + e,$$

where $X_A$ is a vector of variables that affects $A^*$ and $X_B$ is a vector of variables affecting $Q$. It is assumed that $\partial L^*/\partial Q < 0$, $\partial L^*/\partial A^*$, $\partial(Y/L)^*/\partial A^*$ and $\partial(Y/L)^*/\partial Q > 0$. The emphasis is thus on household labor decisions. In a fully specified model, the availability of jobs would be jointly determined by $K^*$ and $A^*$. Though there may be different lags in responding to $A^*$, both capital accumulation and labor allocation depend on it. Capital growth will also interact with labor force growth. If, for example, a region receives a major exogenous influx of labor, perhaps due to immigration from abroad (such as that experienced by New York City and MSAs in California, Florida, New Mexico, and Texas), the increase in labor force will imply a decline in the capital-labor ratio and greater marginal productivity of capital. This may in turn attract additional investment out of the national pool. Investment could thus be induced by exogenous labor force growth. However, given data constraints, most research has not explicitly modeled $K^*$ by MSA, a precedent that is followed here.

### Simple Stylized Facts of MSA Growth

First the stylized facts of metropolitan growth are set out without addressing the causal relations. Regressions are estimated in the following form:

(4-5) $\qquad \text{LMPOP79} = \beta_0 + \beta_1\text{LMPOP70} + \beta_2\text{MPCMY69} +$
$\qquad\qquad\qquad \beta_3 d_1 + \beta_4 d_2 + \beta_5 d_3$

(4-6) $\qquad \text{LMPCYG79} = \beta_0 + \beta_1\text{MPOP70} + \beta_2\text{MPCMY69} +$
$\qquad\qquad\qquad \beta_3 d_1 + \beta_4 d_2 + \beta_5 d_3,$

where LMPOP79 is the log difference in metropolitan population from 1970 to 1990, LMPCYG79 is the log difference in per capita income in MSAs from 1969 to 1989, MPOP70 is population in 1970, MPCMY69 is metropolitan per capita income in 1969, and $d_1$, $d_2$, and $d_3$ are dummy variables for the Northeast, Midwest, and South—the West being the excluded region. Although many researchers use city values as their independent variables, assuming that cities are the major drivers of metropolitan growth, given the very close correlation between growth rates of cities and suburbs within MSAs I believe the MSA to be the more appropriate geographic unit, as many of the determinants of employment growth are related to metropolitan-wide features.[11] Given the results reported in earlier chapters, it is the major differences in MSA growth across the nation that give rise to different growth rates in cities and their suburbs, and MSA growth is the variable of interest. Put another way, the growth of cities and their suburbs is highly correlated with that of their MSA, and differences in growth rates across MSAs are very large.[12]

The estimates of equations 4-5 and 4-6 allow a number of major facts to be sorted, such as the extent of regional differences; the degree to

11. My results are similar to those of Glaeser, Scheinkman, and Shleifer (1995), despite somewhat different coverage. I employ observations for 250 MSAs, whereas their data include 203 cities and 133 MSAs. When I replicate their results for the period 1960–90, the two sets of estimates are quite close.

12. Whether city or MSA variables explain city or MSA growth is ultimately an empirical issue. My estimates using each set of independent variables suggest that both city and MSA variables yield roughly the same explanation of growth.

**Table 4-2.** *Regional Influence on Metropolitan Population and per Capita Income Growth, 1970–90*[a]

| Variable | Equation 4-5 LGMPOP79 | Equation 4-6 LGMPY79 |
|---|---|---|
| Constant | .63 | .20 |
| | (4.20) | (3.52) |
| LMPOP70 | –.026 | .001 |
| | (–1.79) | (.25) |
| MPCMY69 | 1.95E–.05 | 8.81E–.06 |
| | (1.30) | (1.53) |
| Northeast | –.39 | .026 |
| | (–9.00) | (1.59) |
| Midwest | –.37 | –.04 |
| | (–10.39) | (–2.90) |
| South | –.13 | .05 |
| | (–3.38) | (3.54) |
| Adjusted $R^2$ | .38 | .19 |

a. Base period variables are MSA values; numbers in parentheses are *t* values.

which convergence occurs (for example, do smaller MSAs grow faster than large ones); and the importance of convergence in per capita income. The results are presented in table 4-2. These equations indicate that

—There is some evidence of population convergence, that is, the greater the MSA population in 1970, the less it grew over the period 1970–90.

—Per capita income, however, shows some evidence of divergence.

—The direction of the regional variables is clear, population in the West grew more rapidly than in each of the other regions, and each of the regional coefficients is significant at 1 percent or better.

—The coefficients on region in the per capita income equation are somewhat different—per capita incomes in the South grew more rapidly than in the West, and in the Midwest grew significantly less rapidly. The insignificant coefficient for the Northeast region reflects what is noted above, and is estimated below: namely, the very slow growth of per capita incomes in the MSAs of the Northeast in the 1970s but very rapid growth in the 1980s.

Overall, this gross equation does a better job of estimating population growth than per capita income growth, as indicated by the adjusted $R^2$ values of .38 and .19, respectively. These are very preliminary results designed to provide a rough sense of the major trends with respect to population and per capita income. More extensive equations presented below provide considerably more insight into the processes.

I have also estimated identical equations for the 1970s and 1980s, but they are not shown here.

## Growth in Population and Income: An Expanded View

Although the regression estimates in the preceding section help to organize the disparate evidence about the major facts of MSA convergence, and the differences in experience by region, they do not provide insight into the complex determinants of growth. Existing empirical explanations of the determinants of population growth across cities or MSAs are eclectic, empirically based formulations employing some variant of the framework discussed in the preceding two sections. Most studies use a convergence regression adopted with modification from models that attempt to explain differences across countries in the growth of GDP per capita or across states of the United States.[13] The rate of growth of population is assumed to be a function of initial per capita income, initial population, and a set of variables that are related to $A^*$ or $Q$ in equations 4-2 and 4-3. To avoid endogeneity, initial values of $X_A$ and $X_B$ are employed—for example, the levels of education in 1970 for regressions for the 1970–90 period. The change in education levels during the period cannot be used because this might itself be a response to high growth rates of income per person, as discussed in chapter 3. On the other hand, over a period of 20 years, changing education levels might well have had an effect on growth rates, but absent a simultaneous equation model, for which data are not available, such variables are difficult to incorporate.

### Growth in Metropolitan Population and per Capita Income in the 1970s and 1980s

The analysis that follows expands on existing research in a number of ways, employs a considerably larger data set that includes 250 MSAs, and extends the analysis for MSAs. These extensions take several forms: they broaden the analysis for the MSAs, examining metropolitan employment growth and growth in per capita income rather than concentrating on cities; they include a subset of the nine major employment sectors

---

13. Barro and Sala-i-Martin (1991); Mankiw, Romer, and Weil (1991).

based on their role as exporters of goods or services to other MSAs rather than relying solely on the more common manufacturing/nonmanufacturing breakdown; they examine the role of other determinants of growth such as weather and the presence of research universities.

The analysis considers the growth in population and per capita income in MSAs over the two decades 1970–90 as well as for each of the two decades separately. The same equations have been estimated for city growth rates as a function of metropolitan independent variables, as described below for MSAs, and there are virtually no differences between the city and metropolitan equations in signs, magnitude of coefficients, significance levels, or explained variation. Therefore, the city equations are not presented.

As will be seen, the results for 1970–90 differ significantly from those for the two component decades. Two interpretations are possible: either that the factors affecting long-term growth work slowly and the estimates for the two decades together convey an accurate impression about the growth process; or that given the changes in inflation rates, the size of imports, and the changing importance of major sectors (shown in figures 4-1 through 4-3), the forces driving growth apparently changed, and the decadal results provide the more meaningful picture of the sources of evolution of MSAs.

My equations add a number of variables—for example, initial sectoral shares of employment in four sectors—to equations 4-5 and 4-6 that capture some of the forces believed to be important in determining metropolitan growth rates. The dependent variables are log differences in MSA population and income per capita. To test for convergence, base period values of these variables are included.

### Estimating Equation

Equations 4-7 and 4-8 are estimated to explain both population and per capita income growth for the period 1970–90.

$$
\begin{aligned}
(4\text{-}7) \quad \text{LGMPOP79} = {} & \beta_0 + \beta_1(\text{LMPOP70}) + \beta_2(\text{MPCMY69}) + \\
& \beta_3(\text{LGMPOP67}) + \beta_4(\text{PIMANM70}) + \\
& \beta_5(\text{PIFIRM70}) + \beta_6(\text{PIBSRM70}) + \\
& \beta_7(\text{PIPRSM70}) + \beta_8(\text{PCOGRM70}) + \\
& \beta_9(\text{TECH}) + \beta_{10}(\text{JANUARY}) + \\
& \beta_{11}(\text{PUNEMPM7}) + \beta_{14}d_1 + \beta_{15}d_2 + \beta_{16}d_3
\end{aligned}
$$

**Table 4-3.** *Definitions of Variables Used in Equations 4-7 and 4-8*[a]

| Variable | Definition |
|----------|------------|
| LGMPOP79 | Log change in MSA population, 1970–90 |
| LGMPCMY79 | Log change in MSA per capita income, 1970–90 |
| LMPOP70 | Log of MSA population, 1970 |
| MPCMY69 | MSA per capita income, 1969 |
| LGMPOP67 | Log change in MSA population, 1960–70 |
| LMPCMY67 | Log change in MSA per capita income, 1960–70 |
| PIMANM70 | Percentage of MSA labor force in manufacturing, 1970 |
| PIFIRM70 | Percentage of MSA labor force in finance, insurance, real estate, 1970 |
| PIBSRM70 | Percentage of MSA labor force in business services, 1970 |
| PIPRSM70 | Percentage of MSA labor force in professional services, 1970 |
| PCOGRM70 | Percentage of MSA population who are college graduates, 1970 |
| JANUARY | Average temperature in January |
| TECH | Number of university departments ranked among the top 25 in 1998 in biology, computer sciences, or engineering |
| PUNEMPM7 | Percentage of MSA labor force unemployed in 1970 |
| $d_1$ | Northeast |
| $d_2$ | Midwest |
| $d_3$ | South |

a. Similar definitions hold for the 1970–80 and 1980–90 growth equations, with base period variables and changes in previous decade appropriately adjusted.

$$(4\text{-}8) \quad \text{LGMPCMY79} = \beta_0 + \beta_1(\text{MPCMY69}) + \beta_2(\text{LMPCMY67}) + \\ \beta_3(\text{PIMANM70}) + \beta_4(\text{PIFIRM70}) + \\ \beta_5(\text{PIBSRM70}) + \beta_6(\text{PIPRSM70}) + \\ \beta_7(\text{PCOGRM70}) + \beta_8(\text{TECH}) + \\ \beta_9(\text{JANUARY}) + \beta_{10}(\text{PUNEMPM7}) + \\ \beta_{14}d_1 + \beta_{15}d_2 + \beta_{16}d_3.$$

The same equations are also estimated for each of the two decades; for the 1980–90 estimates the value for the base period variables is that for 1980. The dependent variables are the log differences in population and per capita income. Definitions of variables are presented in table 4-3.

CONVERGENCE. Initial per capita income (MPCMY69 or MPCMY79) is included to test for convergence. A negative coefficient would imply that poorer MSAs experience faster population growth or growth in per capita income—that is, that MSAs exploit their relative backwardness. In international studies in which convergence was first put forth as an empirical hypothesis, it was argued that poorer countries could benefit from the (locally) unused backlog of technology available in richer countries. Convergence within the United States would imply that interregional or intermetropolitan gaps in knowledge are reduced over time given the mobility of individuals, good transportation and communication, a dense network of intermediate goods and machinery sales forces, consulting firms, trade associations, periodicals, and university-based knowledge. These factors enable backward regions to tap the knowledge of other regions, although there may be a lag in doing so. These views imply that the initial value of $A$ in equation 4-1 is not identical across MSAs and that $A^*$ may vary inversely with $A$.

Another interpretation of the convergence term is that initial differences in per capita income may represent differences in factor prices that serve as a signal of the potential cost saving to firms if they locate in the region. As seen through this prism, low-income areas at the beginning of a period have been adversely affected by some economic forces that have driven down the price of land or labor to levels attractive to companies that then locate in the region. The investment induced by such opportunities increases $K^*$ and job opportunities, leading to inmigration of workers and hence population growth.

ROLE OF PRODUCTIVITY GROWTH AND SHIFTS IN DEMAND. Equation 4-4 includes the determinants of $A^*$ as an important source of difference in growth performance. A number of variables can be used to measure the likely evolution of $A^*$ across regions. The initial value of per capita income should have some predictive value for $A^*$, because MSAs with lower per capita income may have absorbed less knowledge and can achieve higher growth rates of productivity by borrowing from more advanced ones. Innovation and productivity growth are likely to be enhanced by the presence of a major research university, and a variable is included to capture such potential benefits. In particular the technology variable, TECH, is defined as the number of universities in the MSA ranked among the top 25 in computer sciences, engineering, mathematics, or biology by the National Academy of Sciences in 1998. Earlier rankings were unavailable. TECH may be endogenous if universities were able to attract better researchers in growing MSAs or those in which per capita income was growing. However, given that most universities maintain a national ranking among the top 25 programs, over long periods of time, there is probably little movement in such rankings. Although the TECH variable is the same in both decades, it will be seen that the impact of university research capabilities became important only in the 1980s in determining the growth of per capita income as the shift to higher-technology economic activity accelerated in that period.

Some researchers used the initial manufacturing share of employment, $N_M/N$, as an indicator of potential productivity growth where $N_M$ is employment in manufacturing and $N$ is total employment in the MSA.[14] The assumption is that a high value of $N_M/N$ is likely to be associated with slow productivity growth because a large stock of manufacturing capital measures the potential for obsolescence of the capital stock. The impact of an aging stock would exert a negative effect on $A^*$ due to negative disembodied technical change. An alternate interpretation is that whatever the impact of $N_M/N$ on $A^*$, it also captures the decline in the importance of the sector over the period in question. Even if a region had a high value of $A^*$, the influx of labor would be limited by reduced job opportunities due to shifts in the structure of the economy.

In fact, manufacturing exhibited *higher* rates of growth of total factor productivity nationwide during 1970–90 than did other sectors. However, the lower income elasticity of demand for manufactured goods than for the nonmanufacturing sector combined with the growing levels of imports of some manufactured goods led to a reduction in its aggregate share of employment and GDP from roughly 31 percent to 17 percent between 1960 and 1990.[15] A significant negative coefficient of $N_M/N$ may capture this demand shift effect and may also serve as a proxy for a low value of $A^*$. A high initial value indicates the potential for decline. Over two decades, the decline in manufacturing within a region might have led to decreases in real wages and land prices relative to other regions that should have induced other nonmanufacturing firms to enter. If $N_M/N$ is negative and statistically significant it would imply that such equilibrating mechanisms were not at work or that they work over a period longer than the period of observation.

Variables measuring the potential impact of shifting national demands are introduced to determine whether there were equilibrating forces. Insofar as local economic activity responds to national shifts in demand, it is necessary to include measures that may affect a region's future share of national growth in sectors other than manufacturing. This analysis considers only "export" industries—those that sell to other regions or

14. Glaeser, Scheinkman, and Shleifer (1995).
15. Council of Economic Advisers (1998, table B-46).

countries—because these are most affected by national trends. In contrast, sectors such as retailing, home construction, and personal services expand and decline in response to the increased population or income per capita that is generated by the export industries. In these branches, the growth of employment and the population is an endogenous response to the changing production of the export industries.[16] A change in a region's household income stemming from a decline in manufacturing output or an increase in the finance, insurance, and real estate sector should have roughly the same impact on local retailing and schools in all MSAs. Different labor force movement across regions is generated primarily by the export sectors.

The specific sectoral measures used are the initial share of MSA-wide employment in four export sectors: finance, insurance, and real estate (PIFIR70); business and repairs (PIBSR70); manufacturing (PIMAN70); and professional services (PIPRS70). For the 1980s, the value for 1980 is used. The decline in the national share of manufacturing between 1970 and 1990 implies that regions in which manufacturing loomed large initially might suffer from slower growth, as Glaeser and colleagues found to be true for the period 1960–90.[17] Nevertheless, such a decline could set in motion the entry of firms in new sectors to pick up the slack, thus providing new jobs. Given the possibility of agglomeration economies within broad sectors, it seems more likely that such entry would occur if there were already large numbers of firms and workers in these sectors in 1970. Insofar as learning is cumulative and localized, a sizable initial sector should also result in a higher value of $A^*$ for the region and potentially greater wages.

EDUCATION. There are many ways in which education may affect the rate of productivity growth. One interpretation of the role of college graduates is that a pool of educated workers attracts knowledge-based firms that have high values of $A^*$ or whose terms of trade are improving relative to other sectors. Perhaps the most convincing theoretical link between education and productivity growth is the argument set out by Nelson and Phelps and by Schultz.[18] In their view higher education facilitates the absorption of frontier technology by potential adopters and the

16. Regional input-output tables typically break down economic activity into export and local economic activity. This analysis uses this concept at a considerably more aggregated level.

17. Glaeser, Scheinkman, and Shleifer (1995).

18. Nelson and Phelps (1966); Schultz (1975).

efficient allocation of capital and labor across firms and industries, thus raising the value of $A^*$. A high stock of educated labor force members in a region implies that $A^*$ in a region will be larger as new technologies are adopted and used more efficiently. An alternative view is that of Lucas, who posits that the average level of education increases the level of productivity ($A$ in equation 4-1).[19] Large numbers of educated peers improve the productivity of both labor and capital. In Lucas's model $A$ is replaced by $H^\gamma$, where $H$ is the average years of education, $H$ generating an externality whose magnitude is given by $\gamma$. Lucas's argument can be viewed as being analogous in its effect to agglomeration economies, that is, explaining a level but not a growth effect. If $H$ grows, it generates a growth effect as well.

Because I view the Nelson-Phelps-Schultz model of the role of education to be the most plausible, I include the percentage of college graduates (PCOGR) at the beginning of each period. Insofar as the Nelson-Phelps-Schultz view assumes that the role of education is to facilitate the adoption of heretofore (locally) unused innovations, it implies that the ability to cope with rapid change is relevant; I believe that in the economy that has evolved over the last decades, it is college education that provides such abilities. Earlier studies testing the implications of this model find that college education was important, even in agriculture.[20] Other researchers have used median education, mean years of education, and percentage of high school graduates. If one adopted Lucas's model of externalities, the mean or the median would be appropriate. In the studies by Glaeser and colleagues and others, the coefficient of education is sensitive to the specific measure used. In this study, as will be seen, the impact of college education differs between decades.

NON–LABOR FORCE POPULATION GROWTH. In the two decades considered, there was considerable growth of the retired population, and many retirees relocated from northern states to the Sun Belt. Many of the rapidly growing MSAs are in Arizona, California, Florida, and North Carolina. Hence, this analysis includes one measure of the attractiveness of such areas to retirees, namely, the temperature in JANUARY. This variable may also capture the impact of immigration. The warmer states—including Arizona, California, Florida, New Mexico, and Texas—are close to major sources of immigration such as Mexico, Central America,

19. Lucas (1988).
20. Welch (1970).

and Cuba. Immigrants from Southeast Asia have also been attracted by warmer climates. The inclusion of JANUARY tests whether the impact of weather adds to the explanation provided by measures of economic opportunity.

QUALITY-OF-LIFE INDICATORS. Four variables were considered to capture potential adverse effects on the quality of life: the size of the initial population, LMPOP70 or LMPOP80, to measure the adverse effects of crowding; the percentage of poverty; the percentage of unemployment; and the percentage of non–high school graduates. High values of any of these might discourage inmigration or lead to a demand for compensating wage differentials by those who do migrate. The latter three variables have relatively high correlations, and only unemployment rates, PUNE70 or PUNE80, are used in the reported regressions. An alternative interpretation is that a lower rate of unemployment reflects greater human capital, which is important in generating higher values of $A^*$. In the view of Glaeser and colleagues, lower unemployment is a proxy for greater human capital at the beginning of a period and thus contributes to growth over the ensuing decades.[21]

PERSISTENT GROWTH. The population growth equations are estimated including and excluding the population growth of the preceding decade, measured as the change in the log of population in the previous decade, LGMPOP67 or LGMPOP78. The argument for inclusion stems from a view that MSA growth, like many other economic processes, has some inertial component.[22] Household decisions are based partly on individuals' personal acquaintance with recent migrants to an area. In Sun City, Arizona (founded in 1960), growth was greater in the 1970s because many potential retirees were acquainted with households that moved there during the 1960s or read or heard about the rapid growth and concluded this was a desirable location. Bandwagon effects can occur in location decisions as well as in the purchase of new electronic consumer goods. Potential labor-force migrants as well as immigrants may engage in similar decision processes. Of course inclusion of the previous decade's growth still leaves unexplained why that growth took place. Were the sources serendipitous or systematic?—a question addressed in chapter 5. The argument for including the lagged value of growth is that it may remove the inertial effects and allow a more precise estimate, on

21. Glaeser, Scheinkman, and Shleifer (1995).
22. For historical evidence on this process see Fabricant (1970).

the margin, of the determinants of growth in the succeeding decade. The alternative estimates cannot thus be judged purely on statistical grounds but on the plausibility of the insights provided by each set of estimates.

REGIONAL EFFECTS. As mentioned previously, one motivation for the current set of estimates is that the results seen in earlier chapters showed considerable differences among regions in the growth rate of their MSAs that were much more important than intrametropolitan differences between city and suburban growth rates. In the regressions presented here, the coefficients of the regional dummies are substantially reduced compared with table 4-2. This implies that the other variables included in equations 4-7 and 4-8 differ regionally and that much of the size of the regional dummies shown in table 4-2 can be explained by such variables. Regions matter, but by themselves they assume less importance. The significance of other variables provides clues to the factors that differentiate regions and policies that are associated with faster growth for individual MSAs.

The regional dummy variables may also reflect the fact that there are some ingredients in the growth process that are location specific. For example, Stanford University's engineering and computer science departments were an important part of the growth story in Silicon Valley. In some cases complementary factors strengthen the region-specific initiating force. The high-technology complexes near Stanford and San Diego are clearly made more attractive by the excellent weather.[23] The regional dummy variables capture both the effects of such nonmobile attributes as natural resources or information networks and their reinforcement by physical attractiveness. The growth of Portland, Oregon, as a high-tech area has often been attributed to a combination of its initial lower land cost and the attractiveness of the Pacific Northwest, as well as its proximity (by air) to Silicon Valley.

If such phenomena could be accounted for in cross-section–time series regressions, some of the residual regional effect would be explained. But these would require time series data for MSAs, which are not currently available. The use of regional dummies provides a helpful guide to the proximate determinants of growth but cannot be interpreted as providing the full story. The richer context of which the reduced forms capture only part needs to be kept in mind. The role of Fairchild, Hewlett-Packard,

23. A variable that shows the interaction between JANUARY and TECH, however, is not significant.

and Intel in the Santa Clara Valley and Microsoft in Seattle is not easily captured by unemployment rates or manufacturing employment. Yet such idiosyncratic area-specific phenomena are clearly important, as shown by the significance of regional dummies in the regressions.

### Metropolitan Areas versus Cities

As discussed earlier, MSA-independent variables are used here to explain both MSA population and per capita income growth. This implies that the rate of growth of total factor productivity in an MSA, whether due to local research and development or the ability to identify and absorb developments in another region, is dependent on the level of education in the entire region rather than in the city. Molecular biologists resident in suburbs but employed by pharmaceutical firms in the city generate or adopt research that increases $A*$ and wage levels, and hence attracts workers to the region. The choice of residential locations among new labor-force migrants within the MSA involves such factors as the public goods package, the preference for proximity to cultural institutions, and the availability of medical care. In this view, the major issue is the source of metropolitan growth, which in turn depends on MSA-wide variables.

An alternative viewpoint in the literature, as indicated in chapters 1 and 2, is that the attractiveness of cities is the dominant force in determining MSA growth. Orchestras, museums, hospitals, and a vibrant downtown serve to attract people to a region. The relatively slow population growth of many Northeastern MSAs such as Newark, New York, Philadelphia, and Boston (during the first three postwar decades) and several Midwestern MSAs such as Cleveland and Detroit does not lend intuitive credibility to such views. Boston, Philadelphia, and Cleveland contain three of the "big five" American symphony orchestras. These three and Detroit are the home of major art museums and first-rate university-based teaching hospitals. Assumptions about the centrality of city institutions also ignore the growth of parallel suburban institutions that may be quite good substitutes for those in the city. Finally, many labor-force members commute from the suburbs to the cities but rarely venture into the city for shopping or culture, undermining the argument of the centrality of cities in the growth process.

Even focusing on $A*$ in the growth process, it is not obvious that city-based research firms or educational institutions are the major source of growth. Research is not a self-contained activity. A large pharmaceutical research laboratory in the city may depend on interactions with equipment suppliers located in the suburbs, and its labor force may be largely resident in the suburbs. Given the vast number of interactions reported in the agglomeration and learning literature, the encapsulation of economic activity in cities is implausible.[24]

## Empirical Determinants of Population Growth

Tables 4-4 through 4-6 contain estimates of the determinants of metropolitan population growth for 1970–90, 1970–80, and 1980–90, respectively. Four equations have been estimated for each period. Equations 1 and 2 estimate growth without regional dummies. Equations 1 and 3 exclude the rate of change of variables in the decade preceding the estimate; equations 2 and 4 include these variables to evaluate the extent of dependence between periods.

The first regression for the entire period (table 4-4, equation 1) shows that smaller MSAs grew more rapidly, implying that crowding may have discouraged the growth of larger MSAs. In line with other estimates, a large initial share of employment in manufacturing exerts a negative effect on population growth. The coefficient on the climate variable, JANUARY, is positive and highly significant. Although weather may affect labor-force decisions about migration, it is likely that JANUARY is also capturing the impact of weather on the decisions of retirees and immigrants.

Regression 2, which includes the previous decade's population growth, LGMPOP67, generates a significant positive coefficient for this variable, a typical result in all of the estimated equations. This suggests a persistence effect, reflecting the continuation of inmigration as new potential labor-force members and retirees are more likely to locate in these MSAs for reasons suggested above, namely the familiarity with households that had moved earlier. Potential inmigrants are attracted to areas to which persons like them have moved, providing a community and offering an easier transition. Individuals also move to particular regions as a result of recent growth rates, which may affect their perceptions of the future size of the market and the demand for workers. If this is the case, then the coefficients for the other variables obtained when LGMPOP67 is included provide a better estimate, on the margin, of their impact. For example, compare

24. Saxenian (1994).

**Table 4-4.** *Determinants of MSA Population Growth, 1970–90*[a]

| Variable | Regression equation | | | |
|---|---|---|---|---|
| | *1* | *2* | *3* | *4* |
| Constant | .005 | 0.231 | .362 | .475 |
| | (0.03) | (1.52) | (1.89) | (3.04) |
| LMPOP70 | –.030 | –0.019 | –.019 | –.014 |
| | (–1.97) | (–1.62) | (–1.34) | (–1.22) |
| MPCMY69 | 2.97E–.05 | 2.08E–05 | 4.68E–06 | –3.43E–05 |
| | (1.92) | (–1.58) | (0.28) | (–2.46) |
| LGMPOP67 | ... | 1.063 | ... | .997 |
| | | (11.49) | | (10.92) |
| PIFIRM70 | –.007 | 0.010 | –.003 | .012 |
| | (–0.67) | (1.20) | (–0.35) | (1.43) |
| PIBSRM70 | .019 | 0.018 | .011 | .012 |
| | (1.05) | (1.23) | (0.65) | (0.82) |
| PIMANM0 | –.005 | –0.004 | –.004 | –.003 |
| | (–3.55) | (–3.28) | (–2.52) | (–2.57) |
| PIPRSM70 | .002 | 0.006 | .006 | .009 |
| | (0.54) | (1.97) | (1.42) | (2.57) |
| PCOGRM70. | .007 | –0.011 | .0002 | –.014 |
| | (1.18) | (–2.29) | (0.040) | (–2.90) |
| PUNEMP7 | .007 | 0.008 | –.030 | –.017 |
| | (0.88) | (1.26) | –(2.87) | (–1.96) |
| JANUARY | .010 | 0.007 | .011 | .007 |
| | (9.50) | (7.30) | (7.82) | (6.24) |
| TECH | –.037 | –.006 | –.032 | –.007 |
| | (–2.28) | (–0.49) | –(2.11) | (–0.53) |
| Northeast | ... | ... | –.216 | –.126 |
| | | | (–4.12) | (–2.89) |
| Midwest | ... | ... | –.184 | –.135 |
| | | | –(3.90) | (–3.49) |
| South | ... | ... | –.231 | –.160 |
| | | | (–5.25) | (–4.39) |
| Adjusted $R^2$ | 0.519 | 0.690 | 0.590 | .712 |
| Number of observations | 248 | 248 | 248 | 248 |

a. The dependent variable is the log change in population; numbers in parentheses are *t* values.

equations 1 and 2. In 1, the initial presence of a large manufacturing sector, PIMANM7, is negative and significant, but none of the other sector variables is significant. After allowing for the inertial attraction induced by earlier growth, a high value of initial professional services, PIPRSM70, is estimated to induce further growth, partly offsetting the decline of manufacturing. The national growth in the demand for professional services ben-

Table 4-5. *Determinants of MSA Population Growth, 1970–80*[a]

| Variable | Regression equation | | | |
|---|---|---|---|---|
| | 1 | 2 | 3 | 4 |
| Constant | .226 (2.14) | .350 (4.05) | .411 (3.87) | .472 (5.37) |
| LMPOP70 | −.033 (−3.95) | −.028 (−4.05) | −.027 (−3.32) | −.023 (−3.60) |
| MPCMY69 | 7.02E−.06 (0.81) | −2.07E−.05 (−2.77) | −2.64E−.06 (−0.29) | −2.37E−.05 (−3.02) |
| LGMPOP67 | ... | .583 (11.13) | ... | .539 (10.48) |
| PIFIRM70 | .001 (0.24) | .011 (2.25) | .003 (0.55) | .011 (2.44) |
| PIBSRM70 | .020 (2.02) | .020 (2.42) | .016 (1.62) | .016 (1.98) |
| PIMANM70 | −.002 (−2.54) | −.001 (−2.03) | −.001 (−1.30) | −.001 (−1.07) |
| PIPRSM70 | .002 (0.81) | .004 (2.25) | .004 (2.14) | .006 (3.39) |
| PCOGRM70 | .003 (1.02) | −0.007 (−2.38) | −.002 (−0.57) | −.009 (−3.49) |
| PUNEMP7 | .005 (1.13) | .059 (1.54) | −.016 (−2.74) | −.009 (−1.82) |
| JANUARY | .006 (9.29) | .004 (7.05) | .005 (6.79) | .003 (5.03) |
| TECH | −.025 (−2.82) | −.009 (−1.18) | −.022 (−2.57) | −.008 (−1.12) |
| Northeast | ... | ... | −.153 (−5.25) | −.104 (−4.24) |
| Midwest | ... | ... | −.124 (−4.74) | −.098 (−4.48) |
| South | ... | ... | −.121 (−4.92) | −.082 (−4.01) |
| Adjusted $R^2$ | 0.533 | 0.693 | 0.587 | 0.718 |
| Number of observations | 248 | 248 | 248 | 248 |

a. The dependent variable is the log change in population; numbers in parentheses are *t* values.

efited MSAs that had an initial advantage. Again JANUARY is significant. The precise interpretation of this depends on further disaggregation of the sources of population growth to determine whether this coefficient captures retirement decisions, labor force relocation, or immigrant decisions.

The most complete specification of 1970–90 population growth, equation 4, includes regional dummies and the preceding decade's growth rate.

**Table 4-6.** *Determinants of MSA Population Growth, 1980–90*[a]

| Variable | Regression equation | | | |
|---|---|---|---|---|
| | 1 | 2 | 3 | 4 |
| Constant | −.146 | −.344 | −.009 | −.24 |
| | (−1.30) | (−3.84) | (−0.08) | (−2.78) |
| LMPOP80 | .009 | .028 | .018 | .029 |
| | (1.08) | (4.04) | (2.14) | (4.39) |
| MPCMY79 | −7.02E−.06 | −5.26E−.06 | −1.98E−.05 | −1.29E−.05 |
| | (−0.89) | (−0.86) | (−2.48) | (−2.01) |
| LGMPOP78 | ... | .582 | ... | .570 |
| | | (12.28) | | (11.43) |
| PIFIRM80 | .002 | .0004 | .001 | −.001 |
| | (0.37) | (0.12) | (0.22) | (−0.39) |
| PIBSRM80 | .002 | −.004 | −.007 | −.008 |
| | (0.19) | (−0.50) | (−0.71) | (−1.04) |
| PIMANM80 | −.002 | −.0004 | −.001 | −.001 |
| | (−2.08) | (−0.59) | (−1.62) | (−1.04) |
| PIPRSM80 | −.003 | .001 | −.002 | −.0003 |
| | (−1.37) | (0.36) | (−0.83) | (−0.19) |
| PCOGRM80 | .008 | .002 | .005 | .002 |
| | (3.33) | (0.86) | (2.33) | (1.00) |
| PUNEMPM8 | .0001 | −.002 | −.011 | −.007 |
| | (0.04) | (−0.56) | (−2.98) | (−2.38) |
| JANUARY | .042 | .001 | .006 | .003 |
| | (7.27) | (1.80) | (7.47) | (4.09) |
| TECH | −.010 | .001 | −.012 | .005 |
| | (−1.16) | (1.25) | (−1.46) | (0.75) |
| Northeast | ... | ... | −.059 | .010 |
| | | | (−2.20) | (0.45) |
| Midwest | ... | ... | −.039 | .011 |
| | | | (−1.61) | (0.56) |
| South | ... | ... | −.120 | −.063 |
| | | | (−5.79) | (−3.60) |
| Adjusted $R^2$ | 0.416 | 0.642 | 0.484 | 0.669 |
| Number of observations | 248 | 248 | 248 | 248 |

a. The dependent variable is the log change in population; numbers in parentheses are *t* values.

Inertial forces are strong, the coefficient of LGMPOP67 being large and highly significant. The coefficient of initial per capita income is negative and significant, suggesting the possibility of substantial technological catch-up that allowed more rapid growth in $A^*$ in "backward" MSAs and labor flows induced by the expansion of productivity-driven wage growth. As noted earlier, the significance of MPCMY69 may also result from the firms' investment in low-wage areas. The negative effect of manufacturing is significant and professional services are again positive and significant, suggesting the existence of equilibrating forces. Lower initial unemployment is associated with faster growth. This may reflect the impact of a less negative image of MSAs with lower unemployment, a more flexible or highly skilled labor force, or both. The impact of JANUARY and the regional dummies is significant. Thus some of the factors that lay behind the differences in growth among the regions (accounted for in the earlier equations solely by the regional dummy variables) have been identified.

The main anomalous result is the negative coefficient for PCOGRM70. The reason for the inclusion of college graduates is as a measure of their ability to generate and absorb productivity-enhancing technological development. Higher rates of $A^*$ should generate higher wages in a region and attract more labor. Other studies using average or median years of education sometimes find a positive effect for these measures, education acting as a shift variable, $H^\gamma$, increasing $A^*$. However, if the underlying view is that the role of education is important for the adoption of technology, the coefficient of PCOGRM70 should be positive.[25] However, as can be seen below, this coefficient differs between the two decades, and the estimates for the entire period may be misleading. TECH has no effect, and interacting technology with college education also yields no significant coefficient.

The results for the 1970s and 1980s shown in tables 4-5 and 4-6 demonstrate the difficulties of deriving a definitive explanation of MSA population growth for all periods. Consider again the fourth specification. As in the results for the longer period, in the 1970s the coefficient on initial per capita income is negative. The effect of larger initial population is negative, suggesting crowding. The former implies, as noted above, the possibility that $A^*$ was higher in initially poorer regions, the latter that smaller MSAs grow more rapidly. Persistence, as measured by the coefficient of LGMPOP67, is a major influence on growth. The base-period size of the professional services sector, PIPRSM70, is also a major contributor to growth, whereas the initial size of manufacturing does not exercise a significant effect over this period—in most specifications it is negative but not significant. A large initial financial services sector,

PIFIRM70, was also associated with accelerated growth. A high percentage of "deindustrialization" had occurred by the mid-1970s, and other forces became important. The major impact of the demand shift away from manufacturing had had its major effect during the 1960s, although manufacturing continued to decline during the next two decades. The decline of the Frost Belt is reflected in the larger negative coefficients of the Northeast and Midwest relative to the West. In the 1970s, the dummy for the South was quite similar to that of the two Frost Belt regions, implying that its more rapid growth was due to other favorable factors. Here too, the major anomalous result is the negative coefficient of college graduates, PCOGRM70, although the next set of regressions for the 1980s and those for the determinants of the growth of per capita income may help to put this in perspective.

The results for the 1980s (table 4-6) show that population increased more in the MSAs with low base period per capita income. However, in none of the specifications is there evidence of the adverse effects of crowding. On the contrary, the coefficient of LMPOP80 is positive and significant. Interesting questions of interpretation are raised by the differences between specifications 3 and 4. In specification 3, the effect of PCOGRM80 is positive and significant; in 4 it is insignificant. Not allowing for persistence in population growth may yield unwarranted conclusions about the role of a college-educated population. The initial size of manufacturing is not significant. As anticipated, taking account of the characteristics of the MSAs, particularly in the 1980s, reduces very substantially the residual regional effects. The coefficients of Northeast and Midwest are positive though not significant, whereas the coefficients of the South are negative. Nonetheless, regional differences in metropolitan growth, due to specific characteristics of the MSAs in different regions, are still substantial. As discussed in chapter 1, only one MSA among the fifty with the fastest-growing populations was in the Northeast or Midwest.

What can be concluded about the determinants of population growth? First, the determinants vary between decades, which are themselves not necessarily the most appropriate interval but are determined by census dates. The impetus for growth may change: the sectoral shifts in response to oil prices were important. Even allowing for this, warm weather as measured by JANUARY is important. Retirees, a significant determinant of population growth in some MSAs, are responsive to weather. Region-specific total factor productivity growth may be important if the coefficient of initial per capita income is correctly interpreted here. Initial sectoral shares are important for the 1970s, although it is possible that they are capturing shifts in sectoral demand rather than serving as proxies for productivity growth.

The preceding paragraphs mainly discuss the results of the most comprehensive regression, number 4, for each time period. Equation 4 differs from the first three by including both the change in population from the previous period and regional dummies. The regional dummies are generally significant and have the expected sign. Their inclusion results in some of the other coefficients corresponding more closely to expectations. Thus in regression 4 in table 4-4, PUNEMPM7, which is positive and insignificant in equation 2, is negative and significant. Similarly, the inclusion of the lagged population growth variable, LGMPOP67, leads to changes from regressions 1 to 2. For example, PIPRSM70, which is insignificant in regression 1, becomes positive and significant in regression 2, suggesting that the growth of professional services partly offsets, as expected, the impact of a declining manufacturing sector. As noted earlier, I believe that the persistence phenomenon is important and allows a better estimate of the impact, on the margin, of such variables as initial sectoral concentration.

In a number of regressions, the larger set of variables contained in equation 4 changes the results substantially. For example, in table 4-5, PIMANM7 is negative and PIFIRM70 is insignificant in regression 1. In regression 4, PIMANM7 remains negative but is insignificant, whereas PIFIRM70 is positive and significant. Each of these regressions is useful for its own purpose. Without considering lagged population growth and regions, a large initial manufacturing share is associated with significantly lower rates of population growth, whereas a large presence in finance, insurance, and real estate seems to have had little effect in stimulating population growth. However, the manufacturing effect may have a large regional component—for example, high wages prevailing in a region. After removing this effect, the results indicate that a large manufacturing share was not per se the source of decline—a region-wide effect such as high relative unionization and high relative wages, for example, may have been the source of slower population growth, although PIMANM7 still exerts a negative (but less significant) impact.

The insights to be obtained from each of the four specifications in tables 4-4 through 4-6 are useful for different purposes. However, the greatest insight comes from the most comprehensive results, derived from equation 4 in each table.

## Empirical Determinants of per Capita Income Growth

Tables 4-7 through 4-9 present the results of regressions explaining per capita income growth for 1970–90 and for the 1970s and 1980s, respectively. The results for the entire period and for the two decades differ. The interpretation depends on one's view of whether the initial factors determining the growth in per capita income have an impact within a decade or with a considerable lag. It seems plausible to assume that households respond to changing employment conditions fairly rapidly, because long-term unemployment is difficult to sustain. Businesses search for more favorable business climates rather than accept reductions in profitability in (relatively) declining areas. Increasingly competitive markets including greater competition from abroad exert pressures that cannot be resisted for a period as long as a decade.

The variables used are the same as in equation 4-5 with the exception of lagged population growth. Table 4-7 shows per capita income growth for the entire period 1970–90. Significant convergence in per capita income is found in specifications 1 and 2, as indicated by the negative coefficient on base year per capita income, MPCMY69. This variable becomes insignificant in specifications 3 and 4, suggesting that some of the convergence occurred primarily in the MSAs of one or two regions. Population as a measure of crowding is insignificant. The percentage of college graduates, PCOGRM7, has a positive coefficient, significant at .10 and .05 in the first two specifications. TECH has the expected positive sign in both equations. PUNEMPM7 has the predicted negative sign, significant in specification 1. Higher initial unemployment is associated with slower income growth. PIFIRM70 is positive and significant in both specifications 1 and 2, suggesting that a large initial employment base in some of the high value-added financial service sectors provided an impetus to growth. For the entire period, a high initial value of PIFIRM70 predicts greater per capita income growth (perhaps because this sector had growing remuneration levels, particularly in its financial component). This may be due to high values of $A^*$ within the sector or may represent growing rents associated with the financial boom of the 1980s. JANUARY is positive and significant at .05 in both specifications.

Specifications 3 and 4 differ from the first two by including regional dummies. The Midwest regional dummy variable coefficient is negative and significant. Two of the variables whose coefficients are significant in the first two specifications, MPCMY69 and PUNEMPM7, lose signifi-

Table 4-7. *Determinants of MSA per Capita Income Growth, 1970–90*[a]

| Variable | Regression equation | | | |
| --- | --- | --- | --- | --- |
| | 1 | 2 | 3 | 4 |
| Constant | .354 | .276 | .341 | .299 |
| | (4.24) | (3.38) | (3.94) | (3.56) |
| MPCMY69 | −1.55E−.05 | −1.34E−.05 | −6.27E−.06 | −9.54E−.06 |
| | (−2.24) | (−2.03) | (−0.83) | (−1.48) |
| LMPOP70 | 5.67E−.05 | −.002 | −.002 | −.003 |
| | (0.009) | (−.270) | (−0.31) | (−0.53) |
| LMPCMY67 | ...1 | .39 | ... | .364 |
| | | (4.74) | | (4.33) |
| PIFIRM70 | .009 | .009 | .009 | .009 |
| | (2.05) | (2.03) | (2.04) | (2.11) |
| PIBSRM70 | −.004 | .005 | −.007 | .002 |
| | (−0.52) | (0.62) | (−0.92) | (0.21) |
| PIMANM0 | .001 | 7.12E−.05 | .0003 | −.000 |
| | (0.76) | (0.11) | (0.45) | (−0.12) |
| PIPRSM70 | −.002 | −.004 | −.001 | −.003 |
| | (−1.26) | (−2.08) | (−0.63) | (−1.62) |
| PCOGRM7 | .005 | .005 | .004 | .004 |
| | (1.79) | (2.10) | (1.33) | (1.80) |
| PUNEMPM7 | −.012 | −.005 | −.008 | −.005 |
| | (−3.11) | (−1.42) | (−1.76) | (−1.10) |
| JANUARY | .002 | .001 | .001 | .000 |
| | (3.57) | (1.73) | (1.01) | (0.66) |
| TECH | .016 | .017 | .014 | .015 |
| | (2.21) | (2.52) | (1.98) | (2.23) |
| Northeast | ... | ... | .022 | .025 |
| | | | (0.96) | (1.08) |
| Midwest | ... | ... | −.040 | −.033 |
| | | | (−1.84) | (−1.62) |
| South | ... | ... | .023 | .001 |
| | | | (1.19) | (0.07) |
| Adjusted $R^2$ | 0.169 | 0.238 | 0.225 | 0.279 |
| Number of observations | 248 | 248 | 248 | 248 |

a. The dependent variable is the log change in per capita income; numbers in parentheses are *t* values.

cance in one or both equations. Nevertheless, the general thrust of the equations is similar, namely, PIFIRM70, TECH, and PCOGRM7 were conducive to growth for the entire period. As can be seen below, these variables played a major role in the 1980s, less so in the 1970s. This conforms to expectations given the different profile of macroeconomic performance in the two decades.

**Table 4-8.** *Determinants of MSA per Capita Income Growth, 1970–80*[a]

| Variable | Regression equation | | | |
|---|---|---|---|---|
| | 1 | 2 | 3 | 4 |
| Constant | .458 | .455 | .416 | .423 |
| | (7.20) | (6.99) | (6.75) | (6.83) |
| MPCMY69 | −2.67E−.05 | −2.66E−.05 | −2.10E−.05 | −2.04E−.05 |
| | (−5.10) | (−5.07) | (−3.94) | (−3.81) |
| LMPOP70 | −.014 | −.014 | −.011 | −.011 |
| | (−2.74) | (−2.74) | (−2.36) | (−2.31) |
| LMPCMY67 | ... | .012 | ... | −.064 |
| | | (0.18) | | (−1.03) |
| PIFIRM70 | .003 | .003 | .002 | .003 |
| | (1.01) | (1.00) | (0.89) | (0.89) |
| PIBSRM70 | .018 | .018 | .019 | .017 |
| | (2.96) | (2.91) | (3.40) | (3.02) |
| PIMANM70 | −.001 | −.001 | −.001 | −.001 |
| | (−1.97) | (−1.97) | (−1.18) | (−1.02) |
| PIPRSM70 | −.001 | −.001 | .001 | .001 |
| | (−0.64) | (−0.66) | (0.50) | (0.72) |
| PCOGRM7 | .0002 | .0002 | −.002 | −.002 |
| | (0.094) | (0.10) | (−1.20) | (−1.29) |
| PUNEMPM7 | .004 | .004 | .003 | .002 |
| | (1.37) | (1.34) | (0.89) | (0.71) |
| JANUARY | .0001 | .0001 | −.001 | −.001 |
| | (0.48) | (0.38) | (−1.92) | (−1.82) |
| TECH | −.001 | −.001 | −.003 | .003 |
| | (−0.110) | (−0.10) | (−0.64) | (0.60) |
| Northeast | ... | ... | −.080 | −.080 |
| | | | (−4.73) | (−4.75) |
| Midwest | ... | ... | −.020 | −.018 |
| | | | (0.018) | (−1.16) |
| South | ... | ... | .017 | .021 |
| | | | (1.18) | (1.40) |
| Adjusted $R^2$ | 0.358 | 0.355 | 0.475 | 0.475 |
| Number of observations | 248 | 248 | 248 | 248 |

a. The dependent variable is the log change in per capita income; numbers in parentheses are *t* values.

Turning to the results for the 1970s, table 4-8 shows the impact of convergence; MSAs with initial low income per capita grew more rapidly in the 1970s. The coefficient of LMPOP70 is negative, suggesting that compensating wage premiums did not arise in this period to offset the presumed disadvantages of large MSAs. Perhaps if they had, population growth would have been more rapid in the larger MSAs. In contrast to

Table 4-9. *Determinants of MSA per Capita Income Growth, 1980–90*[a]

| Variable | Regression equation | | | |
|---|---|---|---|---|
| | 1 | 2 | 3 | 4 |
| Constant | –.16 | .140 | –.18 | .037 |
| | (–1.64) | (1.48) | (–2.11) | (0.42) |
| MPCMY79 | –2.64E–.05 | –1.50E–.05 | –1.26E–.05 | –3.45E–.06 |
| | (–3.83) | (–2.40) | (–1.92) | (–0.55) |
| LMPCMY78 | ... | –.66 | ... | –.550 |
| | | (–8.20) | | (–6.70) |
| LMPOP80 | .024 | .010 | .015 | .004 |
| | (3.26) | (1.46) | (2.15) | (0.69) |
| PIFIRM80 | .017 | .015 | .014 | .011 |
| | (4.05) | (2.83) | (3.76) | (3.05) |
| PIBSRM80 | –.012 | –.012 | –.014 | –.012 |
| | (–1.36) | (–1.47) | (–1.68) | (–1.56) |
| PIMANM80 | .004 | .002 | .002 | .001 |
| | (4.62) | (2.48) | (3.04) | (1.79) |
| PIPRSM80 | –.001 | –.002 | –.003 | –.003 |
| | (–0.51) | (–1.19) | (–1.50) | (–1.52) |
| PCOGRM80 | .007 | .005 | .009 | .007 |
| | (3.55) | (3.01) | (4.78) | (3.87) |
| PUNEMPM8 | –.000 | –.005 | .048 | .002 |
| | (–0.06) | (–1.80) | (1.52) | (0.527) |
| JANUARY | .001 | .001 | .001 | .001 |
| | (1.70) | (3.24) | (2.15) | (1.74) |
| TECH | .016 | .011 | .010 | .009 |
| | (2.08) | (1.67) | (1.51) | (1.43) |
| Northeast | ... | ... | .136 | .093 |
| | | | (6.13) | (4.28) |
| Midwest | ... | ... | .016 | –.001 |
| | | | (0.82) | (–0.067) |
| South | ... | ... | .038 | .049 |
| | | | (2.23) | (3.09) |
| Adjusted $R^2$ | 0.428 | 0.426 | 0.426 | 0.517 |
| Number of observations | 248 | 248 | 248 | 248 |

a. The dependent variable is the log change in per capita income; numbers in parentheses are *t* values.

the entire period, business services (PIBSRM70) rather than financial services (PIFIRM70) were conducive to high income growth. The initial share of manufacturing has a negative impact on growth in equations 1 and 2, but this turns insignificant in equations 3 and 4 when regional dummies are introduced, suggesting that the decline captured by PIMANM70 was concentrated in two regions. The impact of JANUARY is negative in equations 3 and 4 for the decade, implying that workers will accept somewhat lower wages to be able to locate in warmer climates. The Northeast dummy is negative and significant, consistent with the image of a severely depressed Northeast in the 1970s.

The results for per capita income growth in the 1980s (table 4-9) are of particular interest, as they underline the rapid changes that can occur even in a period as short as a decade. Many of the disequilibrium phenomena of the 1970s were no longer affecting household and business decisions as more stable economic factors became dominant. Inflation decreased, as did both nominal and real energy prices. Convergence in per capita income continues to be a significant phenomenon in the first three specifications. In the fourth, the inclusion of lagged growth in per capita income, LMPCMY78, reduces the significance of MPCMY79, initial per capita income. Whereas fast growth in the 1960s led to convergence in the 1970s, taking account of that convergence in the 1980s is not a significant phenomenon. Whichever specification is correct, convergence in one form or another is an important phenomenon, a factor that repeatedly arises in descriptions of the evolution of individual MSAs, some of which are briefly described in chapter 5. In particular, lower wages or real estate costs are often cited as an important advantage for attracting new investment. The positive and significant coefficients on LMPOP80 in equations 1 and 3 suggest that the negative effects of large MSAs require greater compensation. PIFIRM80 and PIMANM80 have significant positive coefficients. The presence of a large initial finance, insurance, and real estate sector (PIFIRM80) was conducive to growth. The impact of positive rapid growth of total factor productivity in the manufacturing sector presumably led to higher income growth even if the size of the manufacturing sector was declining. The separation of the growth process into decades underlines the fact that the negative impact of one factor— the initial large share of manufacturing—was exhausted by roughly 1980, and manufacturing may even have played a positive role in the remainder of the decade. The financial sector plays an important role in fostering higher incomes. Shifts in demand to this sector and its high average wage contributed to the growth in per capita income.

PCOGRM80 was a significant positive influence, as the economy increasingly became technology oriented rather than simply adjusting to the transitory phenomena of the 1970s and early 1980s, such as relative price changes and historically unprecedented inflation. The positive coefficient of PCOGRM80 is significant in all four specifications in table 4-9.

This result is consistent with the general impression of the 1980s of an economy increasingly propelled by technological innovation after the slow total factor productivity growth of the 1970s. This shows up more in income per capita than in population growth. TECH is positive and significant in specification 1, although its lack of significance when regional dummies are included may imply that it partly captures regional phenomena. If TECH is viewed as the correlate of growth, it suggests the growing importance of research universities as the source of growth when innovation rather than adjustment to changing relative prices became important. Climate, JANUARY, has a positive effect on per capita income growth, significant in several specifications at .05. This is a puzzling result if it is taken to imply that households require higher wages in addition to good climate. However, if JANUARY is capturing the rapid shift in investment and the demand for labor to the South and West, the positive coefficient may reflect a slow response of labor supply to shifts in the demand for labor.

Reversing the decline of the 1970s (and, not shown, the 1960s), per capita income in the Northeast grows faster than in other regions. Its earlier relative decline may have set in motion equilibrating forces such as lower (skill-adjusted) wage rates and land prices. However, as indicated by the equation, the change in the signs and significance of sectoral variables and TECH indicate that the sources of growth in the 1980s differed from those in the 1970s.

The differences between the decades in explaining per capita income growth highlights the tenuous nature of once-and-for-all explanations of the growth of MSAs. In the earlier period, the results suggest considerable flux as the economy underwent several changes, including "deindustrialization," relative price changes due to the oil price shocks of 1973 and 1979, and the differential impact on various sectors of rapid inflation. In the 1980s, in which longer-term forces exerted their effect, MSA per capita income growth responded to a different environment in which higher-technology manufacturing and advanced services came to the fore. Given the impact of initial characteristics and changing circumstances, growth across MSAs will differ. Those with a more favorable initial constellation of characteristics have more rapid growth in income per capita. Within this context some unmeasured phenomena captured by regional effects may reverse themselves—witness the turnaround in the Northeast in the 1980s compared with the 1970s.

Given the contingent nature of the results for MSAs, attempting to explain the results for city and suburbs separately is not productive.

Household and firm location decisions—insofar as they are affected by weather, the presence of research universities, and relative factor prices—lead to a focus on MSA-wide characteristics. The precise division of population or firm growth between the city and suburb is a different phenomenon given the high correlation between the city and suburb and the positive effect of MSA growth on the well-being of cities and suburbs (chapter 3). Once the relevant characteristics of an MSA have been identified, the decision to move there is the major one; the choice between city and suburb is subsidiary. Just as in the Tiebout model, households are assumed to locate in an MSA and then choose the particular jurisdiction depending on the public goods package and the tax price paid.[26] The initial choice among MSAs is based on factors that transcend the constituent city and suburb. The trajectory of individual cities and their suburbs thus depends on the MSA in which they are located.

26. Tiebout (1956).

CHAPTER FIVE

# Behind the
# Growth Equations

THE STATISTICAL ANALYSIS in chapter 4 provides an ex post description of the factors that were conducive to growth in two very different decades. From the vantage point of policymakers the major question is whether the regressions provide a guide to policies that could improve the performance of individual metropolitan statistical areas (MSAs). The policy issue could be framed as one of fate versus choice. Some of the variables that were found to have important effects on the growth process cannot be altered by policy (for example, the temperature in January). Many of the fastest-growing metropolitan areas in terms of population were relatively warm areas, attractive to both workers and retirees. As shown in this chapter, other MSAs benefited from exogenous factors such as the growth of large universities (Bryan, Texas), the presence of a major regional university (Provo, Utah), or a fortuitous choice by business for the location of a gambling or entertainment center (Las Vegas, Nevada, and Orlando, Florida). In each of these instances, the growth of the metropolitan area was determined by fate, by factors largely outside its sphere of influence. And, even to the extent that a metropolitan area could lobby a state legislature to expand a given campus or a business group to establish an enclave of casinos, this is a zero-sum game at the state or national level. There could not have been a second Las Vegas or three or four additional major campuses of the Texas state university system.[1] Total national investment is limited in any given year, as are state education budgets.

Indeed, the zero-sum aspect also warrants care in discussing metropolitan population and income growth across the country. Given national population growth, determined by the rate of natural increase plus immigration, faster growth in the Northeast and Midwest would have meant slower growth in the South and the West. Nevertheless, somewhat greater growth in the former regions at the expense of the latter could have occurred without greatly slowing the growth of the southern and western metropolitan areas. Similarly, given the aggregate level of national investment and labor force growth, more productive factors going to one area imply fewer in other areas. Unless different allocations of factors across areas lead to greater growth in total factor productivity (for example, if labor moves to areas in which its marginal product is greater or the aggregation of capital and labor in some areas lead to agglomeration economies), growth for the economy as a whole is not affected by the regional allocation of economic activity.

Earlier chapters discussed the concern about the decline, absolute or relative, of the older industrial Frost Belt MSAs—if their performance could have been improved, that of their cities would have also been better given the linkages or correlations between cities and their suburbs shown in chapters 1 through 3. Concern about the generally slower growth in MSAs in the Northeast and Midwest and the effect this may have on social indicators, particularly in the cities, must be viewed in a national context. Assuming a given national growth in gross domestic product, gains in the MSAs of the Northeast and Midwest would necessarily come at the expense of MSAs in the Sun Belt unless marginal products differ across regions or greater agglomeration economies would accrue in MSAs favored by policy. Policies focused on improving MSA growth implicitly assume that the acceleration of growth in one MSA does not occur at the expense of another.

Moving from fate to choice, the population regressions, for example, show that the metropolitan "winners" in each decade benefited from a favorable industrial structure at the beginning of the 1970s or a high ratio

1. The replication of a gambling center in Atlantic City, New Jersey, a quarter century later than the start of accelerated growth in Las Vegas, was also largely outside the purview of the MSA that was chosen. Atlantic City was picked as a new gambling center because of its proximity to the huge population agglomeration between Boston and Washington, its seashore location, and its accessibility by existing interstate highways.

of college graduates at the beginning of the 1980s. But even if the sources of fast growth can be identified ex post, could individual MSA policy-makers (assuming there was an effective regional planning authority) have successfully forecast the future and made the correct policy choices? The regressions suggest that the growth-fostering factors changed between the two decades considered here. Choosing the best sectors to encourage, for example, through tax incentives in the 1970s might have improved the initial position of a metropolitan area for the 1980s, but the main choice variable that had a significant effect for the 1980s was the percentage of college graduates. Only a few planners would have been prescient and identified the correct growth strategy. Nor is it clear what local policy instruments could affect the percentage of college graduates. Very few cities or MSAs fund their own colleges. To the extent that there were explicit growth-promoting policies, most MSAs and cities encouraged light industrial parks, convention centers, and sports arenas through tax and other incentives as well as providing direct tax concessions to individual firms.[2]

Picking strategies for future rapid growth is akin to choosing among individual stocks: it is risky with a low probability of success. And unlike a bad stock choice, sectoral bets resulting from tax incentives are not easily liquidated. A new regional office park will not be torn down if the anticipated tenants and their employees do not arrive as predicted. A convention center or sports complex whose construction is subsidized by the regional governments will simply lie idle or relatively empty—as does an expensive sports arena–convention center in New Haven, Connecticut—there are no put options on buildings. The policy choices are discussed in more detail in chapter 6; this chapter considers the lessons that can be drawn from the regressions of chapter 4.

In this chapter both the fastest-growing and slowest-growing MSAs are examined to extract the lessons of their growth patterns. Growth is measured by both population and per capita income. Whereas the regressions of chapter 4 show that the growth in population in the 1960s was important in determining growth in the 1970s, the growth in the earlier decade was not itself explained. One reason that effort was not undertaken is that the persistence of population growth in the postwar decades is very high, and to complete the explanation of population growth in the 1970s or 1980s would have ultimately required accounting for the

2. For a thorough survey of the measures employed see Wasylenko (1997).

growth of the 1950s. The data required for a systematic econometric explanation of the 1950s are not available.

## The Twenty Fastest-Growing and Slowest-Growing MSAs in Population

The regressions presented in chapter 4 are successful in determining the correlates of rapid growth: the values of $R^2$ are typically quite high. To extract further insights from the data, this chapter considers the performance of some of the fastest-growing and slowest-growing MSAs by looking at their characteristics and then examining, for a number of them, the concrete circumstances that gave rise to the high or low values of the independent variables that are responsible for their observed growth pattern.

First, in an attempt to gain some insight, the twenty MSAs with the fastest and the twenty with the slowest population growth are examined for performance. Although the analysis will be extended to the fifty fastest-growing MSAs in population, a number of important points are more readily apparent from the smaller group. In particular, the extent to which their growth was attributable to fate or choice is examined. The analysis sheds light on the systematic sources of fast and slow growth compared with the idiosyncratic and those totally beyond the reach of local policymakers such as weather and the presence of major research universities.

Table 5-1 shows the twenty fastest-growing and table 5-2 the twenty slowest-growing MSAs in terms of population for the 1970s and 1980s. The concentration of rapidly growing MSAs in regions with warm climates is consistent with the systematic importance of the JANUARY variable in the regressions reported in chapter 4. In some, such as Orlando, Florida, a specific business decision—namely, the establishment of Disney World—generated rapid growth that might just as well have occurred in another MSA in Florida such as Naples. However, Disney World could not have been established in Buffalo or Utica, New York, or in Great Falls, Montana—all slow-growing MSAs in the 1970s—given the need to operate the outdoor park year round. This example suggests that insofar as some of the growth sectors of the economy are responsive to climate, good policies pursued by individual MSAs can affect only the decisions of the sectors that are not dependent on climate. Highly income-elastic activities such as vacation and travel will not expand in some areas regardless

Table 5-1. *Twenty Fastest-Growing MSAs: Population, 1970s and 1980s*

| 1970s | 1980s |
|---|---|
| Austin, Tex.* | Atlanta, Ga. |
| Boise City, Idaho | Austin, Tex.* |
| Brownsville, Tex. | Bakersfield, Calif. |
| Bryan, Tex. | Daytona Beach, Fla.* |
| Daytona Beach, Fla.* | Fort Pierce, Fla.* |
| Fort Collins, Colo. | Fort Worth, Tex. |
| Fort Lauderdale, Fla. | Laredo, Tex. |
| Fort Pierce, Fla.* | Las Cruces, N.Mex. |
| Las Vegas, Nev.* | Las Vegas, Nev.* |
| McAllen, Tex.* | McAllen, Tex.* |
| Orlando, Fla.* | Modesto, Calif. |
| Phoenix, Ariz.* | Orlando, Fla.* |
| Provo, Utah | Phoenix, Ariz.* |
| Reno, Nev. | Riverside, Calif. |
| Santa Cruz, Calif. | Sacramento, Calif. |
| Santa Rosa, Calif. | San Diego, Calif. |
| Sarasota, Fla.* | Sarasota, Fla.* |
| Tampa, Fla. | Stockton, Calif. |
| Tucson, Ariz. | Vallejo, Calif. |
| West Palm Beach, Fla.* | West Palm Beach, Fla.* |

*In both decades.

of how good the school system is or whether industrial parks have been established.

The growth of Bremerton, Washington (which just misses being included in the twenty fastest-growing MSAs), offers another germane example of fate. Microsoft's location there and the huge number of firms that it attracted to the area in the 1980s and 1990s does not reflect any specific attribute of Bremerton other than being close to Bill Gates's place of birth. Indeed, at its inception as the sole purveyor to IBM of the operating system for the IBM personal computer, Microsoft would have been expected to select a location near IBM headquarters in Armonk, New York, as its home.

Many other examples of "growth by luck" can be found in table 5-1. McAllen, Texas, is across the Mexican border from the export processing zone established by the Mexican government that allows firms to import raw materials, process them locally, and export them, without taxes on

**Table 5-2.** *Twenty Slowest-Growing MSAs: Population, 1970s and 1980s*

| 1970s | 1980s |
| --- | --- |
| Akron, Ohio | Casper, Wyo. |
| Binghamton, N.Y. | Charleston, W.Va. |
| Boston, Mass. | Davenport, La. |
| Buffalo, N.Y. | Decatur, Ill. |
| Cleveland, Ohio | Dubuque, Iowa |
| Dayton, Ohio | Duluth, Minn. |
| Detroit, Mich. | Enid, Okla. |
| Elmira, N.Y. | Gary, Ind. |
| Great Falls, Mont. | Huntington, W.Va. |
| Jersey City, N.J. | Johnstown, Pa. |
| New York, N.Y. | Kankakee, Mo. |
| Newark, N.J. | Kokomo, Ind. |
| Norfolk, Va. | Muncie, Ind. |
| Philadelphia, Pa. | Parkersburg, W.Va. |
| Pittsburgh, Pa.* | Peoria, Ill. |
| Pittsfield, Mass. | Pine Bluff, Ark. |
| St. Louis, Mo. | Pittsburgh, Pa.* |
| South Bend, Ind. | Waterloo, Iowa |
| Utica, N.Y. | Wheeling, W.Va. |
| Youngstown, Ohio* | Youngstown, Ohio* |

*In both decades.

imported materials or on exports. Boise City, Idaho, attracted high-technology companies such as Micron and Hewlett-Packard's laser jet production facility because of its proximity to outdoor recreation areas, in addition to initially low housing costs and wages. West Palm Beach, Florida, attracted not only retirees but also such major corporations as Paxson Communications because of the preference of Paxson's chief executive officer for year-round golf.[3] And obviously, the large number of communities in Florida represents the attraction exerted by warm winters on retirees. Other examples of special circumstances are provided in the last section of the chapter.

Figures 5-1 and 5-2 compare the average values of the independent variables contained in the regressions in chapter 4 for the twenty fastest-

3. Tim W. Ferguson and William Heuslein, "Best Places," *Forbes,* May 29, 2000, pp. 136–60.

**Figure 5-1.** *Characteristics of Twenty Fastest-Growing and Slowest-Growing MSAs, Population, 1970–80*

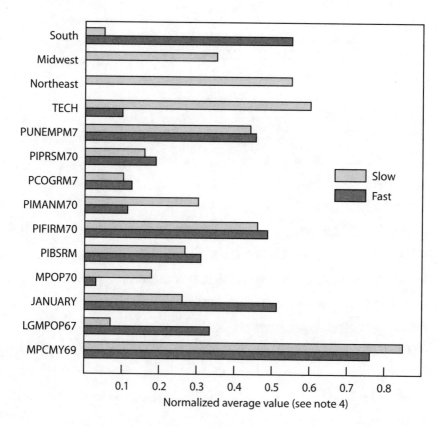

growing and slowest-growing MSAs.[4] Given the changing coefficients and their significance in the regressions reported in chapter 4, these differences imply substantial variations in growth in some specifications, smaller in others. Despite the difficulty of choosing the "best" regressions in chapter 4, the differences in the size of the independent variables provide insight into the variety of growth performance across metropolitan areas.

In contrast to the fastest-growing MSAs, in both decades most of those with the slowest population growth were located in the Northeast and

4. The values of the independent variables shown in figure 5-1 and subsequent figures in this chapter have been obtained by normalizing the original variables so that each is less than one, for convenient representation. For example, metropolitan per capita income has

**Figure 5-2.** *Characteristics of Twenty Fastest-Growing and Slowest-Growing MSAs, Population, 1980–90*

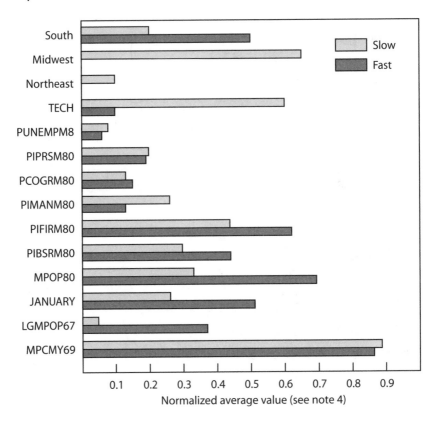

Midwest. There were few MSAs in the South in this group, and none in the West. For the 1970s, important differences exist in five variables in addition to the regional dummy variables: TECH, PIMANM70, JANUARY, MPOP70, and LGMPOP67. MPOP70 and MPOP80 are shown in these figures because the logarithm does not visually convey the size of the differences. These variables are useful in understanding tables 5-1 and 5-2. The slow-growing MSAs had more than three times the population of the fast-growing ones. During the 1970s the large industrial MSAs of the Northeast and Midwest dominated the declines: Boston, Cleveland,

---

been divided by 1,000 and January temperature by 100. The units of the variables have been adjusted to allow them to be compared on the same axis.

Detroit, New York, Philadelphia, and Pittsburgh. Because the size of the population is included to reflect negative effects of crowding such as high housing and commercial real estate prices and long commuting times, it would have been easy to conclude in the early 1980s that the day of the large city had passed. However, in the 1980s (table 5-2) very slow growth was typical in smaller MSAs, Pittsburgh being the only large one in the group. TECH is *higher* for the slower-growing MSAs of the 1970s. The presence of Harvard, MIT, Columbia, the University of Pennsylvania, and Carnegie Mellon University appears to have had limited effects in spurring growth in their MSAs in the 1970s, although growth might have been still lower without, for example, the Route 128 complex near Boston. The large MSAs in which these institutions are located witnessed very slow growth or a decline in population. The association between rapid population growth and major university research centers, Stanford–Silicon Valley being the exemplar, is a rather recent phenomenon. Growth in the 1970s was often based on other factors. Although the slow-growing areas were characterized by much heavier involvement in manufacturing in both decades, the negative impact, given the coefficients of the growth regression, was relatively small. Two other important structural changes become apparent in differentiating fast and slow growth in population in the 1980s. MSAs with rapidly growing populations are characterized by initially larger proportions of employment in the finance, insurance, and real estate sectors and in business services—the former a consumer of high-technology inputs, the latter containing many of the high-technology–producing sectors. Perhaps in the 1980s, the advent of large profit and wage opportunities in high technology overcame the deleterious crowding effects, which only worsened.[5]

Although differences in growth in the 1970s were affected by developments during the 1950s that in turn determined the growth of the 1960s, LGMPOP67, these were exogenous to policymakers in the 1970s. Even if the policies of the 1950s established favorable growth conditions for the 1960s that continued to reverberate during the 1970s, it is exceedingly unlikely that any MSA in the 1980s could have benefited from policies similar to the earlier ones in an economic environment that had changed from dealing with inflation and energy price increases to one that put a

5. The opposing trends are reflected in the developments in the 1990s in which large MSAs, including their central cities such as New York City, witnessed robust growth in per capita income despite extraordinary increases in housing and office space costs. For a good discussion of these opposing trends see Charles J. Bagli, "Office Shortage Imperils Growth in New York City," *New York Times*, September 19, 2000, pp. A1 and B4.

premium on the ability to innovate in a much more competitive world economy.

In attempting to understand the difference between very fast-growing and very slow-growing MSAs, key questions are what is the source of the continuing importance of earlier population growth and what was the initial impetus for growth captured by the previous decade's fast growth. As noted earlier, the original thrust presumably reflected a natural preference for better weather and a search for lower land costs and wage rates in the West and South. Technology and college graduates played limited roles in the 1970s. By the end of the decade the major Frost Belt cities had suffered much of their ultimate decline that then spread to secondary cities such as Akron, Ohio, in the 1980s. There is no single explanation of slow population growth in MSAs. Given the presence of bad weather, high factor prices, an old infrastructure, and industries characterized by slowly growing demand, there were simply no strongly positive characteristics to offset what was, in many dimensions, a natural decline.

The lesson to be drawn from tables 5-1 and 5-2 and figures 5-1 and 5-2 is that even over relatively short periods, the fortunes of individual MSAs, measured by population growth and the presence of a number of employment sectors—finance, insurance and real estate and a variety of business services—can change dramatically. Nevertheless, there are strong long-term regional forces that dominate the evolution of MSAs. Boston and New York, with their extraordinary and diversified human resources and international importance, may be able to avoid a continuation of their relative decline, but Youngstown and Akron, Ohio, Gary, Indiana, and Duluth, Minnesota, cannot overcome the negative impact of their inherited characteristics.[6] These issues will become even clearer when per capita income growth is considered.

## The Fifty Fastest-Growing and Slowest-Growing MSAs in Population

Although the focus on the twenty areas with the fastest growth and the twenty areas with the slowest growth allows the identification of several major issues, it is helpful to expand each list to fifty, as the larger sample is subject to fewer idiosyncratic factors. The differences between the fifty fastest-growing and the fifty slowest-growing MSAs can be seen clearly in

---

6. Pittsburgh, a relatively large MSA and among the slowest-growing MSAs in both decades, is the major exception to the reversal of patterns.

**Figure 5-3.** *Characteristics of Fifty Fastest-Growing and Slowest-Growing MSAs, Population, 1970–80*

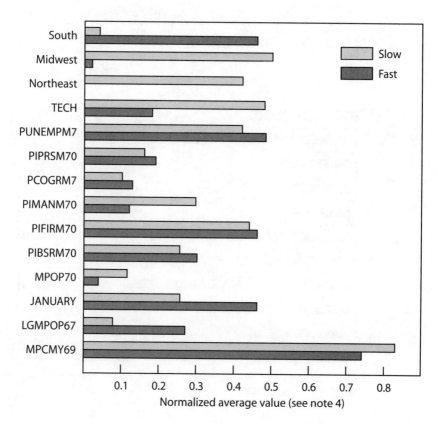

Normalized average value (see note 4)

figure 5-3 for the 1970s and figure 5-4 for the 1980s. The regional dimension continues to stand out with the expansion of each sample from twenty to fifty. With one exception, all of the fifty fastest-growing MSAs in the 1970s are in the South and West, and none are in the Northeast. Conversely, all but two of the slowest-growing MSAs are in the Northeast and Midwest. As in the case of the smaller group, the average population of the slow-growing MSAs was almost three times that of the fastest growers. Warm Januaries and rapid growth in the 1960s again characterize the fifty fastest-growing MSAs of the 1970s. Rapid growers did begin with somewhat lower per capita income—thus growth may have reflected a convergence fueled by the possibility of more rapid growth of productivity as initially poorer MSAs were able to catch up technologically with

**Figure 5-4.** *Characteristics of Fifty Fastest-Growing and Slowest-Growing MSAs, Population, 1980–90*

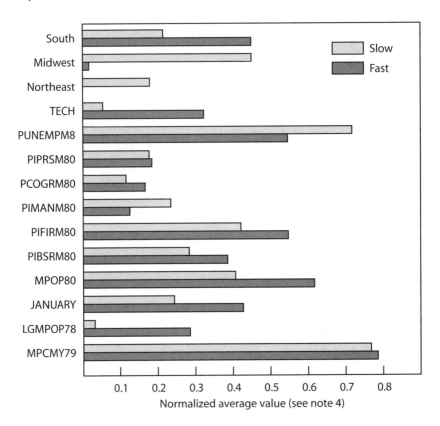

Normalized average value (see note 4)

more productive ones and firms moved to lower-wage areas. High initial shares of manufacturing were associated with low growth. Thus, the patterns that held for the twenty hold for the expanded set. The previous results were not reflecting the slow population growth or decline of a few large metropolitan areas such as New York and Philadelphia, but were broadly characteristic of the more general pattern for the 1970s.

The comparisons for the 1980s indicate that quite different mechanisms were at work in this period. The Northeast and Midwest continued to be the regions in which most of the slow growers and almost none of the fast growers were located, although a few slow-growing MSAs were in the South. However, there was a large difference in the importance of

TECH, the fast-growing regions having roughly five times the measure, unlike the 1970s, when the TECH measure in the rapidly growing MSAs was less than half the size of that in the rapidly growing metropolitan areas. Reinforcing the view that population growth in the 1980s was propelled by innovation and technology, the percentage of college graduates was somewhat greater in the fast-growing MSAs, and the initial share in finance, insurance, and real estate—the high value-added business service sectors—was larger. A high initial manufacturing share continued to be a predictor of further decline. Another reversal of the patterns of the 1970s is the fact that fast-growing MSAs were about 50 percent larger in population and had somewhat greater initial per capita income. In the 1980s the negative effect of crowding appears to have been less than the benefits of agglomeration. Finally, "fate" continued its role. JANUARY and the previous decade's growth were again very different in the fast-growing and slow-growing MSAs.

## Per Capita Income Growth

Comparisons of fast-growing and slow-growing MSAs as measured by per capita income provide a considerably different perspective on growth patterns. Tables 5-3 and 5-4 show the twenty fastest-growing and slowest-growing MSAs in the 1970s and 1980s. As noted in chapter 4, the 1970s were atypical, dominated by adjustment to the huge oil price shocks of the 1970s, high inflation throughout the decade, a major recession in 1973–75, and high unemployment. Fast growth in per capita income in the 1970s was dominated by oil and natural resource–oriented MSAs, whereas slow growth was concentrated in the MSAs of the Northeast and Midwest. The reversal in the 1980s is striking. A considerable number of the fastest-growing MSAs are in the "old" regions. New York, New Haven, and Philadelphia shift from the slowest-growth to the most rapid growth category. More generally, the relation between per capita income growth in the 1970s and the 1980s is negative for the entire sample of 250 MSAs (figure 5-5).[7] Moreover, the most rapid growth in income per capita in the 1980s often occurs in the Northeast, unlike the results for population. Although the variables used to explain population and income per capita are the same, their effects on the two dependent variables are very

---

7. See also the discussion in chapter 1 of these phenomena.

**Table 5-3.** *Twenty Fastest-Growing MSAs: per Capita Income, 1970s and 1980s*

| 1970s | 1980s |
|---|---|
| Abilene, Tex. | Atlanta, Ga. |
| Alexandria, La. | Atlantic City, N.J. |
| Baton Rouge, La. | Bangor, Maine |
| Billings, Mont. | Boston, Mass. |
| Bismarck, N.D. | Burlington, Vt. |
| Brownsville, Tex. | Fort Pierce, Fla. |
| Casper, Wyo. | Hartford, Conn. |
| Charleston, W.Va. | Jersey City, N.J. |
| Enid, Okla. | Lewiston, Maine |
| Florence, Ala. | New Haven, Conn. |
| Fort Pierce, Fla. | New London, Conn. |
| Houston, Tex. | New York, N.Y. |
| Jackson, Miss. | Newark, N.J. |
| Lafayette, La. | Philadelphia, Pa. |
| Lake Charles, La. | Pittsfield, Mass. |
| McAllen, Tex. | Portland, Maine |
| Monroe, La. | Raleigh, N.C. |
| Odessa, Tex. | Sarasota, Fla. |
| Shreveport, La. | Trenton, N.J. |
| Victoria, Tex. | West Palm Beach, Fla. |

different. For small groups and for the entire sample, reversals in per capita income performance in MSAs are typical (figure 5-5), whereas population growth is a persistent phenomenon (figure 5-6).

The presence of major museums, orchestras, theaters, research universities, and a lively urban life were no match in the 1970s for the possibility of, among other things, year-round outdoor living and lower costs of production, especially in the South. Nevertheless, in the 1980s (and 1990s), the presence of cultural and educational institutions is often cited as one of the sources of vitality of MSAs undergoing a renaissance in per capita income growth if not in population. The reinvigoration of MSAs such as Boston and New York in the 1980s and 1990s is often attributed to some of the characteristics that were less important in the 1970s. Faculty experts and graduates of Harvard, MIT, Columbia, and New York University became part of the growth process that was often initiated by firms founded by faculty members and former students. High technology and financial sectors become the drivers of growth in the

**Table 5-4.** *Twenty Slowest-Growing MSAs: per Capita Income, 1970s and 1980s*

| 1970s | 1980s |
|---|---|
| Albany, N.Y. | Beaumont, Tex. |
| Bloomington, Ind. | Billings, Mont. |
| Charlottesville, Va. | Brownsville, Tex. |
| Dayton, Ohio | Casper, Wyo. |
| Elkhart, Ind. | Davenport, La. |
| Hartford, Conn. | Duluth, Minn. |
| Jackson, Mich. | Enid, Okla. |
| Jersey City, N.J. | Gary, Ind. |
| Los Angeles, Calif. | Johnstown, Pa. |
| New Haven, Conn. | Lafayette, La. |
| New York, N.Y. | Lake Charles, La. |
| Newark, N.J. | McAllen, Tex. |
| Philadelphia, Pa. | Odessa, Tex. |
| Pittsfield, Mass. | Peoria, Ill. |
| Providence, R.I. | Pueblo, Colo. |
| Rochester, N.Y. | Shreveport, La. |
| Springfield, Mass. | Waterloo, Iowa |
| Syracuse, N.Y. | Wheeling, W.Va. |
| Utica, N.Y. | Wichita Falls, Tex. |
| Vineland, N.J. | Yakima, Wash. |

Boston and New York MSAs, and this growth was abetted in some instances by the availability of low-cost space. For example, "Silicon Alley," the location of many New York–based high-technology start-ups in the 1980s and continuing in the 1990s, is located in low-cost office buildings and lofts in Manhattan that were abandoned or shifted down to low-value uses during the 1970s and early 1980s and were viewed as one symptom of the decrepit capital stock and absence of modern infrastructure. Simultaneous rewiring of numerous class B and class C office buildings facilitated new agglomeration economies in businesses whose major inputs are highly educated people, low-cost space, and excellent telecommunications infrastructure. Agglomeration economies, perhaps caught by variables such as PIFIRM90 and PCOGRM90 will also probably be significant when data for the 1990s become available.

Figures 5-7 and 5-8 compare the size of the independent variables from equation 4-8 for the 1970s and 1980s for the fifty fastest-growing and slowest-growing MSAs as measured by per capita income. The major

**Figure 5-5.** *Per Capita Income Growth Rates, MSAs, 1970–80 versus 1980–90*

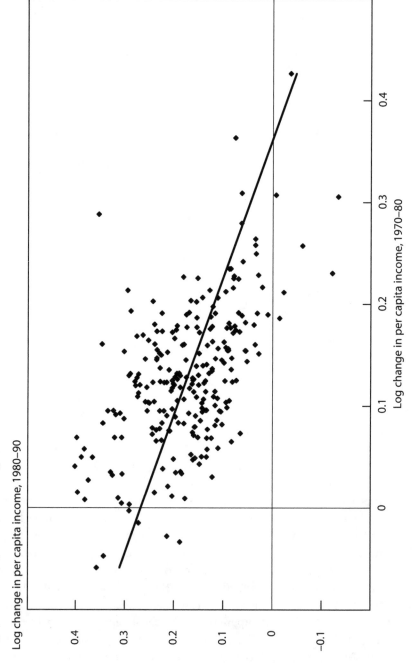

Log change in per capita income, 1980–90

Log change in per capita income, 1970–80

**Figure 5-6. Population Growth Rates, MSAs, 1970–80 versus 1980–90**

Log change in population, 1970–80

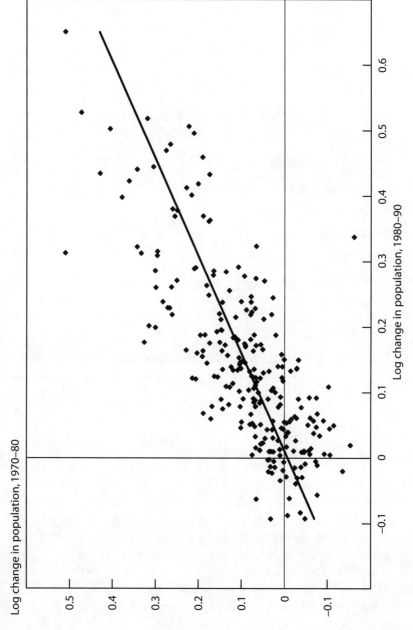

Log change in population, 1980–90

**Figure 5-7.** *Characteristics of Fifty Fastest-Growing and Slowest-Growing MSAs, per Capita Income, 1970–80*

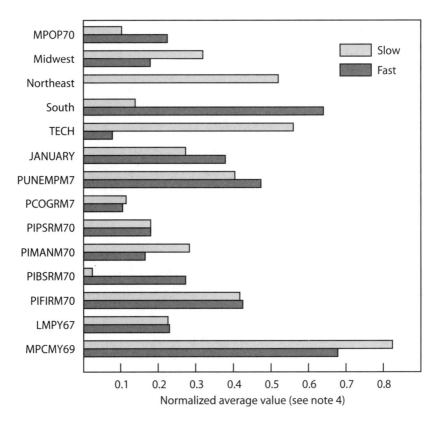

Normalized average value (see note 4)

characteristics for the fast growers in the 1970s are the lower initial per capita income, MPCMY69, the lower initial share of manufacturing, PIMANM70, a much *lower* technology index, TECH, and, not surprisingly given the oil disruptions of the 1970s, the lower January temperature in the slow-growing MSAs. Moreover, 84 percent of the slow-growing MSAs are in the Northeast and Midwest. Unlike the results for population, persistence is not a characteristic of per capita income growth. Indeed, as shown in figure 5-7, the fast-growing MSAs in the 1980s had lower per capita income growth in the 1970s.

Although the theory underlying equation 4-4 suggests that a major source of differential growth, both population and per capita income, among MSAs will be attributable to differences in total factor productiv-

**Figure 5-8.** *Characteristics of Fifty Fastest-Growing and Slowest-Growing MSAs, per Capita Income, 1980–90*

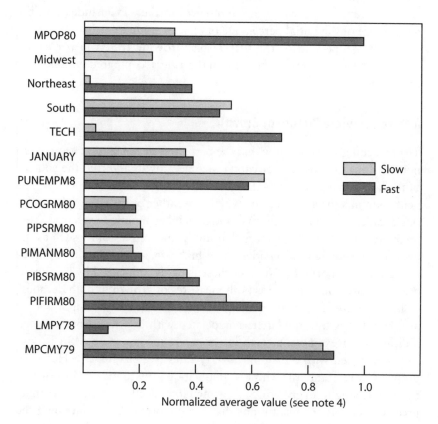

ity growth, in the 1970s a number of the fast-growing MSAs in terms of both per capita income and population were oil-producing areas. The growth in prices in the 1970s was idiosyncratic, and the fall in the 1980s led to the disappearance of most of these MSAs from the list of areas with rapidly growing per capita incomes.

The growth of international trade in the 1970s and the relatively low income elasticities of demand for manufactured goods contributed to the decline of areas with high values of PIMANM70. By the 1980s this was halted, and the fifty most rapidly growing MSAs in terms of per capita income had somewhat greater values of PIMANM80. Similarly, in the 1970s, the fifty fastest-growing MSAs had considerably warmer Januaries. By the 1980s this difference had become negligible. Comparisons of the fastest-growing and slowest-growing MSAs in terms of per capita income suggest the characterization of the 1980s as innovation and education driven, as shown by the differences in the TECH index and the importance of the initial percentage of college graduates.

Finally, 38 percent of the fifty fastest-growing MSAs in per capita income are located in the Northeast in the 1980s, compared with none in the 1970s.

## A More Complete Picture of Growth

The preceding sections show that the correlates of population growth are not the same as those of per capita income growth and that the sources of the latter changed significantly between the 1970s and the 1980s. For per capita income growth, fate, whether weather or growth in the previous decade, is not important. As fundamental economic forces reasserted themselves in the 1980s, factors that imply innovative ability such as the presence of research universities and a high percentage of college graduates grew in importance. None of these is easily influenced by local policymakers. Region matters for both measures of growth in both decades.

Both the size of population and per capita income may be important for an MSA. Growth in the latter is associated with improvements in social indicators; for example, growth in per capita income in an MSA is typically associated with a drop in poverty rates (see chapter 3).[8] However, growing living standards with low population growth may be insufficient to support long-term growth. Slow growth or a decline in population may preclude support for institutions that are important for maintaining the attractiveness of an MSA. Declining usage of hospitals, cultural institutions, and retail stores may lead to their cutback or closure, discouraging further growth. This may occur even if there is a growth in per capita income, concentrated in the upper middle class. Conversely, rapid population growth may not be sustainable without growing per capita income, as some of the same institutions depend on the patronage and the charitable contributions that come mainly from those with growing incomes. Tax revenues may grow slowly if the increase in the tax base is slow due to anemic growth in per capita income.

8. The structure behind this relation is not clear. It could be that growing incomes lead to more spending on education, improving the quality and income of the local labor force.

Growth in both population and per capita income is likely to be necessary for a thriving MSA, although there is not likely to be a single optimum combination for all MSAs. An MSA like Boston may prosper with a slowly growing population and a rapid growth in per capita income. The density of high-income, highly educated residents in the region promotes the financial health of the city and suburban jurisdictions and of the major health and cultural institutions that lie behind the long-term attractiveness of the area. In contrast, in smaller, less well endowed MSAs, a decline in population may result in a declining quality of life that discourages new private-sector investment and the choice of location by highly educated residents, who foster greater innovation and the subsequent growth of investment and per capita income.

Obviously there are no fixed rules. Boston and New York were among the MSAs with the slowest population growth in the 1970s but witnessed rapid growth of per capita income in the 1980s. Most of the industries that fueled the later boom did not leave, nor did the highly skilled workers. However, many of the MSAs that lost population in the 1970s have not turned around in either dimension. There may be threshold effects.

Two patterns of development are possible: extensive and intensive. The former consists of population growth but not necessarily per capita income growth. The latter largely consists of per capita income growth with slowly growing population. The MSAs with growing per capita income in the 1980s often had low growth in population. This pattern can be seen in figures 5-9 and 5-10, which show the relation between population and income growth by region for the 1970s and 1980s. The Northeast and Midwest had the lowest population growth rates in both decades. In the 1970s they also experienced the lowest per capita income growth, but in the 1980s the northeastern MSAs had the highest growth in income per capita but very low population growth rates. Figures 5-9 and 5-10 underline the possibility that American MSAs may bifurcate into two groups, both of which have high income growth rates but one has slower, the other more rapid population growth. As emphasized in chapter 1, in both cities and suburbs in the Midwest and the Northeast population grew relatively slowly in both decades. Even with the resurgent growth of income per capita in the 1980s in the Northeast, its MSAs continued to experience low population growth.

As the structure of production has shifted toward knowledge intensity, growth in income is no longer determined solely by natural resources but

**Figure 5-9.** *Comparison of Population and per Capita Income Growth, by Region, 1970–80*

Percent

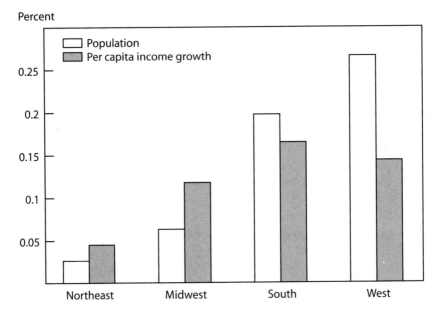

by wages, real estate availability for both offices and residences, the quality of education institutions, and the perceived quality of life. As can be seen in the second column of table 5-3, MSAs in the Northeast are not necessarily at a disadvantage in these respects. Boston, Jersey City, Philadelphia, and others did well in per capita income growth in the 1980s, reflecting favorable combinations of these factors.[9] Yet none of these MSAs experienced large population growth, although wage levels were rising more rapidly than in other MSAs. Major MSA population growth continued to take place in the Sun Belt regions. This pattern suggests that even where there are favorable conditions in place for per capita income growth such as Boston and New York, it may not translate into significant population growth. Population may continue to shift toward warmer areas. The U.S. metropolitan picture may evolve into one in which MSA per capita income growth is associated with knowledge-intensive growth but some MSAs derive a fillip to population growth from the added attraction of better weather or access to outdoor recreation.

9. Frey (1993).

**Figure 5-10.** *Comparison of Population and per Capita Income Growth, by Region, 1980–90*

Percent

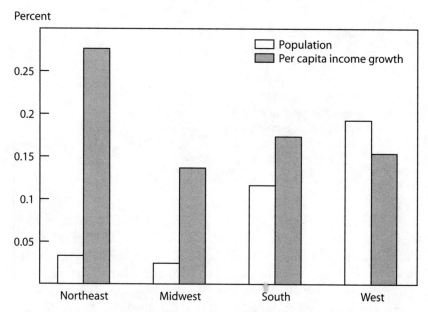

The difference in evolution between Austin, Texas, and Boston is enlightening. Austin benefited from explicit efforts by the public officials and the University of Texas to attract high-technology industry, whereas the Boston area benefited from the presence of several major research universities. Yet Boston's population growth has been very slow, whereas that in Austin has been among the highest. Equal shifts in productivity growth may elicit much greater willingness to relocate to a Sun Belt MSA rather than a northeastern one.

Two major conclusions emerge:

—There are no magic bullets that foster rapid growth; multiple factors are associated with growth, especially in the 1980s.

—Idiosyncratic sources of growth abound.

## Persistent Structures and Changing Success

One characteristic of the underlying data conveys an important message: the correlations between the independent variables used in equations 4-7 and 4-8 are fairly high for the two periods 1970 and 1980 (table 5-5). If

Table 5-5. *Correlation of Exogenous Variables*

| Variable | Correlation coefficient |
| --- | --- |
| MPOP70, MPOP80 | .99 |
| LGMPOP67, LGMPOP78 | .59 |
| MPCMY69, MPCMY79 | .89 |
| PUNEMPM7, PUNEMPM8 | .53 |
| PIPRSM70, PIPRSM80 | .94 |
| PCOGRM7, PCOGRM80 | .97 |
| PIMANM70, PIMANM80 | .97 |
| PIFIRM70, PIFIRM80 | .94 |
| PIBSRM70, PIBSRM80 | .84 |

the underlying forces determining differential growth had been unchanged, then the growth of population and per capita income for individual MSAs should have been similar in both periods. This is in fact the case for population, as shown in figure 5-6. For per capita income, figure 5-5, the relationship is negative. The fortunes of many MSAs do change as a result of the different coefficients of the regressions. If the variations in coefficients are viewed as the result of changes in the world or nation (oil price movements, federal laws), then the fate of MSAs with basically unchanging characteristics can be viewed as being altered by factors largely beyond their control. Of course, as can be seen, the variables are not perfectly correlated; movements do occur and insofar as such changes can be induced by policy and have a favorable impact on growth performance, MSAs have some measure of control over their fates. But it is useful to remember that changes in the basic economic structure in a period as short as a decade can be large, and few MSAs are likely to be able to exploit such changes for their benefit.

## Qualitative Perspectives

Another perspective on the empirical results presented here is fruitful, namely, the qualitative examination of a few of the fast-growing and slow-growing MSAs.[10] As can be seen from the values of $R^2$ reported in

10. The sources for the following discussion include real estate periodicals for individual metropolitan areas, newspaper and magazine articles, and chamber of commerce descriptive materials.

chapter 4, the performance of individual MSAs is generally well explained. Nevertheless, many of the fastest-growing MSAs lie above the 95 percent confidence band, particularly for the population regression, whereas most of the slow-growing MSAs lie within it. As Tolstoy might have put it, the unsuccessful MSAs are all unhappy in a similar manner, but the high performers are cheerful for very different reasons. Although an exhaustive explanation for the unusually successful MSAs cannot be provided here, the special circumstances of a subset of them are enlightening. In addition, the discussion of the extremes leads to perspectives on the rich processes underlying MSA trajectories only some of which can be fully captured in the equations presented in chapter 4.

The experience of Austin, which was among the fastest-growing MSAs in population in both the 1970s and the 1980s (and was outside the confidence band), provides considerable insight into specific local characteristics affecting growth. Although most of Austin's high growth is explained by the variables included in the regressions, the regressions do not capture a number of features that account for its rapid growth. In the 1970s Austin benefited from the rapid rise in energy prices, as did a number of the other metropolitan areas in Texas and Louisiana on the list of fast growth in per capita income (Alexandria, Baton Rouge, Lafayette, Lake Charles, Monroe, and Shreveport, Louisiana; Odessa and Victoria, Texas). The oil price decline in the 1980s removed this source of expansion in per capita income, and many regions in these states suffered a significant reversal in fortune. For example, Lake Charles changed from being among the twenty fastest-growing to being among the twenty slowest-growing MSAs in per capita income. Why was Austin different?

Austin exhibited relatively low-cost land and office space, a factor captured by the level of initial per capita income. The presence of the University of Texas, a major research institution, facilitated continued growth even after the oil price collapse. Its impact is, to some extent, captured by TECH in the regressions. What is not caught by TECH is the intense effort undertaken to attract two major research institutions and the firms that followed in their wake. Sematech, a research group whose goal was to restore the U.S. lead in high technology (which was viewed as having been lost to Japan) was lured to Austin, as was the Microelectronics and Computer Technology Corporation. The endeavor was facilitated by public-sector guarantees coordinated with generous promises from the university and funds from the private sector. $132 million was raised by private donors and the University of Texas, and an additional $32 million was pledged to increase the size and quality of the University of Texas engineering program, thus assuring both these institutions and firms that followed them into the area of a continuing supply of skilled labor. High-technology firms soon moved in large numbers to take advantage of the close proximity to these two research institutions and the expanding high-quality labor pool. The location of these firms was also encouraged by relatively low prices of office and factory space. Thus in addition to the favorable characteristics captured by the independent variables, an imaginative (and expensive) public and private initiative capitalized on these assets.

Raleigh-Durham, North Carolina, one of the fastest-growing MSAs in per capita income in the 1980s, also lies outside the 95 percent confidence interval. Its experience was much like that of Austin. State funding was critical for the establishment of a "research triangle" to attract new higher-technology firms. But the success of the state effort was predicated on the presence of faculty and graduates of three major universities: Duke, the University of North Carolina, and North Carolina State, each with different strengths. The combination of good universities and state activism was helped by the excellent climate and outdoor recreation possibilities of the region. A mental experiment that illustrates the latter point is to imagine a similar public effort by the state of New York to establish a research quadrangle to take advantage of Rensselaer Polytechnic Institute, Cornell University, Syracuse University, and the University of Rochester. The area encompassed by these universities includes some of the most slowly growing MSAs in the country. Although the distances among these universities is greater than in North Carolina, the potential for interactions would nevertheless be considerable and there is a great deal of very low-cost space in cities such as Utica and Syracuse. Although there is some anecdotal evidence of people moving to these areas to take advantage of lower crowding and lower real estate prices, it seems unlikely that the response to a New York Research Quadrangle would be as strong as it was in North Carolina.[11] Nevertheless, weather does not constitute the entire destiny of an MSA. The population growth of Boston in the 1970s was among the slowest in the country, but its rebound in income in the 1980s was remarkable. Clearly people do not

---

11. Another example of an effort to attract high-technology industry that has not generated significant growth is that of Indianapolis, Indiana, which sponsored the Indianapolis Center for Advanced Research and the Aerospace Research Applications Center, begun in 1963.

live by sun alone—income is important. But the remarkable university concentration in Boston is not reproduced in any other area except for the San Francisco Bay region.

The impact of a public role occurs not only on the state or local level, as in Austin or Raleigh. The very rapid growth in per capita income in Houston in the 1970s was a result not only of the oil boom but also of the location of the National Aeronautics and Space Administration (NASA) and the firms that followed it; likewise, the proximity of Cape Canaveral in Florida added to the impetus to growth of the Disney and other resort enterprises in Orlando. The role of federal expenditures has often been cited as an important determinant of economic activity. However, their significance for growth depends on whether they attract private-sector firms that generate growing economic activity. A military base may stimulate local sales from armed forces personnel but does not necessarily encourage growth. In contrast, a NASA facility may induce firms that supply NASA, and who are themselves the source of considerable innovation and growth, to locate close to the NASA operation, stimulating further growth.[12] In terms of equation 4-4, $A^*$ may be greater with some types of federal expenditures. Nevertheless, large military bases may provide stability during periods of transition in the private sector, limiting decline and providing a breathing space during which regeneration occurs. Two air force bases near Sacramento, California, may have provided this type of stabilizer during a period in which other California MSAs of similar size experienced a downturn for a variety of reasons, including the declining importance of agricultural trade centers.

The experience of another Texas MSA, McAllen, among the twenty fastest-growing MSAs in population in both the 1970s and the 1980s, suggests an entirely different set of special circumstances conducive to rapid population growth. This area is contiguous to the Mexican border, and there are extensive interactions with the export processing zone that was established on the Mexican side of the border. U.S. firms that have established plants in Mexico—maquiladoras—set up offices and warehouses to facilitate their business. Moreover, many Mexicans cross the border to shop in McAllen. Nevertheless, despite the rapid population growth of McAllen, partly resulting from substantial legal and illegal immigration, its per capita income remains relatively low and its unemployment rate

12. For a much more thorough discussion of the effects of federal expenditures on regional fortunes see Pack (1980, 1982).

high, underlining the point made above that neither population nor per capita income growth is the sole measure of successful growth.

Brownsville, Texas, another MSA that experienced rapid growth in the 1970s in both population and per capita income, also benefited from its contiguity to the Mexican maquiladoras but also had low per capita income at the end of the decade. The importance of maquiladoras is explicit in the extensive advertising in trade magazines by the Brownsville region of its proximity to the Mexican border area. Brownsville also benefited in an indirect way from the oil boom, as it was a major center for the construction of offshore oil rigs built in its shipyards. When oil prices fell, its position reversed from one of the fastest-growing to one of the slowest-growing MSAs in per capita income. This occurred in several other Gulf Coast MSAs, as noted above. An analogous phenomenon occurred in several other non–Gulf Coast MSAs such as Billings, Montana, Casper, Wyoming, and Enid, Oklahoma. The fate of these MSAs is a partial indicator of the atypical nature of the 1970s and supports the view that the experience of the 1980s is more in tune with long-term forces of growth and decline across MSAs.

Some MSAs experience fast population growth due to contiguity to an expanding MSA whose land and housing prices and commuting times are increasing. Santa Rosa, California (forty miles from San Francisco), Riverside, California (fifty miles from Los Angeles), and Fort Worth, Texas (contiguous to Dallas), all benefited from the crowding in these nearby metropolises, a potential source of growth not included among the variables explaining growth. Although it is more than fifty miles from New York City, the New Haven MSA experienced rapid growth in per capita income as a result of its proximity to New York City and Fairfield County, Connecticut. As housing and office prices continued to rise in New York and Fairfield, households seeking lower housing costs helped turn the MSA around from having one of the lowest growth rates of per capita income to being among the twenty with the most rapid growth rates. Contiguity, however, is not solely a function of distance but of transportation links. New Haven could attract relatively rich "refugees" from Fairfield and New York because it was located next to the major north-south interstate highway, I-95, as well as being on the Amtrak rail line connecting New York and Boston. Similarly, the Newark and Jersey City metropolitan areas received a substantial boost from New York–based financial and service firms seeking lower-cost venues for operation.

Sacramento, California, one of the fastest-growing MSAs in popula-tion in the 1980s, provides another illustration of location spillovers. It is close to the San Francisco–San Jose MSA (and is only a short flight from Los Angeles–Orange County) but is less congested. It has a superb river port and lies on north-south and east-west interstate highway routes and, very importantly, on major rail routes. Thus, it became a major ware-housing and wholesaling center as well as being attractive to firms such as Hewlett-Packard from Silicon Valley that were seeking relatively close but less congested areas.

The role of contiguity to major MSAs experiencing diseconomies of agglomeration is not easy to capture in the equations estimated in chap-ter 4. Correct specification would require inclusion of nearby MSAs, their housing and commercial space costs, wages, and access time between MSAs. Moreover, the growth spillovers are relevant for only a few MSAs. Yet, as just indicated, for some of the MSAs, such factors are quite relevant.

Atlanta, Georgia, which had very fast population and per capita income growth in the 1980s, has a completely different characteristic. Rather than proximity to another MSA, its role is derived from being the major MSA in the rapidly growing southeastern United States. The con-struction of a major airport reinforced its attractiveness to firms given its initially much lower wage and land costs. The "happy" MSA growth sto-ries have very different characteristics. Basic variables are important, but there are often special circumstances.

In looking at the phenomena of population and per capita income growth jointly, one interesting pattern is suggested by the experience of some of the larger MSAs, whose population growth was slow or negative in the 1970s and then witnessed a surge in per capita income (though not in population) growth in the 1980s. Large metropolitan areas with a diversified economic base have a much greater chance of recovery after initial declines. The MSAs centered around Boston, Jersey City, Newark, New York, and Philadelphia were among the most slowly growing MSAs in population in the 1970s. In the 1980s, they were among the twenty MSAs with the most rapid growth in per capita income. Interestingly, the rebound in per capita income growth for these large MSAs is well pre-dicted by their initial variables in 1980. None of their growth rates is out-side of the 95 percent interval.

Large MSAs, whatever their short-term fortunes, have the potential for rapid regeneration, although often in different sectors than those that drove their earlier expansion. For example, in the Philadelphia MSA, population declined in the 1970s due to a loss in manufacturing jobs. This trend was soon redressed by the expansion of high-technology firms along Route 202 in Montgomery County and the rapid growth of pharmaceutical research in several counties—an expansion facilitated by the absolutely large pharmaceutical base that existed in 1980. Whereas the Jersey City and Newark MSAs benefited from proximity to New York, the size and diversity of their economic base was an important part of their ability to recoup. Major financial institutions seeking a lower-cost base for back office operations would not have relocated into smaller MSAs that had no labor pool in relevant occupations nor service firms. On Long Island, part of the New York MSA, layoffs at two defense contractors, Sperry and Grumman, led to the establishment of new firms by recently fired employees—an initiative much easier to undertake in a major metropolitan area with local banks and accounting and financial services than in a smaller region with a paucity of such complementary activities.

Some southwestern MSAs benefited in population growth not only from the oil price boom, which was not sustainable, but also from the continuing influx of immigrants primarily from Mexico. Laredo, Texas, Las Cruces, New Mexico, and to a smaller extent, San Diego, California, all had large inflows of immigrants. However, in the first two instances, the level of per capita income remains quite low. Although the theory underlying the equations of chapter 4 implies population movements in response to the growth of employment, some border communities may grow as a result of large immigration, reflecting the hope that jobs will materialize even if they have not already done so.

In some of the MSAs associated with an influx of retirees there was considerable growth in firms producing products that were exported to other regions rather than simply providing goods and services to retirees. In San Diego, the presence of the University of California, the Scripps Clinic and Research Foundation, and the Salk Institute encouraged many firms to locate in the area. But for many of the retirement havens (Daytona Beach, Fort Lauderdale, Fort Pierce, Sarasota, Tampa, and West Palm Beach, Florida, and Tucson, Arizona), weather was a variable with which more slowly growing areas could not compete. In several instances, the growth of these areas was much more than could be predicted even given the inclusion of average temperature.

Slow growth in some cases is associated with high concentration in one declining industry, for example steel (Gary, Indiana), construction equipment (Peoria, Illinois), steel and automotive parts (Kokomo, Indiana), and heavy manufacturing (Muncie, Indiana). The decline of the U.S. steel industry as lower-cost competitors entered international trade implied that MSAs with high concentrations of employment in this sector would experience serious declines in employment. Somewhat less predictable were the problems encountered by the Caterpillar Corporation, located in Peoria. The growth of a single major competitor, Komatsu, based in Japan, and the increase in the dollar-yen exchange rate reduced the competitiveness of Caterpillar's construction equipment and explains a large part of the slow population growth of Peoria in the 1980s.

Despite these examples, the importance of special factors accounting for fast or slow population or per capita income growth is not typical. The experience of most MSAs is explained well by the fundamental factors included in the equations reported in chapter 4. But the descriptions, especially of thriving MSAs, provide a cautionary tale. Most of the special factors conducive to very fast growth are not easily replicable. Public policy cannot cause a large metropolis to appear next to one's own. The willingness to spend public funds on inducing high-technology firms to locate is unlikely to work without a good or excellent university, and perhaps a good climate. All MSAs cannot relocate to the Mexican border. In terms of the phrasing used earlier, destiny has a large role. Perhaps it is mutable to some extent, but turnarounds of smaller MSAs are rare. And even if they were to turn around, given the nationwide constraint on aggregate growth, the gain of one MSA would necessarily come at the expense of others. In terms of figures 1-5 and 1-6, not all communities can be moved to the high-growth northeast corner of the figure. All cannot be above average.

## CHAPTER SIX

# Regional
# Policy

THE EMPHASIS IN THIS volume has been on interregional differences in growth rates (both population and per capita income), on the resultant shift of the locus of population and economic activity to the South and West of the United States, and on the welfare implications of these growth differentials. On the margin, more rapid growth (particularly of per capita income) is associated with reductions in poverty and unemployment rates and with improvements in educational achievement. Given the differences in growth rates and their apparent associations with desirable welfare outcomes, I have tried to identify the sources of growth differentials.

The basic conclusion of previous chapters is that despite concern over the substantial shifts of population and economic activity out of the Northeast and Midwest to the South and West, welfare measures are moving in the right direction in the last several decades. Although not all regions have seen improvements in all welfare measures, per capita incomes are growing and educational attainment is increasing. Overall, poverty rates and unemployment are largely a function of national macroeconomic conditions, although the more rapidly growing regions and metropolitan areas—particularly those with rapid growth in per capita income—have fared better on these measures than more slowly growing places. The general picture is of convergence: the poorest, most troubled places, in particular the metropolitan areas of the South, have shown the greatest improvement.[1]

Although total income, along with total population, has shifted dramatically toward the South and West, per capita incomes have been converging over time, largely as a result of the sustained increases in the South relative to other regions (figure 6-1).[2] Wide swings in the growth in per capita income are possible from decade to decade within a region (figure 6-1). The loss or slow growth of population does not imply a similar loss or slow growth in per capita income, nor does a rapid growth in per capita income result in an influx of population. In the 1970s when population fell and per capita income grew very slowly in the Northeast, the correlation between the two for all the metropolitan areas was .35. In the 1980s, when there was the enormous increase in the growth in per capita income in the Northeast, there was no similar burst of population growth in the region, and the overall correlation between the two growth rates fell to .30.

Lest it be thought that population growth would take a longer time to respond to the growth in per capita income in the Northeast in the 1980s, it might be noted that the average metropolitan area growth in population in the Northeast between 1990 and 1996 continued to increase, but only from 3 percent to 6 percent. In the South, average metropolitan area population growth continued to increase from 13 percent in the 1980s to 17 percent between 1990 and 1996. In the West, the average growth rate increased slightly from 22 to 24 percent. Thus, although there was some

---

1. This conclusion about convergence requires some qualification. Until the 1980s, it was quite an accurate characterization. In 1980, the difference in average per capita metropolitan income by region was lowest by far, the result of a steady increase in relative per capita incomes in the South and relative declines in the Northeast: the highest average metropolitan area relative per capita incomes were found in the West—about 6.5 percent higher than the national average, compared with the South at about .95 of average; the ratio of the two was about .89. In 1960, the ratio between the low per capita income in the South and the high per capita income in the West was approximately .84, by 1970 it had risen to .90, and as indicated, in 1980, it stood at about .95. However, in 1990, due to the enormous growth in per capita income in the Northeast, the ratio of the South, at the bottom, to the Northeast, at the top, fell back to about .93. Many studies have looked at variants of these data—earnings, household incomes, family incomes, and regional cost-of-living–adjusted incomes—and generally found similar convergence and divergence patterns. The explanations for these patterns differ. Most are considered in chapter 4. See Barro and Sala-i-Martin (1991, 1992); Bishop, Formby, and Thistle (1992, 1994 [on the 1970s]); Eberts (1989); and Farber and Newman (1987).

2. See footnote 1 above.

**Figure 6-1.** *Relative Average per Capita Income, Census Regions, 1960–90*

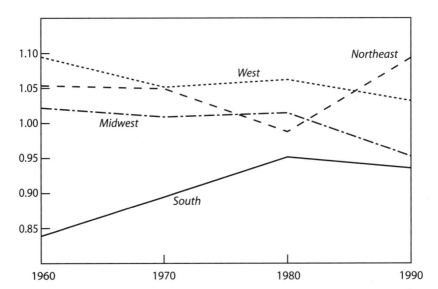

increase in population growth in the Northeast, growth rates in the South and West were still far higher, continuing the overall shift in the regional redistribution of U.S. population from the Northeast and Midwest to the South and West.

Unlike the persistent differences among regions described below in the European Union and the United Kingdom, the enormous mobility of population and capital in the United States appears to be moving the regions of the country to greater similarity in well-being, as indicated by the socioeconomic characteristics of the regions.[3]

## Market Forces, Demographic Change, and Economic Shocks

The big picture of regional convergence in welfare indicators may be viewed as support for the position that a regional policy, or a change in regional policy, is not called for. On the contrary, the market forces that are at work and the public policies that influence regional development

3. Bishop, Formby, and Thistle (1994) also attribute "the convergence of the South to the average distribution of the rest of the country" to "interregional mobility of capital and labor."

appear to have been working in the right direction. Also militating against intervention to influence regional development is the likelihood that the forces behind regional growth are highly susceptible to unforeseeable shocks to the determinants of growth, and therefore policy based on analysis of the 1970s might have been inappropriate for the 1980s.

Chapters 4 and 5 present the conclusion that a substantial policy challenge is posed by the fact that urban growth is a matter not simply of choice (policy or market forces) but also of fate and history. In addition, the underlying systematic elements change over time. One might have been prescient enough to forecast and understand the implications of the aging of the population and the increase in the incomes of the elderly and the relocation of retirees to warmer climates. However, many demographers in the 1960s were predicting that the aging of the suburban population would bring population back to the central cities; that as the suburban population aged, empty-nesters would leave their large suburban homes and relocate in the central cities, where they could live in single-story apartments, use public transportation, and have more convenient access to the cultural life of the city. This prediction was not borne out. Aging suburbanites in the Northeast and Midwest moved South and Southwest or stayed in the suburbs in the new apartment-house developments and retirement communities that had formerly been largely excluded by suburban zoning. Such a demographically motivated intra-metropolitan relocation from suburb to city is once again being predicted and allegedly observed in many places.[4] If such movement is occurring, it does not necessarily mean that cities as a whole are experiencing increases in population. These may be purely downtown increases, with other areas of the city still declining.[5] Most important, a high percentage of retirees will continue to relocate to the South and West.

Still other developments, unlikely to have been captured by earlier models, were the oil price shocks of the 1970s that had such an important

4. For a discussion of new evidence on gentrification in the 1990s, see Wyly and Hammel (1999), and for qualifications and contradictions of the argument and evidence, see the comments on this article by Berry (1999) and Kasarda (1999).

5. A recent article in the real estate section of the *New York Times* describes new construction on the Philadelphia waterfront and cites increases in the downtown population of about 5,000 persons and a pent-up demand for downtown apartments. What it does not indicate is that the city as a whole continues to lose population. According to the U.S. Census Bureau, between 1990 and 1999, the city as a whole lost more than 150,000 residents. Maureen Milford, "On a Pier in Philadelphia, Luxury Apartments," *New York Times,* December 24, 2000, Sec. 11, p. 5.

influence on the growth of the Southwest states. The scarcity and increased price of oil was also widely predicted to foreshadow a movement back to cities from suburbs—another prediction not realized.

Similarly, the enormous increase in the growth in per capita income in the Northeast between the 1970s and 1980s was nowhere predicted in the literature of the 1970s referred to earlier. Looking back it seems obvious that some older metropolitan areas, with their major universities, highly educated populations, and major financial institutions would prosper in the 1980s as a result of the revolution in information technology and the extraordinary growth in the importance of investment banking, commercial banking, and investment services such as brokerages and mutual fund home offices. It would have been less obvious that even their older loft buildings—made obsolete by the postwar technological developments in manufacturing that favored single-story plants on large lots— would become attractive locations for some of the firms involved in the Internet.

## Regional Policy in the United States

There is not, at present, much of a case being made for regional policy in the United States. Urban policies are set out in a variety of reports from the Department of Housing and Urban Development. In the 1980s, the annual reports bore the title *The President's National Urban Policy Report*,[6] but more recent reports are titled *The State of the Cities*.[7] The focus in both analysis and policy prescription has been on cities and intrametropolitan issues, particularly the state of the central cities and how to improve their well-being.[8] Interregional differences have generally received only passing attention.

One would have to go back to the 1970s and early 1980s, to Senator Daniel Patrick Moynihan, to find major advocacy for regional policy in the United States. At that time, Moynihan argued for government inter-

6. U.S. Department of Housing and Urban Development (1984, 1986).
7. U.S. Department of Housing and Urban Development (1997, 1998, 2000).
8. Most current discussions about urban policy and urban policy bias are about intrametropolitan policies. They emphasize policies that are thought to favor suburbs over cities by distorting the true price of suburban development: highway and other infrastructure funding, the federal home mortgage tax deduction, and environmental regulations, particularly those that result in greenfield development. See Brueckner (2000); Voith and Gyourko (2000).

vention to help the North, *without politicizing the process*, without interfering with the free movement of capital and labor, and without diverting
resources to less than optimal uses.[9] Although he acknowledged that
"there is not much government can do to prevent economic change of this
order" (the shifts of population and economic activity to the West and
South) and he argued that "government should not promise to do what
it can't do," he went on to say that *"government must do what it can."*[10]

To bolster his support for government intervention to assist northern
economies, Moynihan pointed to a long history of "successful" regional
policy in the United States—citing policies that fostered "westward
expansion" in the 1800s and the policies to assist the South during the
New Deal.[11] With respect to the New Deal and the South, he approvingly
quotes President Franklin Roosevelt in 1938,

> It is my conviction that the South presents right now the nation's
> number one economic problem—the nation's problem, not merely
> the South's. For we have an economic unbalance in the nation as a
> whole, due to this very condition of the South's. It is an unbalance
> that can and must be righted for the sake of the South and the
> Nation.[12]

In 1978, as indicated above, Moynihan's concern was with "the situation in the North today. . . . True economic decline, an actual diminution
of economic activity."[13] It was the uneven growth pattern among regions,
particularly the loss of population in the North, that troubled him.

The arguments for regional policy in the United States appear to be
grounded largely in considerations of political and economic equity. In
President Roosevelt's statement and Moynihan's arguments, much is
made of the U.S. liberal tradition of regional policy, of caring for lagging
regions, to which the nation should not "suddenly appear to be indifferent." The liberal tradition to which he refers "incorporates an ethic of

9. Moynihan (1978).
10. Moynihan (1978, pp. 8–9, emphasis added).
11. Moynihan (1978, p. 3).
12. Moynihan (1978, p. 4). This is very similar in its rationale for regional policy to that
offered by European nations as described in Begg, Gudgin and Morris (1995): "At the level
of the nation state there has been a general acceptance of the implicit importance of national
equity and cohesion," p. 2.
13. Moynihan (1978, p. 5).

collective provision . . . that has triumphed politically and . . . has triumphed in the goals it set for itself. We are a vastly stronger, more united,
and happier nation thanks to Franklin D. Roosevelt and the ideas he
stood for. . . . [T]he vast outpouring of programs and aid for the South
were for him the expression of a national purpose, which knew little of
regional power, but concentrated greatly on regional need."[14]

In providing more up-to-date background for what became an argument specifically for assistance to New York City, then on the verge of
bankruptcy, Senator Moynihan argued that policy biases, both those
favoring the South and those contributing to the decline of the North,
loom large in observed differences in regional fortunes. "The most con-
spicuous example is that of the heavy concentration of defense facilities in
the South," which he attributes to "a pattern of Congressional influence
. . . that . . . should now be put behind us."[15] The implication is clearly
that these political biases resulted in inefficient, regionally inequitable
location decisions with important economic implications. A second
source of bias according to Moynihan is the federal flow of funds. He
cites Peterson and Muller's study of the regional impact of federal tax
and spending policies.[16] Although they found very great differences in
federal outlays received by different regions of the country (wages of federal employees, purchases of goods and services, and capital investment),
they concluded that these differences were based on efficiency considerations. Despite his recognition of this conclusion, Moynihan argues that
"it may be that the . . . imbalance . . . is *not* dictated by the market."
Rather, "the federal government has been deflating the economy of New
York State."[17] This conclusion is based on his figures showing that federal
outlays going to New York State in 1976 were $26.3 billion, compared
with revenues going from New York to the federal government of
$33.7 billion.[18]

14. Moynihan (1978, pp. 9–10).
15. Moynihan (1978, p. 11).
16. Peterson and Muller (1980).
17. Moynihan (1978, p. 12, emphasis in original). I have argued that such outlay-revenue
imbalances could hardly be otherwise in an economy with a progressive income tax and relatively high incomes in New York State. To require equality between revenues and expenditures would negate the purposes of a progressive income tax system. Pack (1980, 1982).
18. It is notable that in the absence of any change in regional policy over the two
decades, in New York City, the center of Senator Moynihan's concern about regional

Studies emphasizing the net flow of funds on federal account and its impact on local economies embody several assumptions that have limited theoretical basis. They assume that, analogous to the national economy with a given capacity to supply output, changes in taxes and expenditures affect local demand, which is the primary determinant of local income. Local demand then automatically elicits a response in both population and per capita income. Such a view is deficient in a number of dimensions. First, considering an economy made up of large numbers of metropolitan statistical areas (MSAs), the movement of labor and hence of population among them depends on each MSA's rate of productivity growth relative to all others, a view underlying the equations estimated in chapter 4. Growth in per capita income also depends on such differential productivity movements. Moreover, given a metropolitan area's supply ability—determined by its capital stock, labor force, and level of total factor productivity—the MSA's own demand is not critical. A very small percentage of Microsoft's sales occur in the Seattle MSA. Although local service supply sectors such as retailing, entertainment, and most medical services depend on local demand, business "exports" do not. The assumption of flow-of-funds arguments is that a better fiscal position vis-à-vis the federal government that provides more disposable income to the residents of a given state or MSA will result in greater economic growth. Although it may lead to some increase in local retail sales, some of the additional income will inevitably be spent on refrigerators, television sets, movies, and cars produced in other parts of the country or abroad. Moreover, even expenditures on locally produced goods and services do not necessarily generate additional supply unless wages increase relative to other areas and workers are attracted to the area or the rate of return on capital is increased, thus leading to more investment. But both of these scenarios depend on productivity growth in one MSA relative to others. Moving to a fiscal balance in Connecticut has no effect on productivity growth and no necessary implications even for local demand. As noted in chapter 4, movement in the labor force and hence in population may also occur to obtain access to the cultural amenities of an MSA, medical services, and

---

decline, real per capita income increased by 41 percent in the 1980s, although it had declined by 7 percent in the 1970s. This change is well explained by the model set out in chapter 4. Even population, which had declined by 10 percent in the 1970s, showed a small increase in the 1980s, 3.5 percent.

better weather, none of which is affected in an important way by the federal fiscal balance.[19]

Moving away from the flow-of-funds question to the more general issue of the regional impact of federal policies, several have obviously exerted an important influence on the growth patterns of regions and, by extension, of MSAs. In particular the interstate highway system and water projects have had a major effect. The development of the interstate highway system in the post–World War II period had a large defense component. An inevitable side effect was that many regions that were initially difficult to get to by car or truck became accessible, reducing the costs of firms located in those regions and reducing the moving costs of new firms and of households that discerned increasing job opportunities. It thus had the unintended consequence of encouraging movement of firms and households from the Northeast and Midwest to the South and West. The convergence term for initial levels of income in the equations of chapter 4 would probably have been considerably smaller without the construction of the highway system. It can be inferred from population and business movements that the interstate system enhanced efficiency at the national level. The roads ran in both directions, but there were (net) moves in only one direction.

Water projects that subsidized farms, firms, and households in southern California, Arizona, and New Mexico also had beneficial national effects. For example, improving the productivity of huge tracts of land in California shifted the curve of the national supply of food and resulted in lower prices (or a smaller rate of growth of prices) and greater variety for all consumers, regardless of their area of residence. The movement of retirees to warmer climates was also made possible by the availability of water at heavily subsidized rates—rates subsidized largely by residents of other areas. Although this policy could be viewed as having a regional bias, the option of moving to these areas was available to all residents of the United States, and many Minnesotans and Kansans whose taxes paid for the subsidies availed themselves of the option to move.

Thus, the two readily identifiable federal policies that certainly differentially affected regional growth generated benefits for residents of the United States irrespective of their location. Demands for federal inter-

19. There may be minor effects—for example, the building of a Veterans Administration hospital in one MSA rather than another—but these are likely to have a relatively small impact on population movement.

vention to redress such "biases" ignore these widespread national benefits. Given the flaws in the flow-of-funds analysis noted above, a basis for federal intervention to explicitly favor some regions despite the absence of any national benefit is not easy to set forth unless some externalities can be demonstrated that would arguably improve national welfare rather than simply that of the recipient metropolitan areas. Evidence for such externalities has not been provided.

Nonetheless, the latest of these reports on federal flow-of-funds deficits and surpluses was released by the Kennedy School of Government of Harvard University and the office of Senator Daniel Patrick Moynihan in December 2000.[20] It documents the continued net outflow of tax revenues from the Northeast and Great Lakes to the South and West. The authors recognize that it is relative incomes that are largely responsible for the observed patterns—poorer states paying less in taxes—but they still put the matter in terms of "fair shares."

A somewhat different perspective on the extent of regional policy in the United States is set out by Morris Sweet in a recent volume.[21] Sweet points to nineteenth-century proposals for regional development activities in the United States that were largely rejected by congresses that were more concerned with states' rights issues. Although there was no national development plan, "Congress did move forward on development programs throughout the nineteenth century: . . . land grants for railroad construction, river and harbor improvements, and the Homestead Act of 1862, which made it national policy to encourage agricultural development of the West."[22] Sweet makes clear that not until the depression of the 1930s and the coming of the New Deal programs was there substantial interest in regional development. Moreover, the primary initial motive for many of the programs was stimulating aggregate demand in general to cope with the national depression. As New Deal programs developed, regional considerations became important.

In the immediate aftermath of World War II a number of regional problems began to be discussed by policymakers: "A concern for chronically depressed areas, . . . depressed areas created . . . by shifts in product demand, depletion of resources, and technological change. Extensive pockets of poverty such as Appalachia and the pervasive rural poverty of

20. Leonard and Walder (2000).
21. Sweet (1999).
22. Sweet (1999, p. 237).

the South, along with some major industrial areas affected by declining or shifting markets (e.g., coal and textiles), created a new sense of urgency about the dilemma of decline in the midst of the postwar boom." Despite the regional concentration of many of these problem areas, policy emphasis in the United States was, for the most part, macroeconomic policy. The 1946 Employment Act, for example, was not addressed to regions but to national employment. "In the 1950s, the only regional policy instrument of any note was the 1952 executive order known as Defense Manpower Policy 4."[23] Although it proposed to favor firms in areas of high unemployment in the competition for defense contracts, such firms were required to match the lowest bid.

It is by now part of our historical lore that a 1960 visit to Appalachia had a major impact on presidential candidate John F. Kennedy and led to the development of regionally targeted economic programs, which were later reinforced by President Lyndon B. Johnson's War on Poverty. As Sweet points out, this was not a national regional policy but rather one aimed at a few specific areas. By 1965 even this limited "regional" policy came to an end when the Area Redevelopment Administration was abolished.

If one examines the various federal documents on urban policy of the 1980s and 1990s, it is clear that federal policy is (and has been) largely intrametropolitan rather than regional.[24] Sweet reaches a similar conclusion: "The main focus of explicit federal spatial policies in the 1960s was urban and not regional. . . . Typical was the 1966 Model Cities Program." Despite the Sun Belt–Frost Belt debate of the 1970s, federal programs "did not constitute a carefully constructed national or regional economic development plan." Nor was the Carter administration "overly concerned with regional programs, . . . [and] there has been no change in the 1990s."[25] In fact, toward the end of the Carter administration a president's commission concerned with urban policy supported a policy to maintain strong national growth and concentrate on the needs of people, increasing their human capital and their ability to take advantage of opportunities throughout the country, rather than a policy to support declining areas.[26]

23. Sweet (1999, pp. 239, 241).
24. U.S. Department of Housing and Urban Development (1984, 1986, 1998, 2000).
25. Sweet ( 1999, p. 242).
26. President's Commission for a National Agenda for the Eighties (1980). See the discussion below of people policies versus place policies.

There is thus little evidence on which to base a conclusion that the United States has introduced major regional development policies. In the United States the primary sources of convergence have been the market-induced mobility of firms and households—firms responding to lower costs, population moving to economic opportunity—and the aging of the population and the growth of retirement communities in warmer climates, both resulting in the massive shifts in population and economic activity to the South and West documented earlier.

## Regional Policy in Europe

The major justification for regional policy in Europe is similar to the "one nation" argument made by Moynihan. The arguments and evidence are broadly reviewed in a special issue of the *Oxford Review of Economic Policy*.[27] The introduction to the volume, written by Iain Begg, Graham Gudgin, and Derek Morris, begins, "Policies intended to counter disparities between regions in economic performance have been a feature of most European states throughout the post-war period. *These have been rooted in a widespread belief that living standards and employment prospects in any one region or locality should not fall too far behind the national average.*"[28] Elsewhere in the issue, Gudgin writes that in the United Kingdom, "Persistent differences, particularly in unemployment but also in other aspects of economic well-being, have resulted in a policy response aimed at ameliorating the worst regional imbalance problems."[29] The authors of the introduction further state that "at the level of the nation state there has been a general acceptance of the implicit importance of national equity and cohesion. . . . In the European Union the main concern of regional policy has been to promote economic development in regions with low per capita incomes."[30]

Despite considerable public efforts to reduce regional disparities, such disparities continue. Based on studies of regional policy in the European Union, the United Kingdom, and Italy, Begg, Gudgin, and Morris conclude, "Even in the countries where there has been an active regional policy, it has had only limited effect in reducing regional imbalances, and has to a considerable extent now been dismantled. . . . [A] growing body of

27. Gudgin and Morris (1995).
28. Begg, Gudgin, and Morris (1995, p. 1, emphasis added).
29. Gudgin (1995, p. 18).
30. Begg, Gudgin, and Morris (1995, pp. 2–3).

evidence suggests that regional problems are caused by a multiplicity of interrelated factors which makes them much more impervious to policy initiatives than would otherwise be the case."[31] Gudgin nevertheless finds a limited exception to the general rule—regional policy in the United Kingdom has been directed at "persistent differences, particularly in unemployment but also in other aspects of economic well-being. . . . In the period 1960–73, regional policy had been simple and effective: an estimated 250,000 manufacturing jobs were induced to move from the prosperous regions to the assisted regions."[32] When a more general weakness developed in the United Kingdom after 1973, the policy was abandoned and eventually repealed in 1981.

More recent data illustrate the persistent North-South regional divide in Great Britain. In the *New York Times,* Alan Cowell cites Britain's "chronic problem: an economy perilously skewed between an ailing industrial North and a prosperous South dominated by greater London."[33] Despite the booming economy, despite the fact that "inflation . . . is at its lowest level in 36 years; unemployment has been tamed to levels last seen in the 1980s, and the budget is expected to zoom from a projected deficit . . . to a surplus, . . . the North-South gap is growing—in income, average wages and migration." What is of greatest interest insofar as policy is concerned is the argument that it is not regional policy but rather "a broader economic policy" that has exacerbated the division "between ailing manufacturing [in the North] and booming services [in the South]." The policies that cause problems in the North are not regional policies but rather a strong currency that inhibits exports; a policy that derives from "fiscal discipline," which has resulted in "noninflationary growth . . . [but] has itself begun to push up interest rates." And as the general manager of a heavy manufacturing firm says, "When interest rates go up and the pound goes up, we are not competitive." So the "divide between North and South . . . woven into British history" has not only not been closed by massive attempts at regional economic policies to help the North but is widened by sound macroeconomic policies to strengthen the economy—which turn out to have differential regional implications.

31. Begg, Gudgin, and Morris (1995, p. 14).
32. Gudgin (1995, p. 19).
33. Alan Cowell, "This Splintered Isle: Economically, There Have Always Been Two Englands," *New York Times,* October 5, 1999, pp. C1 and C10.

And in Italy, probably everyone's favorite example of the difficulty of producing a successful regional policy, Leonardi (1995) contrasts the success of the Italian North with the "continued backwardness of the southern regions."[34] He argues that these differences are not attributable to "general national policy or . . . specific national development programmes. . . . Instead, evidence shows that regional growth and development in Italy has tended to be strongly dependent upon local factors, such as social norms and community values."[35] Thus, the European countries, despite greater concern with regional differences and many policies to eliminate them, have seen far less convergence than that achieved by the United States' more market-based approach.

## Is There a Need for Regional Policy in the United States?

As has been demonstrated, in the United States regional convergence in socioeconomic conditions of the population has been a major characteristic of the post–World War II period.[36] This convergence appears to have occurred without major systematic policy intervention. The analyses in chapters 4 and 5 also indicate the difficulty of using policy intervention to influence regional—or for that matter local—development, when the forces behind regional growth are highly susceptible to shocks. In the face of such changes, it is unlikely that policies based on analysis of growth in the 1970s would have been appropriate for the 1980s.[37] In 1976, for example, the Joint Economic Committee of Congress forecast slower growth for the 1980s and 1990s.[38] The committee was concerned that the relative economic well-being of the Northeast and Midwest could fall behind that of the South and West. As seen in earlier chapters, this has not been the case; in 1990, per capita income and educational achievement in the metropolitan areas of the Northeast still exceeded those of the

34. Leonardi (1995).
35. Leonardi (1995, p. 165).
36. This was true even in the nineteenth century, although the pace of convergence was far more rapid in the twentieth century. See Pack (1980).
37. Although several examples were cited in chapter 5 of successful local interventions to stimulate growth, these were also places in which other factors conducive to growth were present. As for the possibility of the success of widespread local interventions, the macroeconomic limitations are critical. In the 1980s, when per capita incomes in the Northeast soared, the increases in other regions barely changed. And when dozens of cities build new convention centers, they simply further divide a relatively fixed number of conventions.
38. Olson (1976).

South, and poverty rates and unemployment were lower. The unexpected very rapid growth of the Northeast in the 1980s compared with the 1970s defied expectations. As seen below, the 1990s have probably also been more complex than the experience of the 1970s would have led analysts to expect in terms of future regional development.

### Metropolitan Areas Left Behind

Despite the findings about convergence and the inference that public policy has not played a major role in bringing it about, it may nevertheless be premature to conclude that economies everywhere are moving in the right direction and that policy intervention is neither called for nor likely to be successful.

—What is true on the average may not be true for all metropolitan areas. Notwithstanding the fact that regional welfare indicators are converging, there may be metropolitan areas for which this is not the case. This is the major emphasis in several recent publications of the U.S. Department of Housing and Urban Development. Despite a vigorous national economy that has had widespread beneficial results, there are some places (the reports emphasize cities rather than metropolitan areas) that are not experiencing the general benefits of a vigorous economy and continue to decline and to be characterized by serious negative social welfare outcomes: high poverty rates, high unemployment rates, and declining populations and tax base.[39] It may be that in the midst of the current prosperity, we are at a point similar to that during the post–World War II economic boom, a moment of concern for "places left behind."

—Insofar as per capita income growth in the 1970s and 1980s appears to have been influenced by different factors, it may be that the 1980s provide a better basis for thinking about the future. The 1970s were far too idiosyncratic to disprove the notion that equalizing forces that underlie economic change could be amenable to limited public policy intervention. Indeed, although studies by both the now-defunct Office of Technology Assessment and the Department of Housing and Urban Development concentrate on cities, rather than regions or entire metropolitan areas, both suggest some continuity between the 1980s and the 1990s and beyond as a result of the impact of "the new high-tech, global

39. U.S. Department of Housing and Urban Development (1999, 2000).

economy."[40] These finding are certainly consistent with those of chapter 4, in which it is shown that in the 1980s technology became quite important in influencing per capita income growth—an educated labor force and the presence of highly ranked university departments being associated with the rapidly growing new-technology and technology-intensive industries.[41]

In its 1999 report, *Now Is the Time: Places Left Behind in the New Economy,*[42] the U.S. Department of Housing and Urban Development considers cities left behind despite the vigorous economy of the 1990s. "Places left behind" or "doubly burdened" cities are those with high unemployment (50 percent or more greater than the national average in 1998) and either long-run (for the previous two decades) population loss (5 percent or more) or persistently (between 1980 and 1996) high poverty rates (20 percent or more) or both. But, as shown in earlier chapters, per capita income growth, not population growth, is associated with improvements in the population's well-being. This is true for cities as well as for their suburbs. The correlation between growth rates in population and per capita income for the 250 central cities in the sample used here was only .3 for the period 1960–90. The correlation in the 1960s was .29; in the 1970s, when the Southwest metropolitan areas prospering from the oil boom experienced rapid growth in per capita income as well as continued rapid growth in population, the correlation was .46; but in the 1980s, with the end of the oil boom and the dramatic turnaround in the per capita income growth rates in the Northeast, the correlation declined to .19.

Thus, for purposes of identifying metropolitan areas left behind, highly distressed metropolitan areas are defined here in terms of their poverty,

40. U.S. Congress, Office of Technology Assessment (1995); U.S. Department of Housing and Urban Development (2000). Both of these reports are discussed in some detail below.

41. California continues to recognize the importance of these factors, despite its already strong position. As reported by John Markoff in the *New York Times,* the governor "announced the establishment of three major research institutions dedicated to nanotechnology, biotechnology, and telecommunications and computing." The California Institutes for Science and Innovation will be made up of "joint ventures among campuses in the University of California system." The state will contribute $300 million over four years to support this undertaking to be matched by at least two times that amount from private corporations, including IBM, Sun Microsystems, Qualcomm, and Sony. John Markoff, "California Sets up Three Centers for Basic Scientific Research," *New York Times,* December 8, 2000, p. A30.

42. U.S. Department of Housing and Urban Development (1999).

unemployment rates, and per capita incomes. Specifically, highly distressed metropolitan areas are those in which poverty rates, unemployment rates, and per capita income were all at least one-half standard deviation worse than average in 1990. By this definition, there were thirty-one such metropolitan areas in 1990 (table 6-1). Several patterns can be noted:

—These metropolitan areas are regionally concentrated: twenty-four of the thirty-one are in the South (of eighty-five metropolitan areas in the South);

—Moreover, nineteen of these twenty-four are in only one of the three census divisions that make up the South: the west south central division, consisting of Texas, Louisiana, Oklahoma, and Arkansas;[43]

—Furthermore, within these four states, all but one of the nineteen highly distressed metropolitan areas are in either Texas (ten) or Louisiana (eight).

Several differences can be noted in the location patterns of the highly distressed metropolitan areas and a group of thirty-three that might be termed very well-off metropolitan areas: those with per capita incomes one-half standard deviation above average and unemployment and poverty rates one-half standard deviation below average:

—The very well-off metropolitan areas are less regionally concentrated: nineteen are in the South and West, and fourteen are in the Northeast and Midwest.

—Of the ten in the South, all are along the South Atlantic, with four of the ten in Florida. These characteristics may be compared with those of the nineteen highly distressed Southern metropolitan areas.

There are great differences between the well-off and the distressed metropolitan areas in the variables identified in chapter 4 as being important for per capita income growth in the 1980s (and that apparently continue to be important):

—The differences in educational attainment are enormous: in 1990, 27 percent of the adults in the very well-off metropolitan areas had college degrees and only 18 percent had not graduated from high school. In the highly distressed metropolitan areas the figures were 15 percent with college degrees and 32 percent who had not graduated from high school (table 6-2).

43. Census divisions are listed in appendix A.

Table 6-1. *Severely Distressed Metropolitan Areas, 1990, 1980, 1970*[a]

| Metropolitan area | Census region and division[b] | 1990 | 1980 | 1970 |
|---|---|---|---|---|
| Albany, Ga. | Reg. 3, Div. 3 | x | | |
| Alexandria, La. | Reg. 3, Div. 7 | x | | |
| Anniston, Al. | Reg. 3, Div. 5 | | x | |
| Bakersfield, Calif. | Reg. 4, Div. 9 | x | | |
| Baton Rouge, La. | Reg. 3, Div. 7 | x | | |
| Beaumont–Port Arthur, Tex. | Reg. 3, Div. 7 | x | | |
| Biloxi-Gulfport, Miss. | Reg. 3, Div. 5 | x | | |
| Brownsville, Tex. | Reg. 3, Div. 7 | x | x | x |
| Corpus Christi, Tex. | Reg. 3, Div. 7 | x | | |
| El Paso, Tex. | Reg. 3, Div. 7 | x | | |
| Florence, Al. | Reg. 3, Div. 5 | | x | x |
| Fresno, Calif. | Reg. 4, Div. 9 | x | | |
| Gadsden, Al. | Reg. 3, Div. 5 | x | x | x |
| Huntington-Ashland, W.Va.-Ky.-Ohio | Reg. 3, Div. 5 | x | x | x |
| Jersey City, N.J. | Reg. 1, Div. 2 | | x | |
| Lafayette, La. | Reg. 3, Div. 7 | x | | x |
| Lake Charles, La. | Reg. 3, Div. 7 | x | | x |
| Laredo, Tex. | Reg. 3, Div. 7 | x | | x |
| Las Cruces, N.Mex. | Reg. 4, Div. 8 | x | x | x |
| Longview, Tex. | Reg. 3, Div. 7 | x | | |
| McAllen, Tex. | Reg. 3, Div. 7 | x | x | x |
| Memphis, Tenn.-Ark.-Miss. | Reg. 3, Div. 7 | | x | |
| Mobile, Al. | Reg. 3, Div. 5 | x | | x |
| Monroe, La. | Reg. 3, Div. 7 | x | | |
| Muncie, Ind. | Reg. 2, Div. 4 | x | | x |
| New Orleans, La. | Reg. 3, Div. 7 | x | | |
| Odessa, Tex. | Reg. 3, Div. 7 | x | | |
| Pine Bluff, Ark. | Reg. 3, Div. 7 | x | x | x |
| Pueblo, Colo. | Reg. 4, Div. 8 | x | | |
| San Angelo, Tex. | Reg. 3, Div. 7 | x | | |
| San Antonio, Tex. | Reg. 3, Div. 7 | x | | |
| Shreveport, La. | Reg. 3, Div. 7 | x | | |
| Texarkana, Tex.-Ark. | Reg. 3, Div. 7 | x | | x |
| Tuscaloosa, Al. | Reg. 3, Div. 5 | | x | |
| Vineland-Millville-Bridgeton, N.J. | Reg. 1, Div. 2 | | x | |
| Wheeling, W.Va.-Ohio | Reg. 2, Div. 4 | x | | |
| Yakima, Wash. | Reg. 4, Div. 9 | x | x | x |

a. 1990: per capita income less than $9,455, poverty rate greater than 16.2 percent, unemployment rate greater than 7 percent; 1980: per capita income less than $8,081, poverty rate greater than 14.3 percent, unemployment rate greater than 7.5 percent; 1970: per capita income less than $7,059, poverty rate greater than 16.6 percent, unemployment rate greater than 5.0 percent.

b. Census regions and divisions are listed in appendix A.

**Table 6-2.** *Educational Achievement in Severely Distressed and Well-Off Metropolitan Areas,1970, 1980, and 1990*[a]

Percent of adults

| Educational achievement | Distressed metropolitan areas | Well-off metropolitan areas | All 250 metropolitan areas |
|---|---|---|---|
| *Less than high school* | | | |
| 1970 | 55 | 40 | 46 |
| 1980 | 43 | 26 | 32 |
| 1990 | 32 | 18 | 24 |
| Percentage change, 1970–90 | –42 | –55 | –48 |
| *College graduates* | | | |
| 1970 | 9 | 14 | 11 |
| 1980 | 12 | 21 | 16 |
| 1990 | 15 | 27 | 20 |
| Percentage change, 1970–90 | 67 | 93 | 82 |

a. Distressed metropolitan areas are defined in table 6-1. Well-off metropolitan areas are those with per capita incomes one-half standard deviation or more above average and poverty and unemployment rates at least one-half standard deviation below average.

—For the technology variable—that is, the presence of universities with highly ranked engineering, computer sciences, or biology departments—the average value is .62 for the well-off metropolitan areas and zero for the distressed areas. There are no highly ranked university departments in these fields in the distressed areas.

There is high correlation in socioeconomic variables from decade to decade (see chapter 3) despite the fact that conditions in the South continued to improve absolutely and relative to the rest of the nation. Nonetheless, the number of severely distressed metropolitan areas in 1990 is more than twice that in either 1980 or 1970—an indication that the distribution of socioeconomic characteristics is less compact in 1990 (table 6-1). Every one of the fourteen distressed metropolitan areas in 1970 appears on the distressed list in at least one subsequent period: seven of the fourteen appear on the list in all three years; six are not on the list in 1980 but reappear in 1990; and one appears again in 1980 only. Thus, of the severely distressed metropolitan areas in 1970, all but one are distressed in 1990 as well. I interpret this to indicate that distress is persistent, despite some decade-to-decade variation. Here is yet another indication of the unusual nature of the 1970s: six of the fourteen distressed metropolitan areas in 1970 and 1990 did not appear on the distressed list in 1980.

It has been noted how many more distressed metropolitan areas there were in 1990 than in either of the two previous decades.[44] Given the very low values of educational attainment and technology in the distressed areas in 1990, as well as their concentrated location, the reason for the increased number of distressed areas appears to lie in the greater importance of the education and technology variables in explaining per capita income growth in the 1980s than in the 1970s. These are metropolitan areas that did not have the basis for adjusting to the requirements of the growth industries of the 1980s, although some of them had benefited from the oil boom of the 1970s.

With regard to population growth—which, as has been seen, has less of an impact on the socioeconomic variables that have been used to identify the most troubled places—none of the distressed metropolitan areas in 1990 were among the slowest in population growth in the 1970s, and only four were among the slowest growing in the 1980s. Rapid population growth, particularly when its base is immigration, may contribute, at least in the short term, to high poverty rates, high unemployment rates, and low per capita income. Although only two of the 1990 distressed metropolitan areas were among the most rapidly growing in population in 1970, both were Texas border towns. Of the three 1990 distressed areas that were among the most rapidly growing in population in the 1980s, all were border towns: two in Texas and a third in New Mexico (table 5-1).

In sum, despite the generally positive picture of a nation in which poorer, less economically dynamic, less well-educated regions and metropolitan areas are converging with the rest of the nation, there are clearly metropolitan areas—concentrated in the South—that are experiencing slow per capita income growth and its concomitants. Do these findings justify a regional policy toward the geographically distressed MSAs?

### General Arguments for Regional Policy

Before examining the arguments for regional policy, several points should be reemphasized:

---

44. Of course, in absolute terms these areas have improved in per capita income and education levels but not as fast as other MSAs.

—Nearly all research finds that market forces, including national growth rates, factor price differences, and technical change, rather than government policies, are the major determinants of regional growth patterns. Although it is rarely emphasized in policy discussions, the one clearly important influence on differential regional growth rates has been the state of the macroeconomy. Several studies during the 1970s showed that the differences in growth rates of the Northeast and Midwest compared with the South and West were most severe during recessions.[45] A more recent study shows the differential regional effects of monetary policy.[46]

—Very little evidence exists that even massive state and local public interventions have positive effects, notwithstanding the examples cited in chapter 5.[47]

—Nonetheless arguments for public intervention continue.

There are numerous circumstances that might justify an argument for regional policy. (This section is not intended to consider whether regional policies exist that might be effective correctives.) These bases for intervention fall in three general categories: efficiency, equity, and policy bias.

EFFICIENCY CONSIDERATIONS. If undesirable outcomes result from market inefficiencies, public policies might improve national economic welfare if effective interventions could be implemented. The most obvious regional market failures would include the failure of capital to move to opportunities that increase returns or labor immobility that perpetuates high localized unemployment or poverty rates. One source of such failures might be inadequate information about alternatives. Externalities, both positive and negative, might also cause or result from market forces and result in too much or too little interregional mobility. Given the very high

45. Bretzfelder (1973); Pack (1980); Williamson (1977).

46. Carlino and deFina (1998) find that between 1958 and 1992, "a core of regions—New England, Mideast, Plains, Southeast, and the Far West . . . respond to monetary policy changes in ways that closely approximate the U.S. average response. The core regions accounted for a little more than two-thirds of the aggregate 1980 gross state product in the United States and for 70 percent of the total U.S. population," p. 586. They also identify "three non-core regions" that respond more or less sensitively to monetary policy.

47. A comprehensive review of the literature points to the general ineffectiveness of state and local economic development policy. See Bradbury, Kodrzycki, and Tannenwald (1997). Although pointing to evidence favoring state and local policies, Bartik (1993a) refers to "the zero-sum game argument [as] the strongest argument against state and local economic development policies." He believes that such "competition may produce net national benefits, *but hard empirical evidence for this position is scant*," p. 169 (emphasis added).

rates of population mobility as indicated by the large shifts in population among regions during the last several decades (even taking into account that part of the population growth in several of the most rapidly growing regions is due in part to immigration and in part to retirees), it would be difficult to argue that there are substantial barriers to labor mobility. The major "barrier" to mobility for part of the population may be a lack of skills that would be necessary to make mobility worthwhile.

In a study by the U.S. Office of Technology Assessment, several arguments are made for "why policymakers at the national level should care about metropolitan development patterns."[48] Although the concern in the study is primarily with the impact of newly developing technologies (particularly communication technology) on intrametropolitan development, the study also addresses intermetropolitan issues. In addition, a number of the arguments for national policy to deal with intrametropolitan development carry over to intermetropolitan development disparities. The principal argument made in the report is that "uneven development can reduce the efficiency of the national economy because some places are declining and have excess capacity, while others are growing and spending to add new capacity." The report continues,

> Firms cannot move their buildings, nor can workers move their homes. Public and quasi-public infrastructure, such as hospitals, utility networks, schools, roads, sewers, and bridges, is likewise immobile. . . . This premature writedown or less than full use of public and private resources imposes costs and reduces the efficiency not only of the declining area, but also of the U.S. economy as a whole.[49]

The report goes on to cite the further implications of decline and expansion: in declining areas, increased spending on social services, a smaller tax base, increased tax rates, and reduced spending on other city services can result in "increases in congestion, crime, and other negative externalities, while reducing educational levels and . . . agglomeration economies." The growing areas will "incur costs . . . for new infrastructure ([for example], bigger hospitals, widened roads) [and will find] private resources . . .

48. U.S. Congress, Office of Technology Assessment (1995, p. 27). This was one of the last publications of this agency, which was disbanded on September 29, 1995.
49. U.S. Congress, Office of Technology Assessment (1995, p. 28).

strained as well."[50] This argument, if valid, suggests a market failure in that the full costs of relocation are not borne by the relocating persons and firms.[51] Such views have also been the basis for legislation that requires firms to provide sufficient notice to employees and communities of planned closings.

The argument made for a federal role, not simply state or local policy, is to avoid the resulting competitive impetus to keep taxes and expenditures low and to provide "political cover" for actions that state and local governments "cannot justify . . . politically." In addition, the report argues that "uneven [development] limits the ability of the Federal Reserve Board to lower interest rates and otherwise stimulate the economy as much as it might, because growing places threaten to overheat the economy. The less uneven development, the faster the U.S. economy as a whole can grow."[52] A related point is made in arguing that federal help to distressed urban areas is not necessarily a zero-sum game. The authors of the report take the position that when the economy is strong, making distressed places (those with high unemployment and underutilized capital stock) more attractive "helps the U.S. economy by evening out differences in regional economic capacities and allowing the national economy to grow at a faster rate with less fear of inflation."[53]

The success of this approach depends on the costs of making the distressed places more attractive compared with the costs and benefits of policies that increase the mobility of the unemployed, and on the costs of efficiently maintaining the utilization of older infrastructure in the distressed areas compared with the costs of expanding infrastructure in the growing places. It is a policy recommendation whose success is also dependent on the demand for and supply of a skilled, well-educated labor force. If, as has been shown, the most severely distressed MSAs are those with low levels of human capital and none of the university resources that have been found to be important attractors of technology-driven industries—both those that develop new technology and those that are

50. U.S. Congress, Office of Technology Assessment (1995, p. 28).

51. Winnick (1966) had argued to the contrary, "Even in an economy with an appreciable margin of unemployed resources, an induced shift of economic opportunities is more likely to be reflected in a redistribution of, rather than an increase in, aggregate employment," p. 275. Also cited in Bolton (1992, p. 188).

52. U.S. Congress, Office of Technology Assessment (1995, p. 28).

53. U.S. Congress, Office of Technology Assessment (1995, p. 33). This position was articulated earlier by Bartik (1993b).

heavy users of technological inputs—it is unlikely that incentives to attract industries to "excess-capacity" areas will be successful, and if they are large enough to be successful, they are unlikely to be efficient.

This line of reasoning also warrants qualification. The high-technology private-sector firm is searching for and finding (with some help from state and local government in the form of tax breaks) locations with lower land and labor costs for its support functions. These functions—back-office operations, warehousing, and distribution—are more footloose and have different location and labor requirements than the corporate head-quarters. Some examples are a new TechCity in Kingston, New York, where rents "average $10 to $13 a square foot, compared with $50 to $100 in Manhattan and $30 in Westchester County"; and "EToys, an Internet retailer with headquarters in Santa Monica, California, [which] has established major distribution sites in Blairs, Virginia, in the rural south-central part of the state, and in Ontario, California, 40 miles east of Los Angeles. The sites . . . are in relatively low-cost areas with largely blue-collar work forces."[54]

EQUITY ISSUES. Normal, efficiency-enhancing responses to market forces may raise equity concerns such as growing poverty or unemployment rates in MSAs in decline. Consider, for example, a technological change such as high-speed data communication that makes possible a shift in location for economic sectors, causing a shift of economic activity to the South and Southwest and a loss of firms and population in the Northeast and Midwest. There are no market failures, no biased government policies behind the shifts.

The resulting relocations of population and industry may yield net benefits for the entire nation, but the persons in the areas losing population may be worse off. Those who do not move are the least educated and the least able to succeed in the new economy. The communities losing population have a reduced tax base but do not lose their dependent populations and as a result are less able to maintain public services, including social welfare services that are local responsibilities. In addition, some of them are entry points for new immigrants, who in the early years of their arrival require substantial amounts of public services.[55] The tax burden on the

54. Joel Kotkin, "Finding a Niche as High Tech's Back Office," New York Times, December 17, 2000, Business Section, p. 7.
55. It is important to keep in mind the very different situation of the rapidly growing metropolitan areas that act as entry points for immigrants—those in the Southwest—

remaining upper-income population increases, providing these people with additional incentives for relocation.

Is this a constellation of characteristics that warrants public intervention? Although the population of the nation is better off as a whole, the people and the MSAs that have been left behind are worse off: low-skill jobs in consumer services are more scarce, the higher-income population that was formerly present and financed the public service package is largely gone. Given that the deterioration of the condition of both the people and places left behind is in large measure the result of the negative effects that accompany the efficiency-enhancing relocations of people and firms, there is a widespread belief that an equity argument for public intervention is justified. The equity case rests on the argument that precisely those conditions that have made it attractive for persons and firms to relocate and increase their profits, their income, and their welfare have resulted in a loss of welfare for the persons left behind. Not everyone can move—older persons no longer in the labor force, for example—nor is it desirable that they move. Nor is it desirable that everyone capable of moving should relocate, leaving behind impoverished populations, with local governments incapable of providing adequate public services. As has been shown, this is not the general case given the low correlation between population and per capita income growth for metropolitan areas.

The principal policies on the equity side may already be in place—a macroeconomic policy to maintain a robust national economy, tax policies like the earned income tax credits, and the "unfair" federal flows of funds that reallocate federal revenues from higher-income to lower-income areas, largely as a result of the progressive federal income tax structure. Moreover, despite the citations of market failures—and they undoubtedly exist—there appear to be strong market forces operating that ultimately increase equity. As in the larger story that suffuses this book, the relocation of firms and population, a longer-term adjustment to the shifts that have left some MSAs behind is beginning to emerge. For example, firms in some rapidly growing industries are shifting their support operations to lower-price locations.[56]

---

compared with those in declining or less rapidly growing areas. See U.S. Department of Housing and Urban Development (1999, p. 29) and Daniel (1994).

56. Joel Kotkin, "Finding a Niche as High Tech's Back Office," *New York Times*, December 17, 2000, Business Section, p. 7.

EFFICIENCY AND EQUITY. Increased well-being of individuals and perhaps of metropolitan areas might be hastened by policies that increase the education and the technical skills of the population and that therefore increase productivity in the declining areas. What must be guarded against is the desire to increase equity by assisting distressed areas in ways that reduce overall economic efficiency and perhaps inhibit natural correctives by encouraging people to remain in places at costs well in excess of benefits—even taking a very broad view of benefits. The efficiency argument for public intervention must be made in terms of increasing national income, rather than moving it around. If the existence of excellent universities and a well-educated population are important sources of per capita income growth (as they have been shown to be in the 1980s) and if more rapid per capita income growth is associated with generally improved welfare outcomes, then investments in improving universities and in the education of the population may increase productivity growth and national growth rates. As described in chapter 5 in the Austin example, such investments can have substantial payoffs, but it appears that they are successful only where other factors contributing to growth are also present. As also described in chapter 5, some metropolitan areas (for example, upstate New York) that have good universities and were the home of early high-technology firms (for example, IBM) have nonetheless not fared well in recent years.

REGIONALLY BIASED GOVERNMENT POLICIES. Numerous public actions have differential regional impacts. One of the most frequently cited has been the federal government's location of defense facilities in the South and West (as a stimulus to economic growth in the period of rapidly expanding defense budgets, but perhaps having a contrary effect more recently as the defense budget has been reduced considerably). These location decisions are not necessarily "biased." They may be based on market factors that influence costs: land availability, proximity to universities that fill research and development needs, and weather.[57]

An example of a biased government policy that may be inefficient would be locating government facilities, purely on equity considerations, in economically distressed areas with high unemployment in which defense firms nevertheless had high costs. The question is whether the inefficiency is understood and whether the magnitude of the trade-off is

57. The policy bias view stems from the long-term tenure of southern senators and their positions on the important defense-related committees.

acceptable. Trying to stimulate development in a depressed area through the location of government facilities or steering government contracts to these areas is a demand-side policy that will not contribute to sustained growth unless it attracts firms that are characterized by continuing productivity growth. Although some defense suppliers have such characteristics, many (food purveyors) do not.

On equity grounds it would be difficult to make an argument for a shift of federal funds, particularly from South to North. Lower per capita incomes and higher poverty rates still characterize the South. Both market forces and existing policies have moved welfare outcomes toward convergence rather than divergence and have not done so at the expense of national economic growth. Put even more simply, in the face of a progressive income tax system, it would be surprising if higher-income areas did not pay more in taxes than lower-income areas, and there is no reason to believe that federal flows of funds should undo this intended redistribution.[58]

Members of the Society for American City and Regional Planning History were asked to list the ten major influences on metropolitan areas in the last fifty years and those likely to be important in the next fifty years. The results of the survey provide some interesting views of the role of policy intervention in the past and in the future.[59] Of the top four major influences of the past cited by respondents, three are federal policies: the 1956 Interstate Highway Act, the Federal Housing Administration mortgage financing and subdivision regulation, and the 1949 Housing Act that gave rise to urban renewal, downtown redevelopment, and public housing projects. As the author of the survey comments, "The single most important message of this list is the overwhelming impact of the federal government on the American metropolis."[60] The influence, however, is seen as affecting intraurban development, the movement from city to suburb, not as a factor in the interregional shifts that have characterized this period.

There is less agreement among the survey respondents on the factors likely to be most influential over the next fifty years. In striking contrast to the list of past factors, not one federal policy is expected to have a

58. See Pack (1982) for an extended discussion of this issue.
59. Fishman (2000).
60. Fishman (2000, p. 201).

major influence. The influential factors anticipated for the future include demographic factors (aging of the population and shrinking household size); changing technology (the growth of the Internet); dominance of the suburban political majority and growth of edge cities; growing disparities of wealth. The only policy mentioned is "smart growth," and as the author and respondents recognize, such policies require the kinds of cooperation among "the different levels of government . . . [that] have rarely been met in American cities and regions."[61] Thus, here, too, the only policy mentioned is one to influence intrametropolitan development.

## Conclusions

Given the earlier discussion of regional policy and the findings of convergence in earlier chapters, summarized above, it would appear that a general regional policy is not called for. Nonetheless several issues need to be addressed with respect to the convergence itself and the persistently distressed metropolitan areas.

The regional differences in levels of well-being have been pointed out, as has been the substantial diminution of these differences over time. Yet there are metropolitan areas, concentrated in the South (particularly in Texas and Louisiana), that appear to have been left behind in the general progress. These areas are characterized by persistently low incomes and high poverty and unemployment rates. In addition, they have low levels of educational achievement and lack major universities—two factors that have been found to be important in attracting economic growth, particularly since the 1980s. Thus if there is to be a regional policy—in contrast with a highly targeted and largely city-focused urban policy—it is still to MSAs in the South to which it should be directed.

The focus of much of the policy literature has been on growth rates rather than welfare. The argument here is that this puts the issue backwards. Our concern should be the well-being of the population.[62] An important policy consideration is whether incentives for persons and firms to relocate to low-growth areas would reduce the growth rates elsewhere. The South presents the clearest case for the conflict between a policy based on growth rates versus one based on welfare levels. As has been

61. Fishman (2000, p. 210).
62. Courant (1994).

shown, the South has experienced high growth rates, yet it still lags behind the rest of the nation in most welfare measures. From this it could be concluded that public intervention should concentrate on metropolitan areas with both low levels of per capita income growth (in contrast to the Department of Housing and Urban Development's emphasis on population growth rates) and low levels of welfare as indicated above by low per capita income and high poverty and unemployment rates.[63]

As emphasized above, the major arguments for regional policy both in the United States and Europe are equity arguments. Moreover, they are generally place-based arguments. It would be difficult to argue that the major relocations that have taken place over the last century, in particular since the end of the second world war, have not been efficient and have not been equitable. They have, in general, resulted in vast improvements in welfare in the least well-off places in the nation. The Moynihan argument—and the continuing reports on federal flows of funds, or as Leonard and Walder put it, balance of payments—has its problems as well.[64] Despite all the qualifications reinforcing the basic case that higher-income states have too large a deficit on federal account—that is, they have higher costs of living (not taken into account in the income figures) and high rates of poverty—it is still difficult to make the case that wealthier, higher-income places should either pay less in taxes or receive greater revenues from the federal government.[65] A fair share of expenditures is not easily defined. Is there an efficiency-equity trade-off on the expenditure side? What is it and which regions of the country, which metropolitan areas, would it favor? Both the aggregate regional figures and the more microscopic investigation of metropolitan areas left behind point to the greatest continued need in the Southwest.

63. This discussion may be seen as part of the "people versus place" policy literature. The phrase "place prosperity versus people prosperity" was introduced to the literature by Louis Winnick (1966) and has since become a staple of debates over whether policy should be designed to improve "the welfare of deserving people as individuals, *regardless of where they live*, and the ideal of improving the welfare of *groups* of deserving people defined by their spatial proximity in 'places.'" See Bolton (1992, emphasis in original). Bolton's paper provides a very good summary of the arguments. Winnick clearly did not favor place-based policies. Bolton, however, supports a place-based policy, subject to benefit-cost analysis, "because sense of place is a factor in regional and local identity and is an important form of intangible capital that has positive externalities," p. 185.

64. Leonard and Walder (2000); Moynihan (1978).

65. Estimates of regional costs of living are fraught with theoretical and empirical problems that make comparisons very difficult: do they reflect capitalization of regional ameni-

To summarize the regional policies to be found both in government documents and academic research, the following types of proposals are found:

—Narrowing the state balance of payments with the federal government.

—This might include increasing demand in these areas by changing federal procurement policies in their favor.

—This might include supply-side policies to make the areas more attractive to firms and population, through infrastructure improvements and through investments in universities and research and development facilities;

—Steering private and public economic activity to depressed (excess-capacity?) areas to help those areas and to increase national output.

—Increasing the human capital of persons (in depressed areas only) to make it possible for them to take advantage of economic opportunity wherever it may be found and perhaps to increase the attraction of firms to the places in which these people live.

There are three problems with moving ahead on any or all of these policies:

—The evidence that they would be successful is nonexistent, sparse, or negative. It is unclear even to advocates of public intervention that the policies would be beneficial either for the places they are designed to help or for the nation as a whole.

—In the face of the regional development of the past several decades, it is not clear that such polices are appropriate. The combination of the high rates of mobility of capital and labor in the United States and the progressive tax system appear to have brought about major changes in the right direction insofar as regional development is concerned.

—The Northeast is robust. Its dramatic turnaround in the 1980s, continuing into the 1990s, as measured by per capita income growth, cannot be attributed to policy intervention; quite the contrary in light of the data presented by Leonard and Walder.[66]

Even the urgency for assistance for the places left behind is unclear. The metropolitan areas with slow growth in per capita income, high poverty and unemployment rates, and low levels of human capital (as indicated by educational attainment variables and the absence of universities attractive to the rapidly growing industries) may be able to benefit

---

ties or disamenities; do consumption baskets differ due to differences in tastes, to needs (e.g., weather); do consumption baskets adjust to differences in prices?

66. Leonard and Walder (2000).

from the location patterns of the types of back office operations described earlier.[67]

For the next generation, for those now being educated, it would be difficult to argue against federal assistance to low-income places tied to education. This is not the same as an argument for educational assistance to build the kind of technical infrastructure that would be attractive to knowledge-intensive industries. Rather, it would make persons better able to take advantage of opportunity and might have the ancillary effect of increasing the quality of the labor force sufficiently to attract the types of firms described above.

Insofar as those not in the labor force are concerned—the retired, those unable to work—transfer policies, despite some views of these as inadequate "disaster relief," may be most appropriate.[68]

In sum, the policy prescriptions that follow from the discussion and analysis are, as indicated above, a continuation of federal expenditure and transfer programs, in which net flows of funds are largely determined by a progressive income tax system that transfers income from wealthier to poorer persons and places; a robust economy that lowers unemployment rates and poverty; and a market system that draws firms to places with suitable land and labor markets for efficient production. If anything is to be added to this mix, it is to concentrate attention on the places and persons that are characterized as being severely distressed: those with low income, high poverty and unemployment, and low educational attainment.

67. Joel Kotkin, "Finding a Niche as High Tech's Back Office," *New York Times,* December 17, 2000, Business Section, p. 7.

68. Moynihan in Leonard and Walder (2000, p. 9).

# States by Census Region and Division

*Region 1—Northeast*
Division 1: New England
  Vermont
  New Hampshire
  Massachusetts
  Maine
  Connecticut

Division 2: Mid Atlantic
  Pennsylvania
  New York
  New Jersey

*Region 2—Midwest*
Division 4: East North Central
  West Virginia*
  Wisconsin
  Michigan
  Ohio
  Kentucky*
  Indiana
  Illinois

Division 6: West North Central
  South Dakota
  North Dakota
  Nebraska
  Iowa
  Missouri
  Kansas
  Minnesota

*Region 3—South*
Division 3: South Atlantic
  West Virginia*
  Virginia
  Tennessee*
  South Carolina
  North Carolina
  Maryland
  Georgia
  Florida
  Delaware

* State has metropolitan areas in more than one census division.

*Region 3—South (continued)*
Division 5: East South Central
    West Virginia*
    Tennessee*
    Mississippi
    Kentucky*
    Alabama

Division 7: West South Central
    Texas
    Tennessee*
    Louisiana
    Oklahoma
    Arkansas

*Region 4—West*
Division 8: Mountain
    Wyoming
    Utah
    New Mexico
    Montana
    Idaho
    Colorado
    Arizona

Division 9: Pacific
    Washington
    Oregon
    California

* State has metropolitan areas in more than one census division.

# The Intrametropolitan Linkage Literature: A Brief Summary

THE ESSENTIAL FEATURES of the intrametropolitan perspective on urban development are described in the text. In this appendix the literature on the subject is briefly summarized.

## Positive and Negative Externalities and Spillovers

The major source of city-suburban linkage cited in the literature is attributed to the existence of externalities or spillovers, both positive and negative. Among the positive spillovers are those stemming from the existence of amenities, generally concentrated in cities, that are attractive to suburban residents. Major hospitals, universities, cultural institutions such as symphony halls and museums, and sports arenas and stadiums are thought to be important to most individuals, yet they are rarely found in suburbs. If the quantity or quality of these institutions decreases, the suburbs may become less attractive.[1] Thus one of the examples of metropolitan cooperation—advertising directed at new businesses with

---

1. A contrary view cited below is presented by John Kasarda, director of the Kenan Institute of Private Enterprise at the University of North Carolina, in an article in the *New York Times*. Joel Kotkin, "Grass Roots Business: A Place to Please the Techies," *New York Times*, January 24, 1999, sec. 3, p. 4.

expenses shared by local metropolitan-wide chambers of commerce or utility companies—typically pictures athletes or ballet dancers but not motorized lawn mowers being driven by Land's End models.

The amenity externality—in particular the notion that important amenities are located in central cities—suggests some interesting questions. Given the massive shifts of population and economic activity away from older cities and metropolitan areas in which such amenities are concentrated, did older cities lose these advantages? Can they regain them? Have newer cities captured these advantages, just as they drew population and firms from the older regions? Have they established newly valued amenities? Or, turning the question around, can newer cities develop these types of amenities? If they do not, does their rapid development argue against the importance of such amenities; do the amenities come, if at all, after the growth spurt? Can older cities produce newly valued amenities? Does this explain the ubiquitous attempt of older and newer cities to establish themselves as tourist, convention, and entertainment centers by luring sports teams and building new stadia, arts centers, and convention halls? Or perhaps the important amenities of today are quite different: mountains for skiing and hiking and year-round fair weather increasing possibilities for outdoor activities, for example.

In contrast to a focus on such positive amenities, Adams and colleagues attribute migration to both city and suburb solely to the presence of negative factors in the central city.[2] Their analyses are based on a set of hardship indexes for both cities and suburbs: "These indices were derived from measures of poverty and unemployment rates, per capita income, crowded housing conditions, dependent populations, and educational attainment."[3] Migration to both central cities and their suburbs was found to be negatively related to the central-city hardship indexes for both 1980 and 1990, providing a potential empirical basis for the linkage of cities and suburbs.[4]

2. Adams and Fleeter (1997); Adams and others (1996).
3. Adams and Fleeter (1997).
4. Note that this also provides evidence for the point made by Ihlanfeldt (1995) and Voith (1997) about outsiders' perceptions of regions being a function of their perceptions of its central city.

## Agglomeration Economies

Both Ihlanfeldt and Voith cite the importance of agglomeration economies as a source of linkage between cities and their suburbs.[5] Ihlanfeldt provides an extensive summary of the arguments and the evidence. He distinguishes two types of agglomeration economies: "Localization economies . . . in which production cost savings accrue to firms from locating close to other firms in the same, or a related, industry[,] . . . [and] urbanization economies . . . that . . . generate benefits for all firms, not just those in a particular industry. Because of their more compact development, central cities are thought to have an advantage over suburban areas in both localization or urbanization economies."[6]

Agglomeration economies arise from "labor market economies, scale economies in the production of intermediate inputs, and communication economies."[7] Given labor mobility, Ihlanfeldt rejects the first argument. After summarizing the arguments for and against the other sources of agglomeration economies, and indicating that "there has been insufficient research to settle the debate over the uniqueness of central-city agglomeration economies," he reaches some tentative conclusions:

Suburb-based companies depend heavily on central-city suppliers of corporate services. . . . Face-to-face interactions influence a firm's location decisions, and central cities . . . have an advantage over suburban areas in offering communication economies. Second, *the maturation of the suburbs, especially as manifested in edge cities, has made these areas more competitive with central cities and less dependent and derivative.* Third, even without supporting evidence, the arguments against the proposition that telecommunications will severely erode the role of the central city in the regional economy are persuasive. . . . Fourth, the hypothesis that cities make an important contribution to regional and national economic growth is attractive. . . . *Unfortunately, however, there is no empirical research that has focused explicitly on central cities as possible engines of growth.*[8]

5. Ihlanfeldt (1995); Voith (1998).
6. Ihlanfeldt (1995, p. 128).
7. Ihlanfeldt (1995, p. 139).
8. Ihlanfeldt (1995, p. 139, emphasis added).

Voith, too, cites the centrality of agglomeration economies. "The compact development of cities that is supported by high-density public transportation systems increases the opportunities for agglomeration economies. If city decline results in a decline in agglomeration economies, industries benefiting from them most are likely to suffer, and if they do move, they may well choose locations outside the region with greater agglomeration economies."[9] The need for "face-to-face contacts of community leaders," and the city as the locus of these types of contacts is also the first of Downs's arguments for the importance of central cities.[10]

There is some evidence that the traditional view that agglomeration economies must be concentrated in large, long-established metropolitan areas is less true. Interesting examples of agglomeration economies developing quickly in newer areas abound. Several executives were interviewed on the subject for a recent article in the *New York Times*. Henry T. Nicholas, co-founder and chief executive of Broadcom, explained the decision to move the communications chip and modem firm from Los Angeles to Irvine, California, in terms of push and pull factors (negative externalities from crowding in Los Angeles and rapidly developing agglomeration economies in Irvine). The negative factors were "congestion, expensive housing—and . . . a certain stigma to [Los Angeles]." The article points out that "for technology companies, [Irvine] is everything a traditional urban center should be but isn't: a strategic location where the relevant partners, competitors, money, and know-how are all close at hand." Similarly, Richard Holcomb, a software executive in Raleigh, North Carolina, describes the agglomeration characteristics of the region in terms of the pool of experienced workers available to firms because of the industry concentration and the attractiveness of the area to workers: "You can get a great job and if this one doesn't work out, you can just go down the road." Equally interesting to the argument that such companies want to locate near large cities for their cultural amenities and infrastructure but to avoid their negative characteristics is the statement by John Kasarda (director of the Kenan Institute of Private Enterprise at the University of North Carolina) that although there are no ports or railroad yards, technology work does not require them. There are no venerable art museums or symphony orchestras, but technology workers do not miss

9. Voith (1992, p. 208).
10. Downs (1994).

such amenities. And there are usually no homeless people or derelict buildings in sight. "You get rid of the problems of the city by charging for the exits. . . . For these people, the city is superfluous."[11]

It seems clear that agglomeration economies are fluid. Thus, their power to explain either intrametropolitan linkage between cities and suburbs or differences in interregional growth and urban development patterns requires not only recognition of their importance but also an understanding that they are not static; they evolve over time as a result of technology changes, congestion externalities, demographic shifts. Agglomeration economies develop in an area, attenuate, and surface in other areas as the underlying location determinants change, some becoming less important, others assuming new roles. In chapter 4, it is shown that the same variables receive very different weights in the growth equations in different decades.

## Economies of Scale

The evidence for economies of scale is mixed—there is evidence for and against economies of scale in infrastructure and service provision. Special districts crossing jurisdictional boundaries indicate that there are indeed some public activities in which economies of scale have been important enough to overcome substantial resistance of local governments to cede control over public expenditures to other entities. In an investigation of regionalization efforts in 27 large metropolitan areas, Summers finds that despite substantial "public rhetoric" in support of regionalization, "formal regional governments are a rarity."[12] City-suburban collaborations appear to be based on economies of scale. "Services most commonly *operating* on a regional level are . . . those transparently and grossly inefficient to operate on a local level. . . . [S]haring of police and fire services occurs only when there is total county consolidation."[13]

Duncombe and Yinger investigate returns to scale in fire protection.[14] They distinguish four different sources of economies: technical returns to scale, returns to population scale, returns to quality scale, and economies

11. Joel Kotkin, "Grass Roots Business: A Place to Please the Techies," *New York Times*, January 24, 1999, sec. 3, p. 4.
12. Summers (2000, p. 190).
13. Summers (2000, pp. 186–87).
14. Duncombe and Yinger (1993).

of scope. They provide a brief review of earlier studies. Little can be concluded from the existing studies both because of contradictory findings and serious limitations in each of the studies. In their study of fire protection, they "break fire protection into its two principal components, fire prevention and fire suppression." Of interest here is the finding that "when economies of scope are controlled for[,] . . . returns to population . . . are . . . constant." This finding "implies that consolidating small fire departments will not result in significant cost savings."[15]

It is not possible at this stage to conclude that economies or diseconomies of scale are considerable. Rather, inferences from the type of cooperation found in Summers's study appear to be more persuasive than the contradictory and problematic studies cited by Duncombe and Yinger. It seems safer to assume that there are economies of scale in the functions for which the existence of special districts or other forms of regional cooperation are observed. The assumption that there are no other potential sources of scale economies may not be warranted, but in the absence of compelling evidence, it would be foolhardy to plunge ahead with policies to force consolidations on the assumption that there are substantial unexploited economies to be realized.

## Other Sources of Linkage

In addition, there are other factors that link the parts of the metropolitan area: technological changes that have often made it possible for increased fragmentation also often provide ties that bind. Roads, for example, make it possible to work and live in different jurisdictions and facilitate interaction, work trips, shopping trips, goods movement, and recreation and entertainment trips. Specialization—in particular cities as the locations for the concentration of cultural, entertainment, sports, and health complexes—has also been argued by some to be a major link, although, here too, the growth of suburbs is pulling more of these functions out of the city.[16] Finally, there is a slightly different argument, close to the one made by Hill and colleagues, that the metropolitan area is one labor and housing market and should not even be thought of in terms of city and suburban links.[17] This argument requires further exploration.

15. Duncombe and Yinger (1993, p. 70).
16. Heilbrun (1992).
17. Hill and others (1995).

## Conclusion

The conclusion from the evidence for linkage between growth or well-being of cities and suburbs is based on positive correlations among a variety of variables in cities and their suburbs: growth rates (per capita income, population) and levels (per capita income, office space costs, house prices, poverty rates, unemployment rates). Although the studies that form this literature differ in many important dimensions—the variables for which linkage is considered, the time period covered, the size of the sample of metropolitan areas—the positive correlations appear to be widespread, although they often differ in magnitude. The evidence that suburbs are dependent on their central city is less persuasive. The arguments are appealing, but the evidence is sparse. Too little systematic attention has been paid to the importance of third factors influencing both city and suburbs in a metropolitan area. There is evidence that the state of the national economy and regional shifts in the locus of economic activity play an important part in the explanation; several studies have emphasized or at least included regional variables, but they have not played the central role in the discussion that they may warrant. With respect to the sources of linkage—externalities, agglomeration economies, economies of scale—there is substantial consistency in the arguments made by various investigators, but the evidence is sparse and often contradictory.

# Annexation and
# Urban Development

IN THIS APPENDIX the effects of annexation on city, suburb, and metropolitan growth are examined more closely. In particular, an attempt is
made to separate the effects of annexation from those of region. Rusk
shows that the cities with no annexation are concentrated in the older
urban areas of the Northeast and Midwest, and the high-annexation and
hyperelastic cities are in the South and West.[1] Given the concentration of
annexations in the South and West—regions of high growth—simple
comparisons of metropolitan areas with and without annexation are not
possible. It is difficult to separate annexation from region.[2] It is also

1. Rusk (1995, tables A-1, A-2, and A-3).
2. It would take a complex political economy model to explain why annexations occur
in some areas and not others. The fact that annexation is encouraged by enabling state legislation in some places and not in others may be a reflection of the fact that annexation is
more beneficial in some states than in others. Whether the purported benefits of annexation
derive from annexation or from the initial conditions that resulted in annexation, there are
some obvious characteristics of cities and their suburbs that might be considered important.
For example, annexation may be attractive in low-density metropolitan areas to take advantage of scale economies in infrastructure or public service provision. In high-density areas,
economies of scale may have been exhausted. One might expect annexation to be more
likely where cities and suburbs are relatively similar socioeconomically; in particular where
poverty rates or per capita incomes are not very different, so that redistribution from one to
the other as a result of merger is not a source of resistance by the higher-income area. In fact,
it appears to be the case that annexation occurred more frequently where city incomes

important in interpreting the annexation data and the effects of annexations to take account of the extent of the annexation. It is not simply the case that there are far more annexations in the South and West, but the average amount of land annexed is nearly twice as great in the South and West than in the Midwest (see table 2-5). In the equations that follow, the annexation variable is the increase in land area that resulted from these annexations, rather than a dummy variable indicating annexation or its absence.

To separate the effects of annexation and region and to see how annexation may affect central cities, their suburbs, and the entire metropolitan area, two equations have been estimated that relate population and per capita income growth separately in cities, suburbs, and metropolitan areas to annexation in different time periods and by region.[3] As indicated above, the specification of the annexation variable is the percentage change in the city's land area. This may be an inadequate representation of the size of the population annexed or of their incomes, but it provides more information than a dummy variable for annexation. The estimated equations are as follows:

(C-1)
$$Y_i = a + b_i X_i$$

(C-2)
$$Y_i = a + b_i X_i + c_i d_i,$$

where $Y_i$ is either the percentage change in population or per capita income between 1960 and 1990 in cities, suburbs, and metropolitan areas, and the $X_i$ terms are the annexation variables, namely the percentage change in city land area in each of the decades (the 1960s, 1970s, and

---

exceeded those of their adjacent areas. The ratios of city to suburban incomes in the 1960s were substantially higher before annexation in the cities that subsequently annexed adjacent areas than in those that did not. In the South and West, for example, average city per capita incomes were 11 percent greater than in the suburbs in the annexing group, compared with only 3 percent in the nonannexing group.

3. Annexations are entered separately for each decade, because the anticipated effects of annexation may occur quickly—that is, have only the immediate effect of the shifting of boundaries around population and economic activity—or slowly, if the annexation has longer-term implications for growth. This disaggregation by decade is also directly relevant to the attempt to separate annexation and regional effects due to the fact that the number of annexations differs enormously by decade and that the distribution of annexations across decades differs substantially within regions (see table 2-5).

**Table C-1.** *Percentage Change in Population and per Capita Income, Cities, Suburbs, and Metropolitan Areas, 1960–90*

Percent

| Variable | Cities | | Suburbs | | Metropolitan areas | |
|---|---|---|---|---|---|---|
| | Population | Per capita income | Population | Per capita income | Population | Per capita income |
| | | | *Equation C-1* | | | |
| Constant | −1.22* | 0.25* | 0.14 | 0.66* | 0.67* | 1.61* |
| City land area, 1970/1960 | 0.10* | 0.03* | −0.01 | 0.005 | 0.03* | 0.01* |
| City land area, 1980/1970 | 0.17** | 0.08* | 0.09 | 0.07*** | 0.14*** | 0.05** |
| City land area, 1990/1980 | 1.04* | 0.11* | 0.51 | 0.15** | 0.60* | 0.04 |
| Adjusted $R^2$ | 0.29 | 0.16 | 0.01 | 0.01 | 0.07 | 0.03 |
| | | | *Equation C-2* | | | |
| Constant | −1.09* | 0.32* | 0.39 | 0.70 | 0.88 | 1.72* |
| City land area, 1970/1960 | 0.09* | 0.02* | −0.03*** | −0.001 | 0.02** | 0.01* |
| City land area, 1980/1970 | 0.14** | 0.07* | 0.03 | 0.05 | 0.10 | 0.04 |
| City land area, 1990/1980 | 0.68* | 0.04 | 0.03 | 0.11 | 0.23*** | 0.02 |
| Region 2 | 0.15*** | −0.10* | 0.02 | −0.05 | 0.004 | −0.19* |
| Region 3 | 0.29* | 0.16* | 0.62* | 0.18* | 0.37* | 0.05 |
| Region 4 | 1.07* | −0.03 | 1.02* | −0.1*** | 0.90* | −0.16* |
| Adjusted $R^2$ | 0.51 | 0.37 | 0.17 | 0.13 | 0.29 | 0.25 |

\* Significant at 0.01.
\*\* Significant at 0.05.
\*\*\* Significant at 0.10.

1980s). The $d_i$ term in equation C-2 is the regional dummy variable. The results of estimating equations C-1 and C-2 are shown in table C-1.[4]

The major conclusion that can be drawn from these estimates is that the principal beneficiaries of annexation are the central cities. Moreover,

4. The F-test shows that the coefficients on the changes in land area differ significantly in the regional equations for both population and per capita income compared with the overall equation across all regions for all three geographic areas, cities, suburbs, and metropolitan areas.

when regional variables are added to the annexation variables, whatever small benefits annexation may have had for suburbs or metropolitan areas largely disappear. Even for the central cities, regions have a major impact on growth rates, quite independent of annexation. Given the general lack of significance of annexation for either population or per capita income growth in the suburbs and in the metropolitan area as a whole, the increased growth in the central city may be a purely arithmetic phenomenon. As pointed out earlier, annexing to the city parts of suburban areas makes the city look better in numerous ways but—except for the improvement in tax base—there might be no change in growth rates or public welfare, if these could be calculated for the preannexation city boundary.

Determining the effects of annexation is further complicated by the possibility that annexation is endogenous. Annexations do not occur serendipitously. It is reasonable to assume that they may be most prevalent where there is mutual advantage from annexation—for example, a relatively robust central city with little vacant land adjacent to a similar or less-prosperous suburban area with substantial amounts of vacant land. This is consistent with our earlier finding that in metropolitan areas in which annexations occurred, per capita incomes in the central city were higher than those in the suburbs before the annexation occurred.

# References

Adams, Charles F., and Howard B. Fleeter. 1997. "Patterns of Metropolitan Suburbanization." *Commentary* Fall: 33–37.

Adams, Charles F., Howard B. Fleeter, Yul Kim, Mark Freeman, and Imgon Cho. 1996. "Flight from Blight and Metropolitan Suburbanization Revisited." *Urban Affairs Quarterly* 31 (4): 529–42.

Arrow, Kenneth J. 1962. "The Economic Implications of Learning by Doing." *Review of Economic Studies* June: 29.

Audretsch, David B. 1998. "Agglomeration and the Location of Innovative Activity." *Oxford Review of Economic Policy* 14 (2): 18–29.

Audretsch, David, and M. Feldman. 1996. "R & D Spillovers, and the Geography of Innovation and Production." *American Economic Review* 86 (June): 630–40.

Barro, Robert J., and Xavier Sala-i-Martin. 1991. "Convergence across States and Regions." *Brookings Papers on Economic Activity* 1: 1991, 107–82.

———. 1992. "Convergence." *Journal of Political Economy* 100 (3): 223–51.

Bartik, Timothy J. 1993a. "Federal Policy towards State and Local Economic Development in the 1990s." *Research in Urban Economics* 9: 161–78.

———. 1993b. "Who Benefits from Local Economic Job Growth: Migrants or the Original Residents?" *Regional Studies* 27 (4): 297–311.

Beeson, Patricia. 1987. "Total Factor Productivity Growth and Agglomeration Economies in Manufacturing, 1959–73." *Journal of Regional Science* 27 (2): 183–99.

Begg, Iain, Graham Gudgin, and Derek Morris. 1995. "The Assessment: Regional Policy in the European Union." *Oxford Review of Economic Policy* 11 (2): 1–17.

Berry, Brian J. L. 1999. "Comment on Elvin K. Wyly and Daniel J. Hammel's 'Islands of Decay in Seas of Renewal: Housing Policy and the Resurgence of Gentrification.'" *Housing Policy Debate* 10 (4): 783–88.

Bishop, John A., John P. Formby, and Paul D. Thistle. 1992. "Convergence of the South and Non-South Income Distributions, 1969–79." *American Economic Review* 82 (March): 262–72.

———. 1994. "Convergence and Divergence of Regional Income Distributions and Welfare." *Review of Economics and Statistics* 76 (May): 228-235.

Blanchard, Olivier Jean, and Lawrence F. Katz. 1992. " Regional Evolutions." *Brookings Papers on Economic Activity 1: 1992*, 1–75.

Bolton, Roger. 1992. "Place Prosperity vs. People Prosperity Revisited: An Old Issue with a New Angle." *Urban Studies* 29 (April): 185–203.

Borts, George H., and Jerome L. Stein. 1964. *Economic Growth in a Free Market.* Columbia University Press.

Bradbury, Katharine L., Anthony Downs, and Kenneth Small. 1981. *Futures for a Declining City: Simulations for the Cleveland Area.* Academic Press.

Bradbury, Katharine L., Yolanda K. Kodrzycki, and Robert Tannenwald. 1997. "The Effects of State and Local Public Policies on Economic Development: An Overview." *New England Economic Review* March-April: 1–12.

Bretzfelder, Robert B. 1973. "Sensitivity of State and Regional Income to National Business Cycles." *Survey of Current Business* 53 (4): 30–31.

Brezis, Elise S., and Paul R. Krugman. 1997. "Technology and the Life Cycle of Cities." *Journal of Economic Growth* 2 (December): 369–83.

Brueckner, Jan K. 2001. "Urban Sprawl: Lessons from Urban Economics." In *Brookings-Wharton Papers on Urban Affairs 2001*: 65–89.

Carlino, Gerald, and Robert DeFina. 1998. "The Differential Regional Effects of Monetary Policy." *Review of Economics and Statistics* 80 (November): 572–87.

Carlino, Gerald, and Keith Sill. 2001. "Regional Economic Flucuations: Common Trends and Common Cycles." *Review of Economics and Statistics* 83 (3): 446–58.

Carter Center. 1997. *Linked Future: Building Metropolitan Communities.* Atlanta.

Chiswick, Barry R., and Teresa A. Sullivan. 1995. "The New Immigrants." In *State of the Union: America in the 1990s,* edited by Reynolds Farely, 211–70. New York: Russell Sage Foundation.

Coelen, Stephen P. 1978. "Regional Income Convergence/Divergence Again." *Journal of Regional Science* 18 (December): 447–57.

Council of Economic Advisers. 1998. *Economic Report of the President.* Government Printing Office.

Courant, Paul N. 1994. "How Would You Know a Good Economic Development Policy if You Tripped over One? Hint: Don't Just Count Jobs." *National Tax Journal* 47 (December): 863–81.

Daniel, Kermit. 1994. "Fiscal and Political Implications of the Concentration of Immigration." Working Paper 186. Zell-Lurie Real Estate Center, University of Pennsylvania.

David, Paul, and Joshua Rosenbloom. 1990. "Marshallian Factor Market Externalities and the Dynamics of Industrial Location." *Journal of Urban Economics* 28 (November): 349–70.

Downs, Anthony. 1994. *New Visions for Metropolitan America*. Brookings.

Duncombe, William, and John Yinger. 1993. "An Analysis of Returns to Scale in Public Production, with an Application to Fire Protection." *Journal of Public Economics* 52 (August): 49–72.

Eberts, Randall W. 1989. "Accounting for the Recent Divergence in Regional Wage Differentials." *Economic Review* 3d Quarter: 14–26.

Fabricant, Ruth A. 1970. "An Expectational Model of Migration." *Journal of Regional Science* 10 (1): 13–24.

Farber, Stephen C., and Robert J. Newman. 1987. "Accounting for South/Non-South Real Wage Differentials and for Changes in Those Differentials over Time." *Review of Economics and Statistics* 69 (2): 215–23.

Fisher, Peter S., and Alan H. Peters. 1997. "Tax and Spending Incentives and Enterprise Zones." *New England Economic Review* (March–April): 109–30.

Fishman, Robert. 2000. "The American Metropolis at Century's End: Past and Future Influences." *Housing Policy Debate* 11 (1): 199–213.

Flynn, Patricia M. 1997. "Policy Implications—A Panel Discussion." *New England Economic Review* (March–April): 139–47.

Frey, William H. 1993. "The New Urban Revival in the United States." *Urban Studies* 30 (May): 741–74.

———. 1999. "Beyond Social Security: The Local Aspects of an Aging America." Discussion paper. Brookings Center on Urban and Metropolitan Policy (June).

Glaeser, Edward L., and Bruce Sacerdote. 1999. "Why Is There More Crime in Cities?" *Journal of Political Economy* 107 (6): 225–58.

Glaeser, Edward L., Jose A. Scheinkman, and Andrei Shleifer. 1995. "Economic Growth in a Cross-Section of Cities." *Journal of Monetary Economics* 36 (August): 117–43.

Greenwood, Michael J., and Gary L. Hunt. 1989. "Jobs versus Amenities in the Analysis of Metropolitan Migration." *Journal of Urban Economics* 25 (January): 1–16.

Greenwood, Michael J., Gary L. Hunt, Dan S. Rickman, and George I. Treyz. 1991. "Migration, Regional Equilibrium, and the Estimation of Compensating Differentials." *American Economic Review* 81 (5): 1382–90.

Gudgin, Graham. 1995. "Regional Problems and Policy in the UK." *Oxford Review of Economic Policy* 11 (2): 18–63.

Gudgin, Graham, and Derek Morris, eds. 1995. "Regional Policy." *Oxford Review of Economic Policy* 11 (2).

Gyourko, Joseph, and Todd Sinai. 2000. "The Spatial Distribution of Housing-Related Tax Benefits in the United States." Working Paper 332. Wharton Real Estate Center, University of Pennsylvania (November).

Gyourko, Joseph, and Richard Voith. 2001. "Capitalization of Federal Taxes, the Relative Price of Housing and Urban Form: Density and Sorting Effects." Working paper. Wharton Real Estate Center, University of Pennsylvania (March).

Haveman, Joel, and Rochelle Stanfield. 1977. "A Year Later, the Frostbelt Strikes Back." *National Journal* July 2: 1028–1037.

Heilbrun, James. 1992. "Art and Culture as Central Place Functions." *Urban Studies* 29 (2): 205–15.

Henderson, Vernon, Ari Kuncoro, and Matt Turner 1995. "Industrial Development in Cities." *Journal of Political Economy* 103 (51): 1067–90.

Hill, Edward W., Harold L. Wolman, and Coit Cook Ford III. 1995. "Can Suburbs Survive without Their Cities? Examining the Suburban Dependence Hypothesis." *Urban Affairs Review* 31 (2): 147–74.

Holmer, Martin. 1978. "Preliminary Analysis of the Regional Economic Effects of Federal Procurement." Department of Health and Human Services working paper presented at the Committee on Urban Public Economics Meetings, May 5–6.

Ihlanfeldt, Keith. 1995. "The Importance of the Central City to the Regional and National Economy: A Review of the Arguments and Empirical Evidence." *Cityscape: A Journal of Policy Development & Research* 1 (2): 125–50.

Inman, Robert. 1992. "Can Philadelphia Escape Its Fiscal Crisis with Another Tax Increase?" *Business Review* September/October: 5–20.

Izraeli, Oded. 1987. "The Effect of Environmental Attributes on Earnings and Housing Values." *Journal of Urban Economics* 22 (September): 361–76.

Jaffe, A., M. Trajtenberg, and R. Henderson. 1993. "Geographic Localization of Knowledge Spillovers as Evidence by Patent Citations." *Quarterly Journal of Economics* 108 (3): 577–98.

Jasso, Guillermina, and Mark R. Rosenzweig. 1990. *The New Chosen People: Immigrants in the United States*. New York: Russell Sage.

Jusenius, C. L., and L. C. Ledebur. 1976. *A Myth in the Making: The Southern Economic Challenge and Northern Economic Decline*. U.S. Department of Commerce, Economic Development Administration.

Kasarda, John D. 1999. "Comment on Elvin K. Wyly and Daniel J. Hammel's 'Islands of Decay in Seas of Renewal: Housing Policy and the Resurgence of Gentrification.'" *Housing Policy Debate* 10 (4): 773–87.

Katz, Bruce J. 1998. "Reviving Cities: Think Metropolitan." Policy Brief 33. Brookings.

———, ed. 2000. *Reflections on Regionalism*. Brookings.

Lang, Robert E., and Steven P. Hornburg. 1997. "Planning Portland Style: Pitfalls and Possibilities." *Housing Policy Debate* 8 (1): 1–10.

Ledebur, Larry C., and William R. Barnes. 1992. *City Distress, Metropolitan Disparities and Economic Growth*. Washington: National League of Cities (September).

———. 1993. *All in It Together: Cities, Suburbs and Local Economic Regions*. Washington: National League of Cities (February).

Leonard, Herman B., and Jay H. Walder. 2000. *The Federal Budget and the States Fiscal Year 1999: Who Wins, Who Loses and Why* (with an introduction by Senator Daniel Patrick Moynihan). John F. Kennedy School of Government, Harvard University.

Leonardi, Robert. 1995. "Regional Development in Italy: Social Capital and the Mezzogiorno." *Oxford Review of Economic Policy* 11 (2): 165–79.

Lucas, Robert. 1988. "On the Mechanics of Economic Development." *Journal of Monetary Economics* 22 (1): 3–42.

Madden, Janice F. 2000. *Changes in Income Inequality within U.S. Metropolitan Areas*. Kalamazoo, Mich.: W. E. Upjohn Institute for Employment Research.

Mankiw, G., D. Romer, and D. Weil. 1991. "A Contribution to the Empirics of Economic Growth." *Quarterly Journal of Economics* 107 (May): 407–38.

Marshall, Alfred. 1890. *Principles of Economics*. London: Macmillan.

———. 1920. *Principles of Economics*, 8th ed. London: Macmillan.

Moynihan, Daniel P. 1978. "The Politics and Economics of Regional Growth." *Public Interest* 51 (2): 3–21.

Myers, Dowell. 1999. "Demographic Dynamism and Metropolitan Change: Comparing Los Angeles, New York, Chicago, and Washington, D.C." *Housing Policy Debate* 10 (4): 919–54.

Nelson, Richard R., and Edmund Phelps. 1966. "Investment in Humans, Technological Diffusion, and Economic Growth." *American Economic Review* 56 (May): 69–75.

Nourse, Hugh O. 1968. *Regional Economics: A Study in the Economic Structure, Stability and Growth of Regions*. McGraw-Hill.

Oakland, William H., and Daniel E. Chall. 1978. "Regional Impact of Federal Expenditures." Paper submitted to U.S. Department of Housing and Urban Development.

Olson, Mancur. 1976. "The Political Economy of Comparative Growth Rates: Studies Prepared for Use of the Joint Economic Committee." In *U.S. Economic Growth from 1976 to 1986: Prospects, Problems and Patterns, vol. 2: The Factors and Processes Shaping Long-Run Economic Growth*. Government Printing Office.

Orfield, Myron. 1997. *Metropolitics: A Regional Agenda for Community and Stability*. Brookings and Lincoln Institute of Land Policy.

Pack, Howard, and Janet Rothenberg Pack. 1977. "Metropolitan Fragmentation and Suburban Homogeneity." *Urban Studies* 14 (June): 191–201.

Pack, Janet Rothenberg. 1980. *Regional Growth: Historic Perspective*. U.S. Advisory Commission on Intergovernmental Relations.

———. 1982. "The States' Scramble for Federal Funds." *Journal of Policy Analysis and Management* 1 (2): 175–95.

———. 1998. "Poverty and Urban Public Expenditures." *Urban Studies* 35 (11): 1995–2019.

Perloff, Harvey S., Edgar S. Dunn Jr., Eric R. Lampard, and Richard F. Muth. 1960. *Regions, Resources, and Economic Growth*. University of Nebraska Press.

Perry, David C., and Alfred J. Watkins, eds. 1977. *The Rise of the Sunbelt Cities*. Beverly Hills, Calif.: Sage Publications.

Peterson, George, and Thomas Muller. 1980. "The Regional Impact of Federal Tax and Spending Policies." Washington: Urban Institute.

Peterson, John E. 1977. *Frostbelt vs. Sunbelt, Part I: Key Trends of the Seventies*. Boston, Mass.: First Boston Bank.

Polenske, Karen. 1969. *Shifts in the Regional and Industrial Impact of Federal Government Spending*. U.S. Department of Commerce, Economic Development Administration.

President's Commission for a National Agenda for the Eighties. 1980. *Urban America in the Eighties.* Government Printing Office.

Quigley, John. 1998. "Urban Diversity and Economic Growth." *Journal of Economic Perspectives* 12 (2): 127–38.

Rees, John. 1978. "Regional Industrial Shifts in the U.S. and the Internal Generation of Manufacturing Growth in the Southwest." Paper prepared for the Committee on Urban Public Economics (May).

Romer, Paul M. 1986. "Increasing Returns and Long Run Growth." *Journal of Political Economy* 94 (October): 1002–37.

Rossetti, Michael A., and Barbara S. Eversole. 1993. *Journey-to-Work Trends in the United States and Its Major Metropolitan Areas, 1960–90.* U.S. Department of Transportation, Federal Highway Administration. Publication FHWA-PL-94-012. Government Printing Office.

Rusk, David. 1995. *Cities without Suburbs,* 2nd ed. Washington: Woodrow Wilson Center Press.

———. 1999. *Inside Game/Outside Game: Winning Strategies for Saving Urban America.* Brookings.

Savitch, H. V., David Collins, Daniel Sanders, and John P. Markham. 1993. "Ties that Bind: Central Cities, Suburbs, and the New Metropolitan Region." *Economic Development Quarterly* 7 (4): 341–57.

Saxenian, AnnaLee. 1994. *Regional Advantage: Culture and Competition in Silicon Valley and Route 128.* Harvard University Press.

Schultz, Theodore W. 1975. "The Value of the Ability to Deal with Disequilibria." *Journal of Economic Literature* 13 (September): 827–46.

Sjaastad, Larry. 1962. "The Costs and Returns of Human Migration." *Journal of Political Economy* 70 (February): 80–93.

Summers, Anita A. 2000. "Regionalization Efforts between Big Cities and Their Suburbs: Rhetoric and Reality." In *Urban-Suburban Interdependencies,* edited by Rosalind Greenstein and Wim Wiewel, 181–204. Cambridge, Mass.: Lincoln Institute of Land Policy.

Summers, Anita A., and Lara Jakubowski. 1996. "The Fiscal Burden of Unreimbursed Poverty Expenditures in the City of Philadelphia: 1985–1995." Working Paper 238. Wharton Real Estate Center, University of Pennsylvania.

Sweet, Morris L. 1999. *Regional Economic Development in the European Union and North America.* Westport, Conn.: Praeger.

Tannenwald, Robert. 1997. "State Regulatory Policy and Economic Development." *New England Economic Review* (March/April): 83–98.

Tiebout, Charles. 1956. "A Pure Theory of Local Expenditures." *Journal of Political Economy* 64: 416–24.

Todaro, Michael P. 1969. "A Model of Labor, Migration and Urban Unemployment in Developing Countries." *American Economic Review* 59 (1): 138–48.

Tolley, George S. 1974. "The Welfare Economics of City Bigness." *Journal of Urban Economics* 1 (1): 324–45.

U.S. Congress, Office of Technology Assessment. 1995. *The Technological Reshaping of Metropolitan America.* OTA-ETI-643. Government Printing Office.

U.S. Department of Housing and Urban Development. 1984. *The President's National Urban Policy Report.* Government Printing Office.

———. 1986. *The President's National Urban Policy Report.* Government Printing Office.

———. 1997. *The State of the Cities Report.* Government Printing Office.

———. 1998. *The State of the Cities Report.* Government Printing Office.

———. 1999. *Now Is the Time: Places Left behind in the New Economy.* Government Printing Office.

———. 2000. *The State of the Cities 2000: Megaforces Shaping the Future of the Nation's Cities.* Government Printing Office.

Voith, Richard. 1992. "City and Suburban Growth: Substitutes or Complements?" *Business Review* September/October: 21–33.

———. 1998. "Do Suburbs Need Cities?" *Journal of Regional Science* 38 (3): 445–64.

Wasylenko, Michael. 1997. "Taxation and Economic Development: The State of the Economic Literature." *New England Economic Review* March/April: 37–52.

Weinstein, Bernard L., and Robert E. Firestine. 1978. *Regional Growth and Decline in the United States: The Rise of the Sunbelt and the Decline of the Northeast.* Westport, Conn.: Praeger.

Welch, Finis. 1970. "Education in Production." *Journal of Political Economy* 38 (January/February): 35–59.

Williamson, Jeffrey G. 1977. "Unbalanced Growth, Inequality and Regional Development: Some Lessons from American History." Paper presented at the symposium, "A National Policy toward Regional Change: Alternatives to Confrontation," Austin, Tex., September 24–27.

Winnick, Louis. 1966. "Place Prosperity vs. People Prosperity: Welfare Considerations in the Geographic Redistribution of Economic Activity." In *Essays in Urban Land Economics in Honor of the 65th Birthday of Leo Grebler,* 273–83. Real Estate Research Program, University of California at Los Angeles.

Wyly, Elvin K., and Daniel J. Hammel. 1999. "Islands of Decay in Seas of Renewal: Housing Policy and the Resurgence of Gentrification." *Housing Policy Debate* 10 (4): 711–70.

# Index
## of Authors Cited

# Index

Hewlett-Packard, 105, 149
High-technology firms, 88, 146, 150, 167, 188
Highways, interstate, 17, 19, 32, 148, 160, 178, 190
Holcomb, Richard, 188
Housing: city to suburb movement, 26–27; federal initiatives, 178; metropolitan area as single market, 190
Houston, Tex., 147

Immigration: and educational attainment levels, 80; labor immigration and per capita income levels, 91, 93–94, 150; of minority populations, 22, 80; and poverty rates, 64, 171; and unemployment rates, 74, 171; and warmer climates, 103–04
Imports, 86, 87
Income, per capita: educational attainment and growth in, 79, 80; empirical determinants of growth, 114–20; fastest- versus slowest-growing MSAs, 13–14, 133–40; highly distressed metropolitan areas, 167–68; and persistence, 71–72, 138; regional differences 1970 and 1990, 48–50, 51–56, 60–61, 66, 82; relating to growth and region, 62–75, 82–83, 92–93, 96; reversals in MSA performance, 134. See also Population growth
Inflation, 86, 87, 118
Infrastructure subsidies and movement to suburbs, 19–20
Innovation, 100–02, 133
Insurance sector. See Financial services sector
Intel, 106
Interregional growth rates, 16–18, 24–26, 31–46, 141; and annexation, 41–45, 192–95; and city-suburb linkage literature, 36–40; and cost differences for employers,

33–34; and demographic change, 35–36; and economic maturity of industries, 33; explanations for differences, 32–36; and federal subsidies, 34–35; policy focus, 28–29
Intrametropolitan linkage, 23–24, 27–28; and agglomeration economies, 187–89; and amenities of central cities, 106, 186, 188; cooperation, 28, 185–86; correlation between city and suburban growth rates, 23; and economies of scale, 189–90; literature summary, 36–40, 185–91; and negative factors of central cities, 186; as policy focus, 27–28, 162; population shift, 155; sources of linkage, 190

Jersey City, N.J., 142, 149, 150
Johnson, Lyndon B., 162
Joint Economic Committee of Congress, 165

Kasarda, John D., 155, 185, 188
Kennedy, John F., 162
Kennedy School of Government, Harvard, 161
Knowledge-intensive growth, 141–42
Komatsu, 151

Labor: immigrant and per capita income levels, 91, 93–94, 150; metropolitan area as single market, 190; mobility, 173–74; Sun Belt demand, 36, 119
Las Vegas, Nev., 14, 85, 121
Lawrence, Kans., 13
Location choice for businesses, 18, 85, 120. See also Sun Belt, industry relocation to
Los Angeles, Calif., 64, 188

Macroeconomy and growth, 63, 86–88, 115, 172